American SALVAGE YARD TREASURES

Published by
Amos Press Inc.
911 Vandemark Road
Sidney, Ohio 45365

Publishers of
Cars & Parts
The Voice of the Collector Car Hobby Since 1957

Cars & Parts Collectible Series	**Legend Series**
High Performance Cars	Collectible Trucks
Cars of the '50s	Collector Car Annual
Cars of the '60s	Corvette
Price Guide	

Catalog of American Car ID Numbers 1950-59
Catalog of American Car ID Numbers 1960-69
Catalog of American Car ID Numbers 1970-79
Catalog of Chevy Truck ID Numbers 1946-72
Catalog of Ford Truck ID Numbers 1946-72
Catalog of Chevelle, Malibu & El Camino ID Numbers 1964-87
Catalog of Pontiac GTO ID Numbers 1964-74
Catalog of Corvette ID Numbers 1953-93

Salvage Yard Treasures
A Guide to America's Salvage Yards

Copyright 1993 by Amos Press Inc.

Distribution by Motorbooks International Publishers and Wholesalers
P.O. Box 2, Osceola WI 54020 USA

Printed and bound in the United States of America

Library of Congress Cataloging-In-Publication
ISBN 1-880524-09-0

ACKNOWLEDGEMENTS

The completion of this project would not have been possible without assistance from the following:

AUTHORS
Eric Brockman
Doc Howell
Randy Moser
Dean Shipley
Robert Stevens

DESIGN/LAYOUT
Ken New
Meg Schultz
Teresa Wenrick

EDITING
Jim Cain

WORD PROCESSING
Emily Ellis
Sherry Fair

INTRODUCTION

At the heart of the American love affair with the automobile is "freedom" - the freedom of getting into the automobile and driving anywhere we want to go. We can travel within the U.S. borders, anywhere we wish, without permission from any government agency.

One of my recurring dreams is to "just go see the country." And judging by the response from readers of *Cars & Parts* magazine, many of them wish they could travel to each of the salvage yards we cover. Due to realities of life (we know what they are), I won't be able to do this in the near future and most of our readers won't either. *Cars & Parts* magazine is doing the next best thing: combining the freedom to see the country with America's love affair with the automobile.

American Salvage Yard Treasures is a travelog and scavenger hunt. We've traveled the backroads of the United States to bring you stories and photos of little known salvage yards. American salvage yards are the backbone of the collector car hobby. Creeping suburbs, restrictive zoning and environmental regulations, plus insurance and liability considerations along with the buying and rusting of these relics of the past, are forcing American salvage yards into extinction.

This is our way of immortalizing something that I will want to have as part of my future. Even if I personally don't get the opportunity to "just go see the country," I have a photo journal of what I wanted to see.

So, I hope you will also be pleased with this photo journal: American Salvage Yard Treasures. It is entirely our pleasure that we have been able to research and develop this book. The time and effort were a joy for all who made this project a reality.

TABLE OF CONTENTS

SALVAGE YARD TOUR, Phase IV

SALVAGE YARD TOUR, Phase V

SALVAGE YARD DIRECTORY

SALVAGE YARD TOUR:

WESTERN MONTANA

Phase I

By Doc Howell

1. *Scenic Lake Coeur d' Alene was the starting point of the western Montana salvage yard tour.*

This narrative may sound a bit like a travelogue or a scavenger hunt. I hope so since it is all of that and a lot more. The idea of covering this part of Western Montana is that I would be able to bring to the reader in print and photo some of the hitherto unpublished aspects of ferreting out collectible and restorable cars and unearthing some little-known salvage yards along the way. Too, it enables me to share with you some of the personalities and anecdotes that go with the territory.

Three days is about half the time necessary to adequately cover the various salvage yards and other related sites in Northwest Montana, but yours truly covered a lot of ground trying.

The trek started at Coeur d' Alene, Idaho with Classic Auto Parts, went north on Highway 95 through Sandpoint to Bonners Ferry, Idaho, and across the state line and down the pass through the dense Kootenai Forest area to the Yaak River. Though the subject at hand was restorable vehicles and parts vehicles for collectors and restorers, one needs to carry extra film just for some of the magnificent scenery. The "Big Sky Country" theme is more than just hype emanating from the Montana Tourist Bureau. Coming over the summit before heading downgrade to the Yaak River is a little like donning a clean pair of glasses or better yet, somewhat like removing a worn and soiled plastic cover from a photo or painting. The sky is bluer, clearer, the breeze has a fresh tang to it. Everything appears more crisp and enhanced, whether it's lakes, trees, rocks or wherever you happen to look. Roadsides lack litter, communities are tidier and there is a decidedly rustic or pioneer flavor to everything, including names. Log homes, a novelty elsewhere, are quite common, and many are upgraded from their turn of the century beginnings.

Just before you reach the tidy little community of Troy, Mont., you'll come to a KOA campground where the owner has a line-up of vintage '50s vehicles, all with "For Sale" signs in the windows: two or three '55 Buicks, a '57 Ford Ranchero, a '61 Imperial, a nice '55 Olds and several pickups. It's too early for the owner to be about, but a check with a source in Libby, Mont. revealed that the owner is "quite proud" of his 3 and 4 vehicles, and substantial negotiating would be required. The source also volunteered that none had been sold for a couple of years. Maybe the owner's still reading '88-'89 price guides?

Following up a lead, I proceeded to Libby, Mont. where I located the small (2-3 acre) salvage yard owned by the widow of Mel Bowker. The yard was purported to be chock full of vintage cars and parts destined very soon for the crusher. The rumor was exactly that, and obviously the party who passed it on during a classic car show hadn't actually been there. When I arrived, one fellow was busy rescuing a chassis for an early '50s Jeep Wagon. There was a '34 Chevy pickup in back, last licensed in '75, that someone aspired to turn into a street rod since a 265 V-8 had been installed and only one lonely bucket seat remained. Sheet metal was fair to good, but all of the support wood in the cab would require replacement. There were enough '49-'51 Ford pickups and 1 1/2-ton trucks left to possibly make one complete pickup. The old Federal wrecker standing hipshot by the side road appeared to be the best restoration project. Essentially, this operation appeared to be an elderly man's local junkyard rather than an auto salvage yard. Since the crusher was slated to arrive around the first of June, this location can best be described as R.I.P. and forgotten.

About two miles farther south on Highway 2 is Jim's Auto Wrecking, which used to have quite an abundant supply of square and round T-Birds, as well as some late '50s Cadillacs. According to the owner, a man from over around Elk, Wash., just north of Spokane, came in with money, crew, trucks and trailers and virtually stripped his lot and the neighboring vicinity of all similar vehicles. The cupboard was bare. Good source for late '60s and up parts, but no collector items.

Kalispell, Mont. and the Flathead Valley has to rate five stars with regard to vehicles. About three miles east on Highway 2, I threw out the anchor and made a u-turn to investigate Young's Enterprises, owned and operated by Dennis Young, with assistance from his son Mike and another party. Young's operation is a mixture of small salvage, custom body and mechanical work and some sales and brokering. Though not all of the approximately 75-100 vehicles they have available are on site, those on hand are very interesting. Out front you can't miss the all original '53 Studebaker Champion five-passenger coupe. The trunk is full of disc brake calipers and other essential items from a '64 Studebaker Lark Daytona V-8, whose running gear was destined to replace the venerable six-cylinder engine and existing brakes. Beside it sits a plain-jane '60 Chevy Biscayne two-door sedan which wouldn't ring anyone's bell until the hood was lifted, revealing the 348 tri-power engine. One person was busy working on a '64 Ford Galaxie 500 XL, while son Mike was underneath a Z-28 Camaro he had just traded to someone for some four-wheel ATVs, a trailer and hopefully enough cash to complete the other day-glo green Z-28 out back. For the most part, this enterprise and its inventory started out as several individual projects and just kept growing.

Wisher's Auto Recycling in Kalispell, Mont., which is listed in the back of the last edition of *Salvage Yard Treasures,* could be confusing since there are actually two lots. Wisher's #1, out of deference to the father, Clem Wisher, is located at 807 W. Wyoming St., directly behind and parallel to the northern perimeter of the fairgrounds. In business for 45 years, this site has the choicest

2

selection of pre-'64 vehicles. Not a recluse, but not what one would consider an outgoing person either, Clem more or less does things when he feels like it, and can best be described as "irascible;" so advance contact is highly recommended. This is not a "drive-in" operation with the usual business hours. A nice '60s suicide-door Lincoln and a '60 Cadillac dominate the area immediately behind the gate, while a very decent '38 Buick reposes on the lawn next to the house. The lot is readily visible from Highway 93 as one approaches downtown Kalispell from the north.

Wisher's #2 is located immediately south of Kalispell off Highway 93 about two miles beyond the Kalispell City Airport on Airport Road Southwest. Take the right branch of the "Y" immediately after passing the Buick-Jeep dealership. Size alone dictates that this site be accorded a lot of space on paper. It covers 35 acres, and while passing time until my scheduled appointment with Jerry Wisher, I opted to forgo a fifth cup of coffee and checked out the local Kalispell City Airport across the highway from the salvage yard. The previous afternoon I had noted the sailplanes activity and was intrigued. The Flathead Valley, more or less nestled between the Rocky Mountains to the east and the Salish Mountains to the west, accords some great thermals for these motorless

sailplane enthusiasts. The flight instructor, Larry Baire, who also happens to be a car addict, was not only helpful with information on other salvage yards, but suggested perhaps he could help me by letting me "hitchhike" a ride on board the glider-tug. I jumped at the opportunity, since only an aerial photo would give an idea of the vast amount of ground Wisher's #2 Auto Salvage actually covers. Off we went in a '79 Vintage Bellanca. After a 6,000-foot release of the sailplane, we jinked for a while until we knew exactly where the novice pilots were, then spiraled down where I endeavored to shoot some black and white and color shots of Wisher's #2 salvage lot. Without faster film and a larger zoom lens on hand, it may have been a futile effort, but certainly not lacking in fun. I'll have to see what sort of appreciation I can extend to Strand Aviation of Kalispell and the Glacier Eagle Soaring Club for imposing and adding 200 plus pounds of ballast to their usual climb rate.

Clem's son Jerry is a very congenial person and a well of information. He virtually grew up in the business and like most, had related hobbies with regard to restoring personal vehicles and some hobby stock cars. But it was so completely time-consuming on top of his daily yard routine that it interfered with home life, and he has it tucked

2. *"Big Sky Country," a view of the mountain pass from Bonners Ferry, Idaho.*
3. *In the resort town of Sandpoint, Idaho, the vintage tin is everywhere. This pair of beauties, a Chrysler 300 D flanked by a '55 Chevy Bel Air were a pleasant surprise awaiting me along the curb after a much needed coffee break.*

away in his "round-to-it" file as many of us do. After hiking though the length and width of Wisher's #2 with an eye on the time, I bid adieu and headed down Highway 93 about six miles, where it has a junction with Highway 82.

A left turn and a half-mile later, here is Flathead Salvage, owned and operated by Dick Lawrence, who started it back in the early '80s. While Lawrence was busy supervising the erecting of a new building, I set out to explore and use up film. Approximately six acres, his inventory starts with some late '20s and early '30s vehicles, focuses quite a bit on '40s-'50s and '60s and is partial to Ford. His hobby is racing Nostalgia Class at the 5/8-mile paved Flathead County raceway, as evidenced by the photo of his '33 Plymouth coupe. The shortage of Studebakers in the salvage lots around the area becomes evident after learning the racing group's class rules. All vehicles must be on a Studebaker Champion chassis, body is optional but leans to early '30s coupes, and engine size is limited to 300 cubic inches. This explains why '50s and '60s Studebakers are in short supply in the valley. Of particular note is the brightwork and sheet metal on vehicles in this area. I was fortunate enough to locate some nice door handles there for an acquaintance who is completing a '41 Chevy coupe.

Located about four miles south of the junction of Highway 93 and Highway 35 is another yard, Polson Auto Salvage, which features primarily Chevrolets from circa 1963 and newer. The owner, Duane Olsen, has a real bargain for the affluent collector or restorer. He wants to sell the whole operation. So, if you're a Chevy fan and salvage lot operator desirous of relocating, this might be the place.

Polson Auto Salvage,
54826 Highway 93,
Polson, Mont. 59860
406-883-6860

The next stop is Neal's Wrecking, located in the small town of Ronan, Mont., about 12 miles south of Polson. This one is not easy to locate, and one should definitely call in advance for explicit directions. He's remedying the problem by relocating to the rear of the big Cenex Service operation south of town on Highway 93, so maybe by the time this is in print, he won't be hard to find at all. A frustrating stop at a local ranch revealed it was still there, but "kids" were blamed for removing the sign which would normally let you know where to turn off Highway 211 to get there. If you are a Ford fan and need a piece for one from '50 to '66, odds are pretty good Neal has it. For his own reasons, Neal's interest switched to Mopars in '65 or '66 and his six to eight acre site is literally covered with every imaginable Mopar of that period. Many of them are of the muscle variety.

4. *This Troy, Mont. KOA Campground has more than camp sites for tourists. A nice selection of "weekend cruisers" for sale.*

The last stop before Missoula has to be Kelly's, located on your left, traveling south about one mile from the Arlee, Mont. city limits on Highway 93. Unless you're used to seeing banana-colored '67 Chevrolet Caprices pole sitting on a 25-foot-tall steel pipe, you can't miss Kelly's. Fenced and covering about 12 acres, Kelly's inventory consists of nearly every make and vintage from '63 on up, with some notable exceptions. In his shed is a restorable '39 Buick sedan keeping company with a '55 Packard Clipper and '55 Packard Patrician. There is a good selection of late '60s Olds Toronados, more Opels than I've seen in years, and lots of pickups, which is SOP for Montana, where more often than not, the first car and perhaps even the second family car is a pickup. Inside Kelly's private shop rests a '36 International pickup and a '25 Studebaker coupe, which are restoration projects of the owner. Kelly has been at the business nearly 20 years and if he doesn't have what you need, odds are he knows within a several hundred mile radius who may have what you need. While browsing through the lot, watch your step and keep your eyes peeled for a Minolta Maxxum lens shroud. It's there somewhere!

One of several conclusions I reached while making this run on what I call Phase I of the Montana outing, is that the loop involved makes an ideal trip for people from B.C. Canada who take Highway 93 south to Missoula, west to Coeur d' Alene, Idaho, and then home again up Highway 95. The same goes for people in Oregon, Washington, and Idaho doing the same tour in reverse. In addition to several excellent salvage yards for parts or complete cars, that portion of the run between Kalispell and over to Idaho is ideal for a scavenger hunt. There are more pre-'60s vehicles either by the roadside or gathered around rural farms and houses that are available than are inside the salvage yards. Inquiries proved that the majority are for sale if the searcher and seller can reach some accord.

In one case, when I stopped to take a stretch, (matter of fact, I missed a road and had my map spread across the hood and finally thought I'd better ask someone) I noted several cars and a couple of pickups parked around a barn not far off the highway, so I drove in and caught the owner tinkering with a tractor. I introduced myself, got directions and then inquired if any of the vehicles were for sale. The fellow said, "sure, any one in particular or you want all of 'em." I told him I was primarily interested in the "Old DeSoto," which incidentally happened to be a '58 Fireflite Sportsman, badly sunfaded and one tire with a square side to it. "Ain't been run in a year or so, the muffler's eaten out and the water pump rattles purty fierce, but guess we could see if it'll fire up." Since I just *happened* to have jumper cables and a spray can of starter fluid, I volunteered my assistance and backed my car over to it. After the second priming and fourth or fifth crank over, it belched and literally roared with the muffler dangling on the ground. It sounded like the pits at a hobby stock race during tune-up time. Dust flew, chickens went squawking and the dog found a sheltered spot behind a two-bottom plow. The water pump was definitely shot, but the 361 V-8 ran without missing a lick. With the brake on and a pass through the gears, everything seemed "OK" with normal amount of slop in the U-joints if the 94,000 on the odometer is accurate. The entire car is undented and unscratched except a minor door ding on the twin moldings on the passenger side. The radio, wipers and horn worked. I told him I was definitely interested and wondered if he had a price in mind. When he asked me if I thought $500 was too much, I nearly fell over. While I was pondering and mentally juggling my deficit status, he apparently assumed I was hesitating and said, "you can have it for $400." Not only a "done deal" as vernacular has it, but he's agreed to store it until I can arrange to pick it up. "Lock 'er up and leave her here long as you want, but I hope you get 'er before the snow flies again; she's real skittery on wet or snowy roads." One water pump, tire

and glasspack muffler, tool kit, gas can and trip permit, and I'll drive this one home! Certainly not a Bugatti Royale, nor an SJ Duesenberg by any stretch of the imagination, but like everyone else bitten by the bug for many years, you never know what's in that barn over yonder or down in that birch hollow where the sun glinted off a car window.

People and personalities make it worthwhile, even if the search is futile. Those I met in this part of the country, almost without exception, were warm, congenial and hospitable. Little kindnesses stick with you just like the coffee warm ups in my own mug at the minimarkets. Ten cents! Next stop, I filled my thermos and it was all of fortynine cents! In several instances, when I queried someone about a direction, location or a particular old vehicle, they stopped whatever they were doing and either made a few phone calls, drew maps, checked directories and went out of their way to be cooperative. That's hospitality and something woefully short in too many places. I knew when I reloaded my thermos at the truck stop just short of the freeway headed west, that I was back in civilization whether I wanted to be or not. "That'll be a buck 'n a half, bub." I'll give you a tip, if you've got western boots with walking or roping heels, WEAR THEM. Better yet, have a Resistol or Stetson and find a big belt buckle.

1

MEL BOWKER AUTO SALVAGE

1. *Your next Hyundai in the making. All were slated for crushing by the middle of June, 1993.*

2. *Sadly it's too late to salvage any of the trim and glass from this '52 Chevrolet Styleline Deluxe four-door.*

3. *There were about a half- dozen of these '48-'50 Ford pickups lying around. The key word here is were.*

By Doc Howell

There was a time, not long ago, in fact, when anyone in Libby, Mont. could direct you to Mel Bowker's Salvage Yard. The directions you would get would sound something like: "It's 'bout two miles out on the left on Highway two towards Kalispell—can't miss it." I guess "salvage yard" is a kindly term for what we simply called the "junkyard" when I grew up. Almost a tradition here in Libby over the years; if you wanted a lid to a pot bellied stove, rear axle from a Model A to make a trailer, old galvanized water heater to

saw in half to make watering troughs for the cows, a motor for the old soda fountain milkshake maker, or perhaps an agitator for the long outdated Maytag, Mel's was the place to come.

Unfortunately, Mel passed away in October 1992. His widow, Catherine, sold the yard to an outfit named Pioneer Auto and Wrecking. I learned this subsequent to my initial information, provided by a party from Montana in attendance at a car show in Sandpoint, the picture he painted was a long way from what I found on my arrival. Being advised of a crusher on the way, since the property had been sold, I had

visions of Marmons, Locomobiles, Stutz and maybe even a Brewster-bodied Ford becoming recycled fenders for next years Hyundais. Now my tipster—well, let's just say he'd be right at home sitting around a cracker barrel at the general store swapping fish stories. I can tell you Pioneer eventually moved in, replete with a crusher and began the cycle that takes yesterday's oldies but goodies, and makes them tomorrow's Hyundais. It's all been crushed. But my camera recorded some of the old iron that Mel Bowker had collected over the years. Like Mel himself, his yard has passed away.

2

3

4

5

4. *Last licensed in '75, this '34 Chevy pickup was obviously someone's street rod dream rig and had a 265 V-8 already installed.*

5. *Seemingly just waiting for the new owner to drive away in it, this '65 Buick LeSabre is a pretty straight arrow middleweight. As this went to press, Mrs. Catherine Bowker still had it for sale.*

6. *This old mid-'40s Federal wrecker looks like it has born many burdens. It was sold and was not crushed.*

6

YOUNG'S ENTERPRISES

By Doc Howell

As the business name implies, Dennis Young's operation just three miles East of Kalispell, Montana on Highway 2 consists of several automotive ventures including, Sales, street rod fabrication, power train swaps, Custom Body Shop, small salvage lot, and virtually anything auto related. His personal interest in automobiles which is shared by his son Michael who was beneath a nice customized blue Z/28 Camaro when I arrived. It was this car plus several others which caused me to throw out the anchor and go back to investigate Young's.

Sitting out front was a pea green '53 or '54 Studebaker Champion coupe of the plain jane variety, which appeared all original and in excellent shape, as well as a '60 Chevy Biscayne two door with a primered hood and sans any front bumper. The Stude attracted me immediately since I have a friend who has been looking for that year in a Starlite coupe, and maybe he'd compro-

mise. Dennis confirmed it was all original and viewing the trunk mat and interior eliminated any tongue-in-cheek skepticism on my part. Seeing the mat took some doing since it had a pile of '64 Stude Lark Daytona disc front brake rotors and calipers parked on top. The V-8 engine, transmission and brakes from the Lark were all slated for the

Champion coupe. What really makes even finding one of these in this area a rare event is the fact that one of the regulations governing entrees to the Nostalgia Class Racing at the Flathead County 5/8-mile track is that all vehicles must have a Studebaker Champion chassis. Any body you want and any engine as long as it is 300 CID or less.

1. *This tidy Studebaker Champion two-door coupe is original, solid and runs. It comes with an extra running gear ('64 Lark Daytona) to make a street rod or just add disc brakes.*

2. *The '60 Chevy Biscayne looks like it might have been the county librarian's or the assessor's car, till you pop the hood and check out the 348 Tri-Power sitting there.*

3. *"Lost in the '50s," this popular Bel Air hardtop isn't seen much anymore, but Dennis has an abundance of parts available to restore it.*

4. *A good supply of solid, rust-free parts for the Bel Air hardtop.*

5. *The angle of the shot conceals a crunched rear end, but this '63 Super Sport is nice enough to warrant tracking down the sheetmetal to do the job.*

3

4

This particular chassis was never noted for it's rigidity; in fact is considered somewhat more flexible than really desirable, but evidently that same flexibility on a short track is a definite advantage. I realize I'm dating myself in commenting, but when I was caught up in this sort of thing, two hunks of railroad rail with a Hudson Hornet Twin-H Power engine and a locked spider gear were the two prerequisites for bringing home the Bacon or tin cup. This car runs well, but needs TLC and

5

6

completing, as does the Biscayne. In the rather frumpy GM moss green of dubious popularity back in 1960, there is nothing from an exterior standpoint to really attract one to this vehicle other than an appreciation for seeing a 33-year-old car in such nice shape. That is until you pop the hood and take a gander at the factory-installed 348 Tri-Power beneath. All the Chevrolet specs I have at hand simply state that "the majority" of these power trains were in Impalas.

On the east side of the building below the highway embankment is another row of vintage Chevys from around '50 to '65. Out back are two '47 Cadillacs, one a sedanette and the other a four door, which together would make a nice vintage cruiser, but figure two years hard labor. In a line back next to the creek is another row of Chevys, from '52 to '64. Behind the main bldg. sits the shell of the Daytona Lark stripped

7

6. It may be a plain jane '59 Chevy, but the body on this Colorado fugitive is A-1.

7. More Chevys and a couple of Mopar products for variety. The '50s Dodge pickup doesn't appear to need much to get back into service.

8. I know many people who would buy this whole car just to get the original sun visor and bumper guards off this Chevy.

8

out to accommodate the Loewy designed '53 coupe and a rather innocuous light green '64 Biscayne two door sedan. Well, it was innocent in appearance until I spotted the 409 emblem on the front fender. In the shed, aft of the main building, are a few more surprises. Anoth'r '72 Z/28 Camaro, which I assume is Mike's next project, since he off the blue one for a car trailer, two 4WD ATVs and a hunk of change. Nearly totally hidden behind it, another rare screamer is revealed, this time a black '61 bubble top Impala with the 409 power train. Next to it, a very decent '53 Coupe de Ville in yellow with a black top is one of but four other Cadillacs available, including a '53 Eldorado Biarritz convertible. Also, about two baker's dozens of Corvairs which are available. Back inside is a '66 or '67 Corvette that needs lots of attention. By now, it was obvious that it didn't require the gleaming red and chrome 348 Tri-Power resting on the bench to convince me I was in diehard GM country. Two early to mid '40s one and one half ton Studebaker trucks complete the roundup, with nary a Ford or Mopar in sight.

Since Dennis has been at it over 20 years, I would almost bet that when Mike was about the three cornered pants age, his playpen was a big tractor tire on the shop floor when dad was bending wrenches. Here too, if something is to be found in the Flathead Valley, odds are Dennis knows where it is. A recommended stop.

9

10

9 & 10. These two vintage Cadillacs have ample parts to complete one and my bet would be on the hard-to-find sedanette.

11. A workhorse Studebaker truck. They are quite popular and prevalent in this area.

12. This '62 Bel Air hardtop doesn't appear to need much attention to get back to being a popular cruiser.

13. This Super Sport, with its nose out of the shed, will see the road again, but it sure blocks access to shooting a couple of surprises behind it.

11

12

13

1

WISHER'S #1

By Doc Howell

Out of deference to the owner, Clem Wisher, who pioneered auto salvage lots in Flathead Valley, I've dubbed his operation (45 years in this location) as number one, as opposed to the much larger operation south of Kalispell, operated by his son Jerry. Though listed in last year's *Salvage Yard Treasures*, it is not affiliated with his son's yard on Airport Road south of Kalispell: only the name and family connection have anything in common.

Wisher's #1 is located immediately north of the Kalispell Fairgrounds which is next to Highway 2 (Idaho Street) and the main east-west arterial through Kalispell's vintage downtown area. It covers approximately seven acres and is bordered on the south by W. Wyoming St. and on the north by West Colorado. The yard is highly visible as one comes in from the north on Highway 93 and glances to the right over the edge of the hill. This high visibility, particularly for incoming Canadians who travel this route with regularity, seems to be irritating to the owner who is a staunch believer in pro-

tocol. In other words, unexpected and unannounced visitors are not welcomed with open arms and a Visitors Bureau smile. This lot contains the "creme de la creme" of vintage automobiles and I sorely regret that I was not able to accord it the exposure it certainly warranted.

For reasons known only to Clem, it simply was not convenient that afternoon, nor for that matter the following morning, to tour the lot with camera gear. I did shoot a nice yellow '38 Buick which graces the lawn next to his house, an early '60s Continental and 1960 Cadillac which reposed just inside the gate. Aside from that, the depths of the lot will have to remain a mystery until another time. Without my 500MM lens, I seriously doubt that shots taken from the shoulder of Highway 93 overlooking the lot will provide much more than a teasing view of what's there. According to all of my sources, his son included, the place is full of vintage vehicles, the majority from '30 to '66.

The only "clue" I gleaned from my brief conversation with the inhospitable owner as to his obvious aloofness and irritable indifference, was that at some

time or other, someone (with a camera?) had climbed on a $250 hood and "ruint it." After leaving, I immediately made a coffee stop and availed myself of the mirror in their facilities to determine if all was in order. Nothing amiss, I then proceeded to the son's operation where inquiries revealed that yours truly wasn't treated any differently than anyone else, including his son. He commented that even he didn't have a key nor did he have any leverage with his father. "Just his cantankerous nature I guess, and it's been that way for 40 plus years that I know of," was the considered opinion I received. I have a mental picture of haggling over what a reasonable price might be, but then again, the next person just might find him with the sweetest disposition possible. If I'm willing to try again, then by all means make the effort. I suspect it would really be worthwhile.

Wisher's #1,
Clem Wisher: owner,
807 W. Wyoming St.
Kalispell, Mont. 59901
406-752-1436
Hrs.-His convenience

2

1. *Clem Wisher's seven acres through a 150MM lens from Highway 93, about a mile from Kalispell's main east/west Highway 2 junction. I should have brought a 1000MM lens!*

2. *If this yellow '38 Buick is any example of what lies inside, persistence is the key word, motivating one to keep trying for access.*

3. *The actual salvage yard starts about where the STOP sign is visible. The area just inside the gate is just a teaser.*

4. *The '62 Continental appeared intact except for wheelcovers. I would surmise by the barely visible "For Sale by Owner" signs in this car and the '60 Cadillac Coupe de Ville hidden behind the pickups, that both vehicles are in running condition.*

3

4

WISHER'S AUTO RECYCLING

(or, "Wisher's #2")

By Doc Howell

Owned and operated by Jerry Wisher and located about a mile south of the Kalispell City Airport on Airport Road SW, this has to be one of the largest single location salvage yards in the northwest. I'm aware there are yards with larger numbers, but most are not in one single location nor do they have the cars sitting individually on the ground. I recall very few "stacked" vehicles in the yard. Covering 35 acres in a series of triangles and a square, it bears a strong resemblance to the trailing edge of a stealth bomber from the air. When I first surveyed shooting this yard, it appeared a formidable task.

Thanks to the most generous hospitality of Strand Aviation and the cooperation of the Glacier Eagle Soaring Club, yours truly was able to hitchhike and do a couple of 360s around Wisher's at 1,500 feet in a Bellanca Scout used as a glider tug for the club members. By a fortunate coincidence, the glider release area is almost directly above the yard and it's no trick for the pilot to spiral down, circle the yard and effectively roll right in for his approach to the airport. With a bird's eye view, the layout of the yard became evident and helped immensely later while traversing it on foot. Since the day ended up near 80

degrees, I was relieved to had made arrangements with the owner to do the walk through early in the A.M.

Jerry Wisher, an affable, young 40-ish man, is congenial and helpful. Once into restoration and building up special vehicles, the all consuming hours created havoc on the home front, so he put the extracurricular hobby activities on the back burner for a while. The itch is there though, and from the conversation, I suspect a project or two is in mind. Since his father has been in the business over 45 years and operates what I call Wisher's #1 on the north end of town, Jerry literally grew up in the business. As near as I could tell from a head count, he has about six or eight employees and none were standing around passing the time of day. It's a busy place.

Here, as everywhere else on this Montana trek, the condition of the sheetmetal and brightwork would put rust belt sand blasters and rechroming shops out of business. No salted road rocker panel damage apparent either. Nearly all of the vehicles were bearing Montana plates and Ziebart plugs are rarely if ever seen. Another encouraging thing for people restoring drivers is that the windshields are mostly intact and not dotted with rock chips.

As the inventory sits for now, vehicles for collectors and restorers are here

and there all through the yard. Jerry plans to move all of the vintage cars to one location and sort the balance by years and manufacturer. It's a big job when you consider the number involved here and that the least damaging way is using a sling arrangement to protect rocker sills and moldings. Many yards use forklifts and invariably, the vehicle ends up with two prominent four to six-inch-square slots from the forks, which really require work to eliminate. For those into restoring old pickups, it would be simple to roll a semi flatbed into Wishers and take home a half dozen in order to complete two rigs. From the prices quoted over the phone, it appears to be a very reasonable place to shop. A productive and fun outing and now I know where to start on a couple of projects of my own as well as where to refer a number of people. Nice operation Jerry, and I appreciate your hospitality.

2

1. *Only the fence surrounding this king-sized salvage yard gives any indication of how large it really is, but an aerial shot gives a better idea.*

2. *From 1,500 feet overhead you get a bird's eye view of what 35 acres of cars looks like.*

3. *Somebody already found a front clip that will work and parked it conveniently where it belongs on this '65 Plymouth Fury convertible.*

4. *Many good parts are still on this Super Deluxe '41 Ford.*

3

4

5

6

5. *A fence partially obstructs the view to 35 acres of western Montana rust-free paradise.*

6. *Having tried finding one of these for an interested party for some time, stop and think how long it's been since you've seen another '55 Mercury two-door post sedan.*

7. *I suspect mint chrome taillight shrouds from this '58 Dodge Coronet are somewhere in the vicinity of silver on the current spot market.*

8. *Good street rod material blocking the view of a Mercury Voyager.*

7

8

9

10

11

12

13

14

9. *Excellent sheetmetal and brightwork on the '55 DeSoto Sportsman. Hemi to boot!*

10. *Limo service? This '56 Fleetwood 75 appears to be all there and surprisingly solid.*

11. *This '53 Plymouth wagon is but one of several very solid '50 to '56s dispersed here and there in the huge yard.*

12. *No apologies for the sheetmetal and trim on this '65 Galaxie.*

13. *There's no shortage of parts for early '60s Chevys in this lot.*

14. *Somebody already got the rear bumper, but there's plenty left to work with on this '64 1/2 Ford Galaxie hardtop.*

15. *More '50s by the dozens and a '48 Buick Roadmaster.*

15

16

17

18

19

16. *There are enough of these '60s -'70s Chevys in decent shape around the yard to produce half a dozen complete ones.*

17. *It needs a grille, but check out the rest of this '64 de Ville hardtop.*

18. *A perennial favorite of off-roaders with Chevy V-8 conversions, you can take your choice of several Willy's pickups and wagons.*

19. *Ever try to find parts for the eggcrate '59 Buicks? Call Wisher's.*

20

21

22

23

24

25

20. This little Rambler somehow got lost or misplaced in the pickup section.

21. Hood, trim and abundance of straight, rust-free sheetmetal makes this Chieftain a bonus for early Pontiac fans.

22. If your Christine is bent, there are several '57 to '59 Plymouths as straight as this one.

23. Over in another '50-'60s section, more spotless chrome seems to be the rule rather than the exception in this climate.

24. Skylark, Catalina Wagon, Biscayne—'50s and '60s abound.

25. This Impala won't stick around long after hitting the media even if it isn't a 409.

26. *Another Willys wagon with a solid body shell and chassis.*

27. *No national debt for '57 Chevy mouldings here. Unbelievably, not a ding or a scratch.*

28. *"J" series Chrysler 300 appears to be pretty unscathed—why not do the whole car?*

29. *Someone in Wisconsin called me for one of these and sounded desperate. Not very many '46-'48 New Yorkers are still around, so either read Cars & Parts or call me back.*

26

27

28

30

31

32

33

34

30. *For the lead sled crowd, just try finding mint rear bumpers like this in your neighborhood.*

31. *An excellent rear bumper on the '59 Coupe de Ville.*

32. *Check the rear trim on this hard to find '60 Buick.*

33. *How about a complete cab, grille and headlight rims for another favorite Ford pickup.*

34. *Another '58 from the Mopar Swept Wing era. Good parts, and check out those excellent chrome eyebrows over the headlamps. Tough to find just like the '60 Cadillac strips.*

35. *A very nice '63 de Ville hardtop with great sheetmetal and front end parts.*

35

1

FLATHEAD
SALVAGE

By Doc Howell

Six miles south of the City Airport on Highway 93 outside of Kalispell as you approach a hill, you come upon a junction with a sign indicating Highway 82 and Big Fork. Take a left on 82 and head east for approximately a half mile and you'll see Flathead Salvage on the left. Average in size, about five to six acres and tidily fenced, the inventory is anything but average. The owner, Dick Lawrence, though partial to Fords, has a potpourri of vehicles inside ranging from the late '20s to current. Business is good and Dick was busy supervising the erection of a second 60 x 100 foot steel building, so many of my questions had to be fielded by his employee who was busy minding the phone and counter. Starting from scratch in the early '80s, he canvassed the valley and bought up all the vehicles he could find. Though limited to perhaps about five percent of his inventory, the vintage section exists undoubtedly due to Dick's racing interests, plus the fact that few are kept by other yards. All of these pre-'40s have the distinctive surface rust patina, but a check of several

2

showed surprisingly solid wood in the cab portions. Several Fords of post WW II vintage have very good sheetmetal and excellent trim pieces. A couple of '41 Chevy's which provided a door handle for a collector friend of mine. Out front are several complete and running,

fair to good cars from about '46 to'69. Dick, like most in the business, is licensed for new and used cars, auto recycling, new and used parts, a 24-hr. towing service and, undoubtedly, a good measure of hobby stock fabrication. A nifty and very colorful '33

3

4

5

1. These heavyweights have trim in remarkable condition. If you're a Dagmar fan like me, you'll be pleased that no blemishes were evident.

2. Lots of good sheet metal and trim on this Ranchero.

3. Front fence of the Flathead yard serves as sales display for running vehicles and rolling stock for sale. Licensed for new and used vehicle sales, Dick's operation covers every contingency.

4 & 5. Aside from restoring, this colorful '33 Plymouth Coupe "Weekend Business Card" makes it evident where the owner's interests lie. On a Studebaker Chassis with what appears to be a 268 cid Mopar V-8.

Plymouth coupe sits out front and lets all know he's an active participant and supporter of the Flathead County nostalgia racing group. These are the culprits who make Studebaker Champion frames disappear from the marketplace, and one supports the well executed coupe. I didn't see any Studebaker Preservation Society members picketing the place, and after all, until the Avantis, Hawks and the R-2 engine appeared on the scene, Studebaker's biggest contribution to performance and racing was hauling the family to the track. Near the northwest corner of the yard rests a couple rows of '50s lead sleds, which are definitely restorable and again, I make special mention of the excellent condition of the chrome and brightwork. Take the Dagmars on the front of the Cadillacs for example, or the garish display on the '58 Olds. This yard is more or less the mecca of valley street rodders and racers and their interests are paralled

and endorsed by the owner. It's an excellent place to check for pre-'60 sheetmetal and trim or even entire vehicles, particularly Ford. Having canvassed the valley on more than one occasion for inventory and parts, Dick undoubtedly would also prove to be an invaluable source of information.

6

7

6. *This menagerie of '30s models, all potentials either for street rods or track runners, are a mixture of several brands of the era.*

7. *East fence to the rear of the Flathead yard has an interesting array of Birds, with a pretty solid '51 Victoria tucked in between styling changes.*

8. *Oops, somebody missed a Champion coupe in their search for race car parts, or maybe this one cuddled up to the Larks is Dick's back-up parts car?*

9

10

11

9. *Fords and Chevy's, from '35 to '48, all grazing in the grass and dandelions.*

10. *Bumper, fenders, hood and rear, as well as glass, in this '58, undoubtedly needs an active home elsewhere.*

11. *Nice appearing Chysler hardtop and noted in the yard a couple of back-up parts cars that would ensure longevity.*

12. *From A-Bone to '33 Chevy, '37 Chevy, and more Fords, a little brown with surface rust but no major rot.*

12

13

14

15

13. *If you're restoring any Ford up to about circa '51, this is the place to call or visit.*

14. *Very underrated car and with styling ahead of the marketplace, this '36 Chrysler Airflow just isn't seen much outside of museums and car books.*

15. *This Studebaker Commander probably owes its continued intact condition to the fact that the chassis doesn't meet the specs for the Flathead County nostalgia class which requires Champion frames only.*

16

16. *Not as sought after or as rare and valuable as the Super convertible, this '49 Buick Super sedanette isn't seen at the local laundromat every weekend either. Aside from a little corrective dental work, it appears eminently restorable.*

17. *Very good stuff on this '46 two door Ford Super Deluxe.*

18. *Like the Victoria, this '41 Chevy just happened to like this spot in between T-Birds. Very solid and with a lot of unpitted and excellent brightwork. Even the tiny chrome parking lights mounted on the sheetmetal between bumper and fenders are excellent.*

17

18

NEAL'S WRECKING

By Doc Howell

Ronan, Montana? Never heard of it! That was my original response. This small community servicing the numerous ranches in this area about 22 miles south of Flathead Lake and Polson may not be on the fashionable tour guide lists, but rest assured, there is an abundance of collectors and restorers of special interest vehicles in this neck of the woods who do know where it is. Particularly those working on '50 to '66 Fords and Mopar muscle cars from '66 to '76, and who, if given their druthers, would selfishly prefer not seeing same publicized in *Cars & Parts* or anywhere else for that matter. It was like their private parts depot. Until I had made it known I was making a "salvage ya rd tour" of western Montana and a few knowledgeable collectors aware of it alerted me, I probably would have whizzed right through this tiny ranch community and bypassed Neal's, totally unaware that I was missing one of the choicest parts sources in the northwest. Just prior to departure, a contact with a collector car auction mentioned that he needed to

give Neal Talsma a call and secure a set of seats for his '50s vintage Ford Victoria. So, it went to the top of my "to do" list.

Getting there is the tough part. If you follow instructions carefully as I thought I was, you might find it. After 30 miles of cruising back and forth on Round Butte Road looking either for evidence

of a salvage yard or any signs, and I was on the ropes. Three separate locals gave me directions and all were wrong. Actually there were four, but when that old boy waved his arm in a general southwest direction, said it was, "over yonder a piece and I couldn't miss it," I counted him out. Belatedly, I discovered the elusive Hughes Road is not five

1. This photo was taken from the back of the yard looking toward the office. It shows a good selection of Mopars from '60s and '70s with a smattering of Fords.

2. The right side of narrow lane leading to Neal's shop and office gives the visitor a hint of what lies in store with late '60s and early '70s performance cars overlooking from the bordering banks.

3. Entrance to the yard really doesn't prepare one for the contents therein. The dogleg created by the path of the stream in the bottom of the gully prevents a good view of the entire yard.

3

4
5

4. A covey of Barracudas and Dart GTs, Darts, Swingers and Demons nestled down in the blackberry bushes and teasels bordering the creek.

5. When you take a good look at the open sided shed with muscle cars and collector cars sheltered there, it's easy to see where Neal's interest lies and what the operation's focus is. The shed has two rows, eight cars in length and they are packed like sardines.

6

7

6. *Our man Neal certainly loves those Mopars, to which these Chargers testify.*

7. *The shed shelters some of Neal's "special keepers," like this '71 Charger R/T.*

8. *This '46 Plymouth coupe appeared very straight.*

9. *Chargers and Roadrunners dominate the yard's landscape.*

8

9

10. *This particular section is Ford country, but not exclusively so. I'm not certain whether the $398 price on the '64 Ford Galaxie windshield is Neal's or the former owner's.*

11. *More Fords—this solid Ranchero was one of very few vehicles I saw that was stacked. For the most part, all have their own ground space.*

12. *The remarkably straight '57 Chevy two-door sedan looks rather out of place among its yard brethren. The trim is gone, but the remainder of the 210 model has potential.*

10

11

12

miles from town, just three. There used to be a road sign, but no longer. I'll try to make it simpler. Whether entering Ronan from north or south on Highway 93, turn west on Round Butte Road at the traffic light. (Since the only stop light in that end of the country hangs over the intersection of Round Butte Road and Highway 93, I know you can't miss it.) Then go west for approximately three miles. Better yet, take the first gravel road to your left after you pass the local golf course. This road will take you south for about two miles and then curves around to the right to head due west again. When you get to the end, about another one and one half miles, you really can't miss it since it dead ends at Neal's.

I suggest you park on the main road and walk down the narrow lane to the shop building, since there is no turn-around. Mopar front and rear ends overlook the narrow lane on both sides. On your left as you near the shop, sits an open sided shed which contains two rows of about eight cars each installed sardine style. Chargers, Barracudas, Challenger RT/SEs, T/As, Darts, Swingers, Super Bees, Demons, 300s, Road Runners and a few early '50s Fords. At the end is a '54 Canadian Mercury Sun Valley. But, it appears to be all there and rust free. Another sort of lean-to shed is attached to the south end of the main shop building and contains another half dozen cars, but the only one I had eyes for was the '56 Pontiac Safari wagon clear at the rear. Adrenalin time!

Inside, you'll generally find the owner, Neal Talsma, on the phone. Neal is a younger man, perhaps in his mid-'30s who has been operating the lot for about 18 years. As with most affiliated in the salvage or wrecking business, he admits that he used to enjoy building up

13

14

15

16

18

19

13. *Here's a Torino Ranchero with Ford and Mopar backups.*

14. *Quite a few late '50s and early '60s Ford pickups, which will probably never lose their popularity.*

15. *Top row on the West bank of "Mopar Gulch" as I dubbed it, contains more than one Ford surprise.*

16 & 17. *I'd almost forgotten how "scoopy" Chrysler Corporation's cars were back in the '60s and '70s, but this inventory brings it to the forefront immediately.*

18. *I always liked the smooth styling of the '71-'72 years and this Fury III with the hidden headlamps is a solid example.*

19. *I had to shoot over the top of more Mopars just to reach a corner full of GM and Ford cars.*

20. *This is just a portion of "Mopar Gulch" and definitely more impressive when viewed in color.*

21. *Someone put some work into this Sunbeam Alpine and then stopped. I'm sure there are a lot of Tiger owners out there who'd love to have the extra panels.*

20

stock cars and bending a few fenders on the oval now and then, but he's mellowed and now his interests lean more toward restoration. I counted nearly forty cars in fair to good condition, which would make a healthy start on a retail collector car outlet. Ahead of me, he advised me he already has a new location right in town about a block off Highway 93 almost directly behind the big Cenex Service operation. There were several cars there already. All of the inventory is to be moved, and as some of the pictures reveal, they really have their work cut out for them transporting the entire inventory.

His crew of three or four, who seemed to be a congenial bunch, even younger

21

22

23

22-24. Mopars are famous for their colors from the '50s through the '70s; and the snowcapped Rockies in the background enhanced the scene.

25.-26. "Plymouth Panorama" or "Dodge Dynasty"? Look closer, the two prints are not duplicates-just hordes of similar vehicles.

27. Here are a couple of the driveables which have been transported to Neal's new location in town, one block east of Highway 93 and a quarter mile south of the only traffic light in Ronan

than Neal, were busy putting pieces together or taking others apart while another was at the new location. The phone is persistently ringing and I made my own way out through the gully and up the hill for a better vantage point, shooting as I went. Currently dabbling with some Mopars, one pass up through the small canyon area of Neal's, which covers approximately six to seven acres, and I was afflicted with a sudden wish attack. Nothing serious—just an unlimited Gold Card and three personal six to eight car carrier trucks! Ford convertibles here, T-Birds there, here a GT Dart, and then on top looking down; a veritable carpet of Mopars. There are more here than one would initially

guess simply due to the terrain and layout. The property slopes off abruptly behind the shop into a gully with a lazy little rill and forms a bowl and then curves around to the north in a dog leg fashion, so actually only about one-eighth of the inventory is visible from the lane to the shop. Chrome and brightwork on most is bright and untarnished as it was in every location visited in the Flathead Valley. Few if any bumpers exhibited the usual dings one encounters. Up here, unlike the metro areas, the people obviously don't park by sound. I don't recall seeing any appreciable sheetmetal rust or at least any that steel wool and WD-40 couldn't handle. It is evident from the inventory

that from '66 to at least '73, Chrysler products obviously dominated the market place and the muscle cars in particular. How much pilfering and vandalism prevails up in this country is something I didn't have the opportunity to ask Neal, but rest assured, a number of locations with this sort of inventory would require an electrified twelve-foot-high chain link fence, concertina wire on top and two Dobermans with a preference for two-legged rare meat of the moving type. I suspect the new location with it's proximity to the main highway is going to pose some heretofore unnecessary precautions. Possibly with such a small community, such troubles aren't the sort he need be

24

25

26

overly concerned with and I certainly hope so. On the plus side, these people all know and communicate with each other and I seriously doubt that if anyone who'd been sporting around in a slant six Dart Swinger suddenly came smoking down the road behind a 440 six-pak transplant, they wouldn't remain anonymous very long.

So, if you need anything Ford or Mopar within the years listed, give Neal a jingle. From what I saw, I can assure you he'll be shipping top notch used parts compared to numerous other locations I've visited.

27

**Neal's Wrecking,
Neal Talsma: owner,
4300 Songer Road,
Ronan, Mont. 59864**
406-676-8111 or 676-8112,
Hrs. Mon.-Sat. 9 am to 6 pm

1

KELLY AUTO SALVAGE

2

By Doc Howell

Arlee, Mont. is another small community about 23 miles north of Missoula on Highway 93, you might unwittingly zip past Kelly's salvage yard while gawking at the beautiful scenery, were it not for Kelly's unique sign. It isn't every day you see a complete banana yellow '67 Chevy Caprice sedan roosting atop a 25-foot steel pole. Though intact, it isn't nearly as attractive as his wife's beautifully restored '69 Chevelle SS 396 sport sedan which, though exhibiting a "For Sale" sign, is sort of an off again, on again proposition. For the size of the community this is a big yard, my first guess would be twelve to fifteen acres, but Kelly services quite an area with his tow trucks. In fact, he was on a wrecker call when I arrived. I made myself at home as per our prearranged phone calls. Kelly is definitely into restoration when time permits. Inside the tidy shop sits a '25 Studebaker coupe and a '36 IHC pickup,

3

4

5

6

1. With the Rockies in the background, Kelly's headquarters conceals a nifty '25 Studebaker opera coupe and a '36 IHC pickup which are his ongoing restoration projects.

2. A pair of vintage Ford pickups, and if memory serves me correctly, a box for the '40 was over near a fence.

3. A colorful and stodgy pair of '55 Packards relunctantly share the building with the shadowy '39 Buick.

4. Surprised to see a decent solid little Olds F-85. Most and its cousins the small Buicks had the aluminum V-8's pirated and the rest discarded.

5. Termites really did a number on this '46 Ford Woodie, but the metal parts don't even show teeth marks.

6. Two long rows of these Mavericks and Mercury Comet sisters in both six and V-8.

7

8

7. *More of the Ford part of the pasture, ranging from '59 to '73.*

8. *Too many Ford pickups to count. In this country, they have priority over passenger cars.*

9. *This '65 Merc has a lot of great parts left, despite some early bird grabbing the ever vulnerable fender end parking lamps.*

10. *At one of the yards back up the road, there was a twin to this one that sorely needed this excellent grille.*

11. *Trim on this Seneca wagon is A-1, but as you can see, the left taillight assembly already has a new home.*

12. *Looking as if it's ready to haul the '33-'34 IHC pickup pieces on the back off to the resto shop, this remarkably intact old '36 cornbinder looks like it could still haul it's share of hay.*

13. *Check the trim and option pieces on this '49 Olds and '40 Plymouth. Back then, sunshades and visors served in lieu of tinted glass. Both were solid.*

both under long term restoration. Across the drive and under another open ended steel building are three more likely subjects for the same treatment, but Kelly said these were for sale: A '39 Buick sedan, a ''55 Packard Clipper and a '55 Packard Patrician. Of the three, the Buick obviously needed the most attention, but was still a long way from being a rust bucket write-off. Actually, the Packards appeared capable of being fired up and driven out.

L-shaped, the large lot contains approximately 1,500 vehicles, of which about one third are '69 and older. The section north of the house and shop has an abundance of Ford and Chevy pick-ups of late '50s-'60s vintage

along with assorted pre-'60s vehicles, as well as acres of straight, nearly rust free sheetmetal and again, pristine brightwork. As you hike around through the orderly rows of vehicles, you'll see complete sections devoted to different makes. The northeast corner of the eastern portion of the lot is reserved for GM's heavies, from early '60s Cads to several late '60s Toronados. In the center is Mopar, and the south side is devoted to AMC. The southwest corner of this section could best be described as the "International Section" and contains one of the largest assortments of Opels I've run across in several years, from GT's, Manta's to wagons, another row has earlier

Datsuns with Z cars, and the cute little 1100 coupes and Toyotas. Here and there, an oddity sticks out, like a rather battered '55 Mercury Monterey which still has a lot of good pieces, and an older FC-150 Jeep pickup which isn't seen much anymore. Kelly does have some older vintage chassis and body parts here and there, but without his capable assistance, I wouldn't even venture a guess to the make or year. I would say overall that the yard is predominently GM and mostly Chevrolet with Ford running a distant third. Not so many years ago, this was the favorite hunting grounds for the Missoulans to find mid-'50s vehicles for their street rods. Those same '50s cars being of

9

10

11

12

13

14

14. *This is AMC country and there are quite a few examples available.*

15. *Two rows of very decent '50s Chevy pickups with surprisingly good fenders, hoods, cabs, trim and glass.*

16. *Heavies monopolize this corner of the east end of the yard. This photo shows how good the trim and sheetmetal really are.*

17. *One corner and side is imports, but look at the Opels! GT on top won't last long after any street rodders spot it. Also, several cute Datsun 1100 coupes, some Zs and older Toyotas.*

15

finite supply and getting more expensive by the day, interest has progressed to the '60s models.

As this is the final stop on a trek that has covered the Flathead Valley, it is interesting to note that virtually none of the yards or operations visited even bother with any of the '80s models. The consensus is they simply are too expensive to attempt repairing or restoring, once hit, the damage is generally so extensive, their greatest worth is in an intact engine or a completely intact front or rear "clip" and relegate the rest to the crusher and smelter. About the only exception to this evident anywhere,

16

17

18

19

20

18. *Still a lot of good parts on this '55 Mercury Montclair. Just don't count on a front end.*

19. *Where else can you find immaculate front ends and hub caps like this '69 Cadillac is sporting?*

20. *This is pickup country and it always surprises me to find so many solid hoods and fenders like the ones on these '60 C-10 and '64 C-10 Chevys.*

21. *The engines in these old Chevys have fell silent, in harmony with the peaceful countryside.*

22. *Venerable Ford coupe has seen better days, but it is all supposed to be on board here.*

23. *Here's a find for those fans of the '70 Gran Prix Pontiacs. Check the trim on this one.*

21

22

23

was later model light trucks and some of the downsized 4 x 4's. The interest and activity in the '70s models hasn't hit its stride yet, but with the emphasis on "disposable" everything, their turn is coming along with perhaps the end of the "shadetree" mechanic and rebuilder era.

24

25

26

27

28

30

24. *From the number of cars on hand, it's pretty obvious that the Falcon and Comet specialty stores haven't visited here yet.*

25. *All Chevelles and the popular models and years.*

26. *Purists always seem to favor the '56 Ford pickup, but this '55 looks as if it could fire up and go home with someone who might have a '56 grille and not be so fussy.*

27. *Old Willys pickups like these never seem to go away or die. They sorta hang around and wait for someone who appreciates them.*

28. *Studebaker trucks from the '40s and '50s were very popular ranch rig workhorses in Post WW II days.*

29. *This '40-'41 Buick is loaded with good parts.*

30. *Unfortunately for the Hudson fans, this Terraplane really doesn't have much to offer other than some body parts and a chassis.*

31. *Last but not least, several '66 to '72 Oldsmobile Toronados share some of the Cadillac corner of the east end.*

32. *How much did you say you paid for '56 Chevy side trim?*

33. *I don't know anyone anxious for the half-an-ambulance in the background, but I know of several '60 Buick folk who would sure appreciate knowing about this smoothie.*

31

32

33

SALVAGE YARD TOUR:
WESTERN MONTANA
Phase II

By Doc Howell

O n the first leg of this tour to bring collectors and restorers a first hand report on some of the various yards and the restorable contents that await them in Western Montana, the biggest single distraction in the area covered was the scenery. On this leg, it was definitely water and fishing. With one eye on the road and the other checking pools and riffles in the Clark Fork River, the Bitterroot River and lastly, the Shalhako River wending its way toward Hamilton to join the Bitterroot, I discovered I've developed a semi-permanent kink in my neck along with a spastic tic in one arm that suspiciously resembles the twitch used in casting with my graphite rod. The water looks so good, my imagination even convinces me that I can hear the Rainbows and German Browns challenging me. I'm certain any self-respecting analyst would advocate purging myself of these repressed and craven desires and it sure sounds like a plan to me, but the only one I know said he'd insist upon accompanying me to conduct a first hand field "clinical study!" Now I know why I call him "slick."

Again, I can't overemphasize the hospitality and courtesy extended by the people in this part of the state, and I don't mean the artificial and carnivorous sort usually associated with hotshot stereotyped Los Angeles auto salesmen. I even received a citation for exceeding the daytime speed limit from a gracious lady trooper who obviously attended a Montana Charm school. I was so impressed, I think the state should add a decal to the door reading "Hospitality Greeter, Hostess" or some such. Having missed a rest stop on top of the pass coming down into the Bitterroot valley, I was urgently looking for-

ward to the next available convenience stop and let the needle creep up to 80. Not hard to do on Highway 90, which I'm sure was partially engineered by a Gran Prix driver. I suspect had I been driving something on the lines of what I used to in SCCA days of yore, the citation might well have been for a substantially greater velocity since even a vintage Austin-Healey could manage every curve between Coeur d' Alene, Idaho and Missoula, Mont. at over 100 MPH quite comfortably with no coffee spillage or any tire squealing. But, at the end of a long sweeping curve just west of Frenchville, the lady trooper was parked in the median strip taking my picture and one glance at the speedo had me flicking on my signal lights for a gradual pull over. Though I may have slightly exaggerated when I pantomimed my distress, she understood immediately, gave me directions and followed me to where I completed my distress call. Gratefully, I accepted my citation and paid my $5 bail forfeiture. I can name you several places where you would have ended up spread eagle across your car for lesser offenses. I sincerely thanked her, and proceeded to keep a date with Otis Gilliland, or "Gil" at Medicine Bow Motors in South Missoula.

Having called in advance, Gil allocated time to conduct me on a guided tour of Medicine Bow Motors. Outwardly, the premises, with the rustic building and rough high fence was quite reminiscent of a frontier fort and in keeping with the locale. Some of the names, excuse me, "handles" people attach to various things around here, like the "Stagger Inn," "Critter Way," and several other colorful titles, all somehow seem to fit. Medicine Bow specializes in

1. *This view looks abit like a step backward in time. Medicine Bow has been around quite awhile.*

vintage Ford parts (a few Chevys too) from day one with Henry to about 1948. The Hershey brown patina of surface rust on most of the vehicles comes as no surprise, given their vintage and exposure to the elements. Since the Bitterroot River forms the rear boundary of the roughly two and one half acres, nocturnal hub cap snatching is best done by a Zodiac with an electric motor. Despite the proximity of the river, there was very little rot through on any of the visible sheetmetal. As Gil commented with regard to rust, "we never get enough rain and we're too poor to salt the roads." We made one quick tour and then did another with cameras, escorted by the yard's vicious attack cat. Insurance forbids the use of Rottweilers, Dobermans, German Police dogs and Pit Bulls, so this cat serves duty with its throaty murmurs which reminded me of a Chris Craft rumbling away at idle in the water. This cat has a motor and a half!

Some really hard-to-find parts and trim items are there and it's evident that not too much has been added to the vintage Ford inventory recently. Gil concedes that more sheet metal, rather than mechanical parts, comprises the bulk of his orders and mostly from professional restorers and street rod builders. Despite an abundant supply of flathead engines, sales of steel fenders, running boards, doors, etc., to fit '30s vintage vehicles, along with radiator shells and trim items, comprise the majority of the business. Active and enthusiastic at

retirement age, the pace suits Gil, who is comfortable with it. Gil came west to Montana back in the mid-'80s after thirty plus years with Boeing in Kansas; he discovered that all of the U.S. was not flat and seems to have no regrets. His interest in old cars seems to have been acquired by osmosis from his brother who has an Auburn-Cord-Duesenberg Restoration Service back in Kansas. I suspect Gil might even be able to accommodate you with a phone number for his brother if you need information or parts on the marques in which he specializes.

Gil's neighbor, Michael Earbolies, who owns the yard next door, specializes in Chevy parts from '48 to about '66. The business name of his operation is the Hare & Tortoise, 406-251-2502, just in case you need a part and on the outside chance that he might answer the phone. Definitely not a publicity hound, I could not even locate a listing in either the white or yellow pages of the two-year--old Missoula directory I keep in the office. Indifferent and aloof is the fairest description I can give, considering the brief personal contact, and I suspect the low profile sign gracing the entrance to the fenced yard is but a token observance of commercial zoning laws for the area. I definitely came away with the feeling that it is his personal hobbyist endeavor and he isn't the least bit interested in promoting his business or furthering other hobbyist's or restorer's activities and interests. Chances are, he would probably prefer

any location other than this busy stretch of Highway 93 on the southern outskirts of Missoula. But back in the mid-'80s, when the former salvage yard which included this inventory and Medicine Bow Motors was up for bankruptcy liquidation, he and Gil agreed to purchase the halves they currently operate. What with various ordinances, the EPA, property values, grandfather clauses etc., it may not be feasible or practical to relocate to a more isolated and less public location. I have been assured that his inventory does contain some very desirable pieces. Perhaps if this reticent owner takes a liking to you or he's in need of half a beef, he might be amenable to dealing on a nice '55 or '56 Chevy bumper or grille.

From Missoula, following up on leads, rumors and hearsay provided by vintage auto clubs and hobbyists, I aimed the hood ornament on the "whale" south towards Hamilton, Mont., and two pleasant surprises. If activity on both sides of the highway between Stevensville and Hamilton is any indication, everyone here is in the log home building business. Every size, shape and style imaginable taking its prefabbed shape in the numerous production lots. Whether in these assembly lots or on a homesite, they appear to belong to the landscape and environment. Driving through Hamilton is a treat. Like many frontier towns of old, the streets are very wide and leave room for three or four lanes of traffic with diagonal parking yet! Harking back to frontier times, this made sense since, with mostly false fronted wooden buildings at the time, a fire with a tail wind then had a hard time jumping the wide avenues and destroying the whole town. Too, it left ample room for herds of cattle to move through town without intruding up onto the boardwalks which usually fronted the buildings along with hitching rails. Latter day "cruising" could get spendy in Hamilton since the main thoroughfare,

Highway 93 or "First Street," is several miles long. And speaking of gasoline, I couldn't get a straight answer from anyone in the area why it should be higher in Montana where it is refined, than it is 204 miles away in Coeur d' Alene. Average for regular seemed to be about $1.20 as opposed to $1.08 to $1.11. Too, for some reason the regular is higher than the unleaded.

Continuing through town to a junction three miles south of Hamilton, where state Highway 43, or "Skalkaho Highway," branches off to head East to locate my next stop. The trick here is to keep one eye on the road and the other on mail boxes since I'm looking for box number 1195. Either very thoughful residents or a training ground for U.S. Postal Service rural carriers, since all of the boxes are prominently numbered. Eight miles east of the junction, I arrive at the little eden that Marshall and Polly Sanders call home. It is an idyllic spot on the bank of the Skalkaho River which parallels the highway and lends the road its name. Little is really visible from the road, and only after entering the gate does one benefit from the idyllic retreat they have created. First thing you see is a three car open garage with vintage cars and another to the right, then a lovely garden with a pre-pie rhubarb plant nearly dominating the vintage gas pump bordering the drive. Then two vintage restored Model A trucks, and behind them, a small rustic building with a sign reading "Marshallville" below the eaves, which contains a complete model railroader's dream with a Kalamazoo number one, an H.O. gauge and another. To the right, a unique motor home which looked vaguely familiar and rightly so, since it started out life as a 1946 Spartan house trailer; the lightest and most aerodynamic trailer of its time. On closer examination, it is something else. My host, a congenial silver haired and affable gentleman with twenty-one years experience with Ford

3. *Medicine Bow has cars, that once upon a time, may have been called heaps. That's while they were still running. When they quit running, they are stacked in heaps..*

Engineering in Detroit before he hung it up, converted this trailer to an Olds Toronado front drive powertrain custom motorhome and had the bugs worked out before GM introduced its fiberglass coach. Ironically, GM sent a couple of engineers out to study how Marshall had overcome some steering anomalies they encountered. With all the current electronic amenities, this hybrid can very casually exceed all the legal speed limits in comfort and microwave some mesquite chicken while doing it to the strains of Debussy over the sound system. With so much to absorb, I neglected to ask him how he managed to stretch the '68 Pontiac grille to accomodate the extra width, but given the fact that he'd already mentioned handmaking the grille for the '34 Dodge from stainless, I assume cutting, splicing and rechroming the bumper was a piece of cake by comparison. The restoration shop/residence combination is unique. Patterned after New England-style barns and even with the door latches duplicated and handcrafted from photos, it is a work of art and obviously a labor of love. The couple lives upstairs, while the complete restoration shop occupies the ground level. Currently, the shop houses a rare yellow and black '57 Dodge D-500 convertible and an even rarer '34 Dodge humpback, both nearing completion. Next to the house, naturally stands a small silo which houses the circular stairway to the "hayloft" residence. Originally an open, circular stairway, Montana winters dictated the silo enclosure. To the west of the house is another long shed and open area which contains his micro salvage and collector yard, none of which is visible either from the highway or the driveway. Led to believe initially that there was a "whole pasture" full of restorable vehicles constituting at least a mini-salvage yard on the order of Medicine Bow Motors, I arbitrarily reclassified it as a micro only due to the numbers. The quality and type of vehicles which are definitely restorable raises the interest factor well

above that of many lots with 10 times the space and number of vehicles. Here a '46 Mercury coupe, a '64 Lark Daytona with the rare sunroof, behind the fence a '40 Studebaker Commander, a '47 Ford two door, a Silver Hawk Studebaker in the corner (sorry it's sold) and an abundance of parts. Marshall, at this time, is only interested in one more restoration project, that being a Studebaker Golden Hawk his wife admires and would enjoy having. If you have one to spare, or if you want some select vehicles, some parts, or good technical expertise on orphan vehicles as well as street rods, here's a unique source. Marshall takes his '34 Plymouth coupe with the full race 360 V-8 to local car and club outingss behind his '38 Studebaker five-ton shortened and customized cabover truck powered by a full race Avanti V-8. Wanna race? At 72 years young, Marshall personifies and reflects the perennial youth factor that all of the dedicated car addicts I've known or met seem to have. If it isn't there, something is missing. Anyway, some are not for sale, like the '38 Studebaker coupe pickup express or the '70 Hurst 300 sitting quietly in the corner, which he's owned since it was but 6 mos. old.

Using the hand drawn map and information graciously provided by Mr. Sanders, I backtracked to Hamilton and turned left on Main Street, traveled west across the bridge over the Bitterroot River and turned North on Ricketts Road in search of Allan Dutton and a supposed treasure trove of restorable Cadillacs and parts cars. The number given in the phone directory just happened to be a pasture, so I backtracked and asked someone in the neighborhood. Seems someone in their infinite wisdom opted to renumber all the residences and what was number 187 is now number 179. From the street, there was no indication of the many vehicles reported to be there. I knocked and introduced myself to the congenial gentleman who answered the door and after a brief conversation he took me in tow to the

4. *Here's a plum waiting to be plucked: a '46 Ford that appears complete down to the hubcaps.*

5. *The Marshallville cache includes a '46 Studebaker.*

6. *Dutton's enormous shed looms like a cave laden with "buried" automotive treasure. One needs only to plumb its depths to find that lost "gem."*

4

rear of his house and started opening shed doors. The innocent sheds concealed everything from a 1917 Dodge Roadster, and '11 or '12 Brass Ts, to a '60 Eldorado Biarritz convertible, '62 T-Bird convertible, '62 Eldorado convertible, '60 T-Bird coupe and more. Through this building, we exited a back door which exposed an even larger steel building and up went that door. Again, filled with vintagee cars, with the first on hand being a very nicely restored '34 Ford Deluxe two door and more

Cadillacs. Behind this building, a long, open faced storage building, again with nearly all Cadillacs. As we got closer, I realized these were double rows, from, '53 to '63 with an occasional '64 and '66 thrown in for good measure. Rear fence to the west, south and east of the lot was lined with vehicles and more in the middle for good measure and again, nearly all Cadillacs. The other end of the lot had its share of Mustang parts cars and complete restorable '50s vintage Fords. All tallied, something like

6

160-170 cars, only two dozen of which could really be considered parts cars. Most of the finned-era Cadillacs appeared as if a jump start and windshield wash would see you on your way. More '59's and '60's than any lead sled addict could dream of finding in one spot. I simply had to dash back out and grab a flash unit, though I'm certain only studio type lighting would do the covered cars justice. Maybe readers will at least get an inkling of what is here. Allan indicated that of all those present, he is only considering restoring the '60 Biarritz convertible, the '62 T-Bird convertible and one of the '53s, "but if someone wants them worse than I do, I may reconsider." A '54 DeVille convertible is currently under restoration in another separate smaller building. Virtually all the rest are for sale and unless a parts vehicle to start with, he's only interested in selling complete units. With my interest in big old Caddies, a winning lottery ticket would find me sitting impatiently in front of his house with a convoy truck capable of carrying eight vehicles! Really has to be seen to be believed and preserve the pictures since the "greenies" would dearly love to eradicate even such hidden scenes from our landscape and history. Allan has been dabbling with cars since he was fifteen and got serious about get-

ting as many of these vintage models as possible about twenty plus years ago when he acquired the extra property behind him, so my guess puts him in his mid-'50s. Refurbishing a number of homes he has acquired keeps him rather busy and certainly too much so to ever consider doing all of his vehicles, but he assured me he's usually around, so it is first come-first served! If you've always wanted a big '50s or '60s Cadillac, better grab the phone and call. Or better yet, just hook up the car trailer and go for it. There has to be one or more that will fit your dream and pocketbook, but just for proprieties sake, call first when you arrive in town. I checked with the Cadillac dealer and two parts houses on my first pass through town and nobody knew anyone with a collection of old Cadillacs!

Thus ends Phase II of the Montana tour. "Whale"" shows the wear and my tail lets me know I've been down the road. But given the pleasure of meeting so many nice people and seeing so many vehicles relegates any physical discomfort to passing afterthoughts.

MEDICINE BOW MOTORS

1

By Doc Howell

Other than the dark brown 12 foot wood fence on the southern outskirts of Missoula, Mont., Medicine Bow Motors bears little resemblance to the average salvage yard. Decidedly rustic, the layout has a fleeting resemblance to some of the rustic frontier forts which dotted the landscape in the Montana Territory a little over a century ago. I have no doubt that the architects had that association in mind, but they dropped the ball and should have used 4 or 6-inch diameter pointed poles rather than flat-milled lumber to give it more impact. Only the king sized blue and white vintage script Ford V-8 trademark and the sign indicate any automotive association. Once inside the gate, which leads to the office, you're subjected to a nostalgia assault. The rear wall of the fence is covered with radiator shells and grilles from '20s and '30s vehicles as is the north wall of the building. A handful of colorful Camaros, Firebirds, a 50's Packard, and what once was obviously a show car '55

2

1. Not much doubt when approaching Medicine Bow Motor's location that you may have found the place for your vintage Ford parts. Architect had fun lending a "Frontier Fort" air to the rustic building.

2. Another view giving a better idea of the scope of Medicine Bow's operation, which is probably the neatest and tidiest of any the writer has had the pleasure of visiting.

3. An assortment of 20's and 30's doors along with wheel covers, and other parts awaits a lift upstairs to the "premium loft."

4. The owner, Otis "Gil" Gilliland shows off a '37 Ford grille, just a sample of one of the many pristine parts he has available.

3

4

Chevy parked just inside the gate strikes a rather discordant note. A little out of place, given the main forte of the dedicated salvage yard, but it is after all, a salvage yard and it still has to pay the overhead.

The owner, Otis "Gil" Gilliland, who rescued this half of the original operation back in the mid '80s when all was under the hammer on a bankruptcy sale, probably put more than a few miles on '30s vintage cars in his youth, but is in a spritely, active number two condition compared to the number six-parts cars in the yard. After 30 some years with Boeing Aircraft at their Kansas operation, Gil opted for the "Go West young man" advice and seems quite content with the change.

The "lobby" of the building is literally crammed with small, hard-to-find original trim parts, and glass cases hold a variety of original emblems, whose scarcity has created an active replica industry. The office is to the right rear and the split log staircase goes up to a loft loaded with premium rust-free parts; doors, bumpers, window frames, headlamps, grilles, etc. Through a doorway, one enters what once was a proprietary restoration shop, but now is leased out to a young fellow who is industriously working on a yellow Packard 110 sedan for a local customer. Outside to the rear of the main building, a roof and rear wall cover an area between the main building and a couple of storage buildings which provide cover for a number of complete flathead V-8s. Overhead, a loft area provides storage for hinged hoods in better condition than those in the yard. The first storage building contains an unfinished '35 Ford coupe, which really doesn't have that much left to go and another early '30s or late '29 coupe. No longer in the restoration business, Gil said these were available for sale.

Only 2.3 acres in size, stacking of body shells is the solution, but all are in somewhat orderly fashion. For the most part, all of the sheetmetal appears to be solid and a light sand blasting away from priming. This would definitely be

the place for someone not wanting a '29 to '32 roadster or coupe with a glass body, but obviously a lot of work involved. Piles of axles and differentials, bare frames, fenders, doors—it's all here. Though dedicated in the sense that the primary emphasis is on Fords to 1948, there are also several early and mid '30s Chevys and Dodge and Plymouth body shells evident. For original parts for older cars, Gil has the supply and a call will usually find the crank handle for that '37 Deluxe, the headlamp cross bar for that '28 Phaeton or the right rear door for the '31 Model A four door.

Gil maintains regular office hours from 8:30 AM to 6 PM and Saturdays by appointment. He offers mail order and is always happy to tour the yard with customers.

Footnote: Just before press time, Otis Gilliland sold Medicine Bow Motors. The new owners are Charles and Candi Jerke. The restoration end of the business is being revived and the inventory entered on a computer.

**Medicine Bow Motors,
5120 Highway 93
So. Missoula, Mont. 59801,
406-251-2244**

5

7

8

9

5. *Missing a radiator shell for your classic or street rod? Just give Gil a call and let him know how many to ship and where. You'll also note a substantial quantity of radiators as well.*

6. *Looking northeast from the gate area, you soon get an idea of just how many Fords and a few Chevys, Dodges and Plymouths really are out in this yard. Actually, three to four deep in places.*

7. *This '28 Model A two door in the center, having reached the top of the pile, more or less rules the roost so to speak, but probably not for long after some street rodder or restorer spots it.*

8. *Hated to mention it to Gil, but this '33 pickup bears a remarkable resemblance to the old "Dodge Brothers" we used to have back on the ranch when I was in short pants.*

9. *This is Gil's vicious attack cat, hired as a stand-in since Dobermans, Pit-bulls, and such are proscribed by Gil's underwriters. I understand he reads Garfield religiously every morning before he gets his Friskies.*

10. *Makes it rather nice not to need a back fence due to having the Bitterroot River at the rear door, and just guess what I'd be having for lunch every day courtesy of Browning or Fenwick?*

10

11

11. Peeled logs, a stairway cut from quarters of twelve-inch logs enhance the rustic fort appearance inside. Cases all contain cloissane and a many hued variety of vintage auto emblems and every conceivable square foot available has something hanging, sitting or leaning on it. The loft up the stairway to the left contains several truck loads of premium items like grille shells, bumpers and any choice pieces to accord dry storage and avoid any further weathering.

12

13

14

12. *Another big pile of '20s and '30s body shells and an abundance of '35 and '36 doors which most will recognize.*

13. *Well on the way towards completion, this '35 Ford coupe is for sale "as is" along with the "A" Model in the background since they no longer do restorations and those facilities have been leased out to a younger fellow.*

14. *Along with axles, wishbones and all sorts of hard-to-find parts, sits an even harder item to find, a "steel" roadster body. Hmmm, some Candy Apple Red paint, a chassis with a powertrain, where will this end up?*

15. *Axles? Well, since we look like a fort anyway, let's just stack them back by the fence "musket style" with the splined ends up.*

16. *No shortage of vintage wire wheels around here. Sandblast, paint and let's get them rolling again.*

17. *If you're one of those unfortunate enough to have a family member with the bad habit of parking by "sound," maybe you should consider having a couple of spare front fenders handy for replacement. Just give them a call.*

15

16

17

1

2

1. *This is the first view one gets when driving into Marshall Sanders' little eden on the bank of the Shalkaho River south of Hamilton, Mont. toward the tortured landscape of Anaconda, Mont. The yellow '34 Plymouth on the right has a rather surprising full-race 360 V-8 under the hood. A mint '58 Crown Imperial coupe is for sale or swap, a '69 AMC AMX with the 'big bad' 390 optional engine isn't for sale nor is the gorgeous '41 Studebaker Commander sedan.*

2. *Owner, Marshall Sanders takes a break from being tour guide for the writer and scans through the last edition of "Salvage Yard Treasures." The Model A truck belongs to a friend for whom Marshall did some work. The house is a handbuilt log one patterned somewhat after New England barns and is a delight.*

3. *Over the red "A" pickup's hood can be seen the silo which artfully conceals the circular stairway to the residence second floor of the "barn." The hand-made latch handles were copied from photos of historical buildings. To the rear of the stairway silo, one can see the Skalkaho River or Marshall's potential "Breakfast Bar." Though he concedes he's not much of a fisherman, the stream is loaded with rainbows.*

MARSHALLVILLE

By Doc Howell

Marshallville is as much a state of mind as it is a real place. The name, after the owner Marshall Sanders, graces the front of his personal railroad station which contains several miniature electric trains which would be the envy of any railroad nut. Given the manner in which the owner does everything else, trust me, it's a confident understatement, despite not having investigated in detail.

A dedicated car addict, tinkerer, hot-rodder of the '50s persuasion, inventor, restorer, gardener, his activities belie his 72 years, and I envy his little touch of eden on the bank of the Shalkaho River. He has a small number of complete running vehicles, cars under construction amd restoration, restorables for sale, some parts and parts vehicles for sale, and maybe even a couple for horsetrading. Given his Ford engineering background and having witnessed some of his handiwork, there is very little I would question with regard to what he has done or what he may endeavor to accomplish where cars are concerned.

When complete, the two Dodges currently in his restoration shop will be most certainly either in excellent or show condition or better. The yellow and black '57 Dodge D-500 convertible is rare enough, but the '34 humpback virtually doesn't exist anymore. My father drove an identical one until 1948 when new vehicles were no longer available on an "under the table only" basis, but it gave good service for many years.

Marshall is cleaning house at his "micro yard" and he has several interesting vehicles, which many collectors

3

4

5

6

7

4. This Stude Starline coupe has been "tweaked" in Marshall style. An avowed hot-rodder, Marshall's 20 plus years with Ford Engineering stand him in good stead despite his enchantment with Studebaker and Mopar vehicles.

5. Not too many '57Cs around as straight as this outside of collections, but this one is for sale if the man from Utah changed his mind or didn't show up. The Charger with its tail hanging out is a 383 version and very restorable.

6. I thought this was a '64 Corvair van with another of the same grafted on the tail end and a Stude Daytona Lark nose job. I suspect when finished, it will probably be powered by a 289 Stude engine, one of Marshall's favorites, and be a really unique tow vehicle for hauling his show cars to events. More than Polly's rhubarb-apple or strawberry pie, I want a picture of this when

complete and a detailed report.

7. The building behind the Model A trucks is the "Marshallville" railroad depot. The contents would drive any electric railroader bananas.

8

10

8. *The place is landscaped with vintage automotive memorabilia including this glass topped hand gas pump. With a Marshall custom touch, it has become a driveway lamp. Check that rhubarb!!*

9. *Here's an overview of the garden showing one of the storage buildings and a glimpse of a Marshall original — a Toronado powered motor home built a couple years before GM got around to it.*

10. *With "A Dream" custom license plate, I'm sure it was back when it was fabricated from the original 1946 aluminum trailer home. Novel application of the '68 Bonneville grille and bumper combo, but haven't quite figured out what rear bumper contributed to the extensions. Capable of cruising at 90 plus, this unique bit of engineering brought GM out to study how he overcame torque steer and other steering*

11

and restorers are seeking, in as solid condition as these. He admits he would like to find and redo a restorable Studebaker Golden Hawk and might even be amenable to accepting a decent '57 or '58 Plymouth or Dodge in trade for the impressive '58 Chrysler Crown Imperial hardtop coupe shown in one of the photos. The '40 Studebaker Commander partially hidden behind the fence could be a real find as either a parts car or a restorable for some. One desirable Studebaker Lark Daytona with the retractable sun roof is very rare anymore and this one has only 50K

original miles. Several seen in the photos aren't for sale unless he has a sudden change of heart, but the '70 Hurst 300 and the AMC muscle car next to the Crown Imperial should make more than a few antsy and hopeful that change materializes. Very knowledgeable regarding Studebaker and Mopars, Marshall would be a recommended source of restoration advice and information on vehicles or parts even if he doesn't have what you need.

A gracious host and a pleasure to talk to, I'm certain he will welcome your calls. Being quite partial to "orphan"

and niche performance vehicles, I'm certain he can spare some pertinent information of interest. Though I neglected to ask what was going to power the unique custom Corvair pickup seen with the Studebaker Lark grille I'm sure it will be awesome when complete.

**Marshall Sanders,
Box 1195 Shalkaho Highway,
Hamilton, Mont. 59840
406-363-5328**

anomalies which with they were stumped.

11. *Now for rarity, try a '38 Studebaker coupe express! Everything forward of the cabs' rear window was '38 Studebaker Commander Model 37A with a double-walled 16 ga. all steel pickup box on the back. Dual sidemount spares were generally only seen on the top of the line President sedan, and due to a shorter front end and restyled front fenders, these spares sat higher than previous models. And you always thought the Ford Ranchero was an original idea.*

12. *Another surprise is Marshall's car hauler truck which usually tows the full-race '34 Plymouth to events. A shortened five-ton "pug-nose" '38 Studebaker truck with many unique features, such as the handfinished and clearcoated hardwood bed. I'm sure whizzing up Montana hills past some really baffled motorists, with the full-race, punched-out Avanti V-8 purring through dual chrome stacks has sent more than one tyro scrambling for their car books. A show stopper at any event.*

13. *Obviously needing some dental work up front and a bumper, this '46 Mercury coupe is a born street rod just looking for an owner.*

14. *The '49 Studebaker is all there and certainly would prove to be a very rare piece for any show.*

15. *This '63 Lark Daytona coupe in very good shape is a rare bird. The total production for two-door hardtops, both 6 and V-8, was less than 4,000.*

13

14

15

1

DUTTON'S RESTORABLES

By Doc Howell

No signs, no 12-foot fences, unknown to most of the residents and even many of the commercial automotive businesses like parts and paint stores, Allan Dutton maintains a rather low profile in the southwest city of Hamilton, Mont. In fact, had it not been for a local member of a vintage auto club from the area, it might have been missed completely. Until very recently, his collection of restorable vehicles and parts cars weren't really for sale, so the reader of this is getting first shot at what is a golden opportunity to acquire a solid, possibly running, and rapidly disappearing number of excellent '50s and '60s cars. With 160 to 170 total vehicles, mostly Cadillacs, it's difficult to understand how this many have escaped the attention of the local population and avoided the hobbyist and restorer grapevine.

1. *Wondering where all the Cadillacs were, I didn't have long to wait when the owner opened the second storage shed door. The '60 Eldorado convertible is a "keeper" unless someone wants it worse than Allan.*

2. *More Cadillacs and someone slipped a '60 square bird and a '69 Karmann-Ghia in while he wasn't looking.*

3. *A '65 Mustang coupe is definitely outgunned by the '39 Buick, '37 Ford four-door and the '59 Cadillac six-window sedan.*

3

4. *In the center, some parts cars and two restorable '53 Buicks. One Special with the straight eight and the Super with the first year of the OHV 322 cid V-8 nailhead engine.*

5. *All parts cars, they definitely have an abundance of decent sheetmetal and great brightwork.*

4

5

6

7

Located across the Bitterroot River from the main part of town, virtually nothing is visible from the road and advertising is non-existent other than by word of mouth and his personalized business cards which feature the aft portion of a '59 Cadillac. Since there must be in the neighborhood of 50 or more of the finned '59 and '60 coupes, sedans and convertibles in inventory, and all in good to fair condition, the logo is appropriate. In fact, with a few strays tossed in like a restored '34 Ford Deluxe two door, a Metropolitan convertible, a few '50s Fords, his inventory is approximately 85 percent Cadillacs from '53 to '69.

Except for about 40 or so, all are under cover. Of that total, only about two dozen could actually be considered "parts cars." These are Cadillacs, Buicks, Fords and a few Mustangs. With only these few exceptions, he is only interested in selling complete restorable vehicles and some, like the '60 Eldorado Biarritz convertible and the '62 T-Bird convertible might require more than a little monetary persuasion to obtain.

Allan has been an avid car bug since he was fifteen and obviously partial to the lead sleds as many of us are. He likes the '59 and '60 finned boats the most. Having had a restored '60 myself, I concur with his leanings towards the '60. Though his son's tastes or selections might differ a bit from dad's, his interest and enthusiasm for all cars is evidently as strong and he does restorations.

All of the vehicles present are in remarkably good shape with rust free sheet metal and excellent trim. Most appear to be capable of being driven away and Allan assures me that most were driven in from places as close as Salmon, Idaho and distances like Kearney, Neb. The photos of the exposed cars can attest to condition to some degree, but rest assured, those

under cover which may not reproduce well on film due to lighting deficiencies are considerably superior. Now that the market for all of the special interest and collector vehicles has gotten more realistic, restoring most of these to mint condition doesn't appear to require mortgaging the homestead. Having been simply collecting up to this point, Allan is a bit uncertain of pricing and is acquiring price guides as well as advice from several restorers, but he isn't deaf to serious offers. He doesn't wish to be considered a bandit by any means, he simply wants a fair price for the car in question considering the present market, but at the same time, has no desire to be robbed blind. Obviously, the proceeds will be rolled over to restoring several he'd prefer to keep.

This may prove to be a once in a lifetime opportunity to get a first pick at a select inventory of particularly choice vehicles and rest assured, the supply is finite and represents about 25 years of personal collecting on the owner's part. No doubt in my mind at all that once publicized, Allan will have to put his house refurbishing on the back burner until all the dust has settled from the mad rush.

9

10

Dutton's Restorables,
Allan Dutton, owner,
179 Ricketts Road,
Hamilton, Mont. 59840,
406-363-3380

11

12

6. *Stepping out the back door of the shed, I really wasn't expecting to be assaulted by so many very straight restorable and parts vehicles. The '65 Ford convertible and '37 Ford pickup both would be Ford restorers' delights.*

7. *Four definite restorables, though the '59 Coupe de Ville is hiding behind the '60 Square Bird. Despite over 40,000 '66 Toronados being built, you don't see many around and even fewer '35 Ford pickups.*

8. *Most of these are restorables, except for a '60 Chevy pickup and an early '50s Chevy coupe. Parts vehicles slipped into this lineup.*

9. & 11. *Just try finding front and rear chrome for '59 and '60 Cadillacs like this. These cars can be restored and are well worth the effort.*

10. *This '66 Sedan de Ville drove in and appears it wouldn't take more than a* jump-start to drive out. There's also a '65 Coupe deVille that only needs a driver's door to be a match for this one.

12. *Nice Impala, but it was no match for this '60 Bird that was so hot, it literally melted the taillamp lenses!*

13

13. *More Cadillacs in front of the '46 Roadmaster and a glimpse of the '36 Ford one and a half ton truck and the '46 Chevy pickup.*

14. *Another view of the parts vehicles along the east-side fence and a peek at the '39 Chevy pickup.*

15. *The large closed storage building hides some gems like this '34 Ford Deluxe four door, which was restored 10 or 12 years ago. All original!*

16. *Rear view of the '34 Ford keeping company with a bunch of Mustangs and a restorable '58 Cadillac convertible.*

17. *The '46 Roadmaster looks like it has an advanced case of leprosy, but fortunately, the sheetmetal is solid and the chrome is great. Very hard to find and only half the sedan production that year went into the two-door sedanette.*

18. *Just a paint job on this '59 Sedan de Ville, thank you, and don't get any on the '63 T-Bird, the '63 Coupe de Ville or the '39 Ford standard coupe while you're at it.*

19. *Not quite sure how something as "new" as this '67 Coupe de Ville got in with the fins, but it's very nice and keeps the Mustang kids in the back row from going out to play. The '67 in the*

14

15

17

18

19

20

21

22

middle looks like it's ready for a Friday night on the town.

20. *This little orphan, a sunburst yellow and white '59 Metropolitan convertible was restored a few years ago and only needs a wash and wax to be in contention at the next "Show & Shine" event. The much sought-after convertible with its 1498cc Austin engine was by no means any muscle car. With 0 to 60 times somewhere between 19.5 and 22 seconds, the former time requiring a fly-weight driver and a tailwind, but it did squeeze a gallon of gas for 30 to 32 city and 37 to 40 highway. The Continental kit was standard and this year was the first for vent windows and trunk lid.*

21. *The south end of the same shed has a majority of Cadillacs too, but shares with a '41 Lincoln Zephyr coupe, '63 Pontiac convertible, '58 Olds 98*

Holiday coupe, '39 Ford coupe, a '39 Olds four door, '46 Hudson sedan, a '40 Plymouth pickup, a couple of '60 Buick sedans and two '69 Mercedes 200D sedans. Like I said, and you can readily see, it's a looooong shed.

22. *Except for an "orphan" kid sister '40 Chevy four door, this north end of the long open front storage shed is dominated by finned Cadillacs.*

SALVAGE YARD TOUR:
WASHINGTON, OREGON, IDAHO

Phase III

By Doc Howell

Perhaps no other portion of my touring in search of different and unpublicized salvage yards and collections of vintage restorable vehicles offers such dramatic contrasts in territory or scenery as does this phase. It starts in the lake and forest area of Coeur d' Alene, Idaho, west through the Spokane Valley and over through the potholes area of eastern Wash. via U. S. 90 to Ritzville, Wash., where Highway 395 takes a southerly turn through the fringe of the Palouse country bread basket. Potholes, is named for its many ponds and micro lakes, which are busy places this time of year with anglers for Bass and Crappie. The Palouse is world famous for grain and hundreds of square miles of wheat fields, which close to harvest time, take on the appearance of a vast undulating golden inland sea. Highway 395 roughly bisects the two agricultural mainstays of this area with dry land grain on the east, and corn, grapes and other irrigated crops on the west. Due to climatic conditions, it's also ideal for scavenging solid restorable rust-free vehicles or parts vehicles and principally, older pickups of the '40s and '50s vintage. One restorer in the Moses Lake area currently has three five-window GM pickups of the '48 to '52

vintage underway, and commented that he could spend the next 40 years doing the same models and never make a dent in the supply. As one approaches the outskirts of the Tri-City area, (Pasco-Kennewick-Richland, Wash.) you get a graphic demonstration of what sandy loam soil can produce given ample water. Acres and acres of lush green crops benefitting from the Columbia irrigation project which the Corps of Engineers started back in the '50s. In the early '50s, most of the area here and extending on over into the central high desert area of Oregon, was limited to planting stakes for Burma-Shave and Stinker Station signs. One which sticks in my memory, informed the drivers they were in "Sagebrush National Forest, and Jackrabbits have the right-of-way." Most attribute the lack of rabbits today to Tularemia, but I suspect their suicidal dashes across the highways also hastened their depletion.

My first stop on this trip is Dan's Garage, located in Kennewick, Wash., across the Columbia River from Pasco, Wash. His salvage yard specializes in GM sporty and muscle cars of the '60s and '70s vintage. Dan Stafford has been tinkering with cars since his early teens and about 12 years ago began toying with Camaros and Firebirds in

1. *Starting out from Lake Coeur d'Alene at six A.M. indicates a sky warranting reloading with faster film.*

2. *Another view of Mount Hood from on top, this time from the southeast. Below the tree line at the bottom left lies the famous Timberline Lodge.*

earnest. Before long he had accumulated a sizeable supply of spare parts for those and for Chevelles. When the owner of the wrecking yard behind him was ready to call it quits, Dan came to the conclusion that he'd always wanted a wrecking yard, so he bought it. The prior owner had scrapped out everything in sight, so Dan had to start with a bare yard and refill it. Now stacked three deep in places, it is overdue for what the owner calls a "spring cleaning," and many in the back row will go as scrap metal.

It's rather ironic that yours truly made a very good living back in the early and mid '60s putting a large number of these very same vehicles on the road as an auto salesman here. In '65, '66, and '67, I would put my GTO or Buick GS demo to extracurricular use dusting off aspiring drag racers at unsanctioned forays on Friday and Saturday night, utilizing a nearby abandoned Navy training airfield. Then on Monday morning the losers would "take a number" and wait in line to pick a GTO or Sprint hardtop or convertible. We simply couldn't get enough vehicles to satisfy them all and many settled for Cougars, Chevelles, Mustangs and Olds 442s. I always wondered where they disappeared to, and now I know. In fact, the black '64 Grand Prix resting beside the building in Dan's "restorables" section once belonged to a gentleman who owned a local clothing store and traded the Grand Prix in on a '66 2+2. Now, though missing its original 421 engine and four-speed transmission, this car could still make an excellent project. Though limited in area, the lot contains a surprising total number of vehicles and I suspect, given the background and middle '30s age of the owner, more than a few of the Camaro and Firebird cars will be lapping the local track in hobby stock racing later this year or next year.

Bidding adieu to Dan and his able assistant Dave, it's time to head over Horse Heaven Hills to McNary Dam and across the Columbia River to Oregon and on to the freeway. McNary Lake, behind the dam, stretches up around the bend clear back to the Tri-City area I just departed. Irrigation pumps from here have transformed much of the former dry pasture and cattle grazing land of this high desert area into an abundant producer of potatos, melons, corn, tomatos, cucumbers and onions. Proceeding west down Highway 84 on the Oregon side isn't considered much of a scenic drive except for occasional glimpses of the river with tugs and barges loaded with grain heading for Portland. The port of Morrow County at Boardman slips by on the right and all of the potato processing plants seem to be running full steam to cope with the demand for french fries and tater tots for which the area is

3 - 8. *These are some of the extremely nice Chevys owned by Will Carey, an attorney and city judge in Hood River. This former fruit storage shed is filled with vintage cars in various conditions and represents a cooperative venture between Will and several other vintage car buffs in the area. Well protected with alarm systems, it's not the sort of place to be prowling around after dark.*

noted. Boardman, a new/old town, replaced the previous by moving lock, stock and barrel when the John Day Dam was completed. Same with the highway, the railroad and the small town of Arlington.

Another hour cruising down the gorge viewing the monotonous walls of sage, bunch grass and rock would probably have the average stranger wondering if all the travel information was pure imagination when it came to describing the scenic Columbia Gorge. The gorge begins close to the Hood River where the slopes of the Cascade Mountain range meet the Columbia River.Back in

1948 B.D. (before dams) this was a fascinating drive and people used to park for hours just to watch the Celilo indians fish from their rickety platforms with dip nets. Now just a memory and collection of historical information, that portion of the river is an inland lake behind the Dalles Dam which backs up to the John Day Dam, another lake dotted with boats and steelhead fishermen. The City of The Dalles comes into view around a prominent rock outcropping, and no matter how many times one sees it, the Dalles Dam is impressive. This city, which got its name from the French-Canadian fur trappers who dubbed it "the narrows" after the rock rimmed chute at the west

9. - 11. *Though John van Ras is a die-hard Ford man from way back, he acknowledges that a few premium cars such as the Olds convertible and the '63 Chevy Super Sport in original condition are worth restoration, and make good show cars. For the most part, he collects Mustangs and has nearly a dozen on hand. Also, not shown is a mint Torino Cobra GT with under 20,000 miles. It's red too!*

9

10

11

end of the river bend, used to have three major industries; a Martin-Marietta aluminum plant, a large Union Pacific yard with round-house and tie plant, and canneries running full tilt processing cherries. Now it appears the maraschino cherry plant is the only one still running strong, making certain the garnish for Manhattans and bits for Christmas fruit cakes are available. A quick check of Brace Brothers Wrecking on the west end of town reveals that my suspicions were correct and they'd been virtually picked clean by parts chasers from the nearby Portland area. Another 19 miles and Hood River appears around the corner. The valley, noted for world famous fruit, is a lush green carpet from the Columbia River up the valley to the Mount Hood snow line and is a drastic contrast to the terrain just covered. In recent years, it seems the community has virtually been overtaken by the youth group devoted to windsailing. Still on the cool side though, that activity hasn't begun yet this season. Time for a quiet dinner with my elderly mother, a good night's rest and then a run up the valley the next morning.

An early morning stop on Tucker Road on the west side of the valley reveals my former classmate, John Van Ras still has a back yard of Mustangs, ranging from a fair '65 blue convertible to a very nice red '67 convertible. All are for sale and would make a good gift item for that student headed for college next fall. Looking John up just

might solve your shopping dilemma. Across the valley, on the east side, lies a large former apple packing shed which is bulging with restored and restorable vehicles. Most are owned by a local attorney, Will Carey, a dedicated Chevy man who isn't interested in selling anything he's had for ten years or more, and definitely not the his and hers '57 Chevrolet Bel Air convertibles. He does, however, have numerous restorable vehicles and a quantity of extra 396 and 409 big block engines available for sale. Collector, enthusiast, restorer and hobbyist, Will also happens to be the local judge, so make certain your check is A-l if you negotiate a deal.

A stop at Mount Hood Auto Wrecking reveals its been thoroughly scavenged by parts chasers. At one time though, years ago, early Ford and Chevy parts were its bread and butter.

The trip over the mountain on Oregon Highway 35 is beautiful; dry roads and very little traffic. A stop or two to shoot a couple of pictures is mandatory. One taken along this route is of the bed of the White River which many movie buffs might recognize as the site of the film "Bend of the River" starring Jimmy Stewart. Mount Hood and much of the Bend/Redmond, Ore. area has been used quite often by the major movie producers.

Down the southeast slope of the mountain, now on Highway 26, the heavy timber gives way to dry

12. - 16. *These are just a few shots of some of the 150 plus vehicles at "Bundy's Corral," outside of Bend. A collector, restorer and hobbyist, Bill has a surplus of choice vehicles on hand, particularly Cadillac convertibles. I have dibs on the red Eldorado, but then again, I may not win the lottery soon enough to suit Bill.*

12

13

14

15

16

land, sagebrush and Juniper trees. It's a downhill run until one gets to the famous Deschutes River winding its circuitous route to the Columbia River. Here, on the edge of the Warm Springs Indian Reservation, fishermen line the banks of the deep pool in pursuit of steelhead. Back on top of the plateau, it's readily apparent you're in hay and cattle country. Also around Madras, Ore., my next stop, are many acres devoted to potatoes, grain and mint. About a mile south of the city core, a rusting vintage vehicle on the east side of the highway supports a sign which advises that "Ira's Sales and Service" is but a quarter of a mile down Merritt Lane. Once there, it's evident the owner, Ira Merritt, is definitely into the scrap and salvage business. No hobby stocks, dirt track cars, or restoration jobs grace the eight acre premises; everything from 18 wheelers to schoolbuses to late model vehicles. This husky 60-plus-year-old owner has been at this location since '57, and

converted the land from a wheat ranch. Given the plight of wheat ranchers I've known over the years, I surmise Ira made a rather astute decision. One corner is devoted to '70s and older vehicles and he is in the process of re-arranging the entire seven to eight acres, where all the collectibles will be situated by themselves.

From Ira's, the trip to Brad's Auto and Truck Parts in Redmond, Ore. is a leisurely half hour drive depending upon the tourist traffic. About two miles south of the city center on Highway 97, you arrive at the only traffic light between Redmond and Bend, Odem Medo Road. This calls for a turn east and a definite stop at the railroad tracks. Those who don't stop are liable to involuntarily contribute to Brad's inventory, given the pace trains maintain across this non-signal bearing crossing. Cross the tracks, and any parts junkie is in for a surprise. If any salvage yard can be described as being the neatest, cleanest and best organized, this has to be it. My guide, Ron Cutter, who has worked for the owner, Brad Carrell and his wife Sharon, for over 11 years, informed me they had even received a national award for just those reasons. Everything has its place and everything is in its place. Complete with satellite hot line and computerized inventory, it only takes a moment to let you know if your needed part is on hand and precisely where. Sons Mark and Brett Carrell, and Brad Severson man the desk, and shipments routinely are directed throughout the US, Canada, Mexico and overseas. Located on a former mill site, only the old sawdust burner indicates what stood here before, and that Brad's hasn't been here quite 10 years yet. Here, even the "teepee" style burner has a function, serving both a historic landmark role as well as back-up support for a circular rack of front and rear clips.

Brad is a dedicated car nut, and his two main passions both start with a capital "P"; Pontiacs and Performance. A couple of mint Panteras, a GT at work and another at home, fall in the latter category. The acres of pre '70 vehicles outdoors and undercover outside town, and adjacent to his residence, reflect his interests and tastes. Any parts or vehicles from this "semi-public" assortment would of necessity have to be arranged strictly by mail, since the two operations are separate entities and none of the vehicles or parts are even listed with the main store. The employees there have their hands full every day coping with the main store business, and collector car or parts calls merely confuse issues.

Brad started years ago with a body shop. Rebuilding and detailing vehicles just naturally resulted in a collection of parts vehicles and ultimately, the decision to capitalize on his existing inventory and the lack of a really organized salvage yard operation in the area led to Brad's Auto & Truck Parts. Then too, the abundance of rust free old cars in the area played a big role, but he still makes buying trips all over the northwest, both for inventory, and his collecting/restoring hobby. If you think you have a '50s or '60s vehicle he might be interested in, by all means drop him a card, but please don't call the store. Covering this location and his isolated "vintage area" located outside of town uses up a day rapidly and the sinking sun indicates it is time to locate a motel and drive to Bend just 19 miles away.

The following morning finds me a few miles out into the eastern fringe area of Bend, going through Bill Bundy's "Corral." A rough count indicates nearly 150 vehicles ranging from a '28 Rolls Royce undergoing restoration, a '40s vintage Diamond T truck, rows of early '70s Chevrolet Monte Carlos, boat tail Rivieras, and many early and middle '60s Pontiac and Cadillac convertibles. I think one in particular would look quite good on me; a bright red '66 Eldorado convertible, which a

cut and polish would have parade ready. There are also two or three Chevy Cameo pickups in various degrees of completion, a pair of Adenauer Mercedes 300s and an orphan Lancia coupe under the trees. Bill is a developer and his hobbies include horse racing and old cars. As often seems to be the case when the means are at hand, he seems to have "overindulged" and acquired more than he'd ever have time to really restore, so about two-thirds are available for purchase or trade. Only a few at the west end of the four to five acre horse corral could be called parts cars. The rest, with urging via hot batteries and starting fluid will all start and more than likely make their own way onto a car carrier or trailer. As with many in the hobbyist field, Bill is neither a dealer nor a full time restorer. A large quantity of very desirable and restorable vehicles of various makes and models is available and he makes appointments only with serious people via personal or phone contact. A good place not to miss if you're in the area looking and can catch him on the phone. Weekends after 10 A.M. or weekday evenings are by far the best bet.

Having run out of black-and-white film before reaching Bill's, I make a dash to a local camera store and restock, then point my land barge towards Prineville, Ore., some 20 miles due east on Highway 26 to check out a yard that used to contain a number of '50s and '60s cars. Unfortunately, nobody's home, and a good scan of what was evident revealed very little of either a collectible or a restorable nature. Primarily a lumber and cattle town, the most prominent features as one enters the community are the huge light blue steel buildings which house the heart and home of the Les Schwab Tire Co. Covering approximately 60 acres in downtown Prineville, I would be remiss in not mentioning it. Founded back in 1952 with a one horse OK Tire Welders recap shop. Les has become one of the nation's largest tire retailers with over 200 stores covering every inch of the territory, Oregon, Washington, Idaho, Montana and California.

A stranger might scratch his head and wonder why Les would choose to locate such a big operation in a small, off-the-beaten-path area. It's really quite simple—this is his home and where he started. All native Oregonians from the eastern part of the state have an abundance of respect and admiration for Les Schwab and his accomplishments in the past 40 years. With the emphasis on service and a credo of, "if we can't guarantee it, we won't sell it," his distinctive tire stores dominate the northwest area.

Failing to find anything worthy of reporting in Mitchell, I continue on Highway 26 to the John Day Valley, the west end of which is a paleontologists playground, full of fossils, and the balance definitely hay and cattle. Several large active lumber mills still work around the clock trying to cope with the seemingly insatiable demand for lumber, but the economy is primarily cattle. After a quick coffee stop and fruitless check on a former yard in John Day, I head over the Blue Mountains and run into a snow storm, which lasts well into the high desert country, on the eastern border of Oregon. Finally, at Unity Lake, the snow ceases, and I get a 20 mile respite until it begins to hail. It's slow going almost into Vale, Ore. with at least a half inch of 3/8-inch hail stones covering the highway. Actually, the weather was a blessing in disguise since the scenery on the long haul is about as fascinating as the stretch between Ely and Tonopah, Nev. Here too, it behooves one to make sure certain tools, extra fanbelts etc., are on board, and definitely some extra water, particularly during the summer months. The owner of the wrecking yard on the west end of Vale, Ore. informs me he'd been picked clean for nearly a year and only had two or three old '40s pickups left, but if I hurried, I could still catch Les Hopkins at Hopkins Antique Autos & Parts over in Caldwell, Idaho before he closed. Not actually in Caldwell, one must take Highway 20-26 to where it meets U.S. 84, take 84 north to the Middleton exit, and then follow old Highway 30 north, paralleling the freeway for about two-and-a-half miles. For old parts vehicles from 1918 to the early '60s, this is a gold mine. Les decided to start buying up old cars and NOS parts about 1972 when he was planning his retirement from farming. Now he and his sons, Don and Bob, have a full time job coping with the people wanting bits and pieces of the 700 plus antique vehicles that cover about seven and a half acres behind the barns and farmhouse. Full of enthusiasm, even at the end of the day, Les thought using his vintage tall forklift to hoist me 30 feet up in the air, giving readers a real birds-eye view of his lot, was the greatest thing since Crackerjacks. With some gusts of 30 to 40 knots at the top, it took some juggling with two cameras and one leg cocked around a vertical bar, but the pictures were worth it. Les is another of the people I am constantly meeting, in and around the automobile collecting and restoration scene, who possess the ingredient I like to call "perennial youth."

People who know of the existence of Hopkins' yard travel long distances to get hard to find parts. Two fellows from Seattle were busy loading a number of '37 Ford coupe parts on a small trailer while I was completing a photo circuit of the property. Another man and his son were grinning ear to ear after scavenging through the lot and finding a pair of very nice '55 Ford tail light lenses. With over 400 miles on the odometer for the day and the clock ticking down, I know I can't make my next stop today, so I call Lynn Morris in Indian Valley from here and make certain he will be available early Saturday morning. No problem, so with a cheerful farewell from Les, I head for the freeway north and make my way to the Payette-Weiser, Idaho off ramp and Highway 95N.

The rustic small town of Cambridge is far enough for one day, and after a delightful dinner at a converted blacksmith shop now dubbed the "Pioneer," I retire to the "Frontier" motel and review my notes. The local store closed at 6 p.m., so lacking reading material, I made some of my own.

Early the next morning, I again head north up Highway 95 about 13 to 14 miles to a country store called "Alpine." A scant quarter mile north of the store is a small sign indicating "Indian Valley Road." East on this road for about two miles brings you to another old building with a sign, advising it is the "Indian Valley Market." Take the road beside the store and travel south for about two-and-three-quarter miles and it takes a bend east again. By now, you can see a blanket of cars and trucks in the distance covering a pasture. Another quarter mile and you'll see an old military armored scout parked by a long lane. You have now arrived at Morris' Antique & Classic Cars and Parts. The owner, Lynn Morris, is a modest and retiring fellow who has been with the Forest Service for over 25 years. By his own admission, an avowed car nut since he was 14 or 15 years old. About 15 years ago, he just started acquiring vehicles, and has kept it up. Nearly 700 adorn the pasture at present. When time permits, he parts out the vehicles selectively, and annually makes about two swap meets per year. Usually one in Spokane, Wash., and "Hot August Nights" in Reno, Nev. Vintages run from the early teens up to about '60, and are predominantly Chrysler Products. By no means limited to these, though he's partial to Dodge, there are a number of GM cars, as well as many of the orphan variety, such as Studebakers, Nashs, Packards, Kaisers/Frazers and some early Corvairs. Knee high grass wet with morning dew soon had Lynn, myself and his two dogs soaked through and through, but undaunted, we covered the complete field. Other than contacts through swap meets, and a few other vintage parts dealers, few people are aware of his inventory.

Time to point north for home and the drive along the Salmon River with wall to wall fishermen all seeking the big one. I didn't check, but it looked like opening day. Later in the season, this area will be invaded by people chartering rides on the many rafts and boats operated by the white water guides, for the exciting run down the Salmon River to where it connects with the Snake, at the lower end of the Hells Canyon Recreation area. Rugged country and a lot of history.

Now, a long uphill haul through the mountainous Nez Perce Indian country with the heater going strong, and I finally get dried out around Grangeville, the heart of the legendary Chief Joseph country. Pronounced either "Nay Percy" or "Nezz Purse", the entire area from here up along the Salmon River to Lewiston, Idaho was the home ground of this famous chief and his tribe. The highway is dotted with historical signs relating the saga of his long trek and eventual surrender to the "yellow legs." An overview from the top of the lofty Lewiston grade, gives a panoramic view of the country and a great history lesson. Few are aware that Lewiston, Idaho, and its' sister city, Clarkston, Wash., are inland ports, and steamboats plied these waters for many years. They are very active ports today, with tugs and barges hauling great loads of lumber and grain down the river and through the locks to join the Columbia.

Through Moscow, and on up over the remaining hills, and back to Coeur d' Alene, it's always nice to head for home and a familiar bed. Seventeen hundred and fifty-nine miles and four days later, the question is always, "was it worth the effort?" I say "yes" because it reveals a number of sources of parts and vehicles to many outside of the immediate vicinity, and gives them an idea of what the owners are like and, perhaps, induces an itch for many to come see for themselves. Travel costs are reasonable given this time of the year, but I always chafe at the bit in some locales, where gas

prices are concerned. Nearly all gasoline here in the inland area is trucked in from either Ferndale, Wash., or from the refinery in Montana. When you find an isolated "convenience" store or handi-mart in a place like the John Day Valley that blatantly displays a sign for regular at $1.549 per gallon, and then less than 20 miles down the road there's another selling the same for $1.339, it has a tendency to "frost you." The disparity can only be chalked up to greed, and anyone with a thirsty motorhome who didn't top off in Bend or Redmond will certainly "pay the piper" when he hits Dayville, Ore.

I didn't find exactly what I was looking for, but I have a stack of postcards to mail out to a number of friends and acquaintances who need many of the items I located. Hopefully, many of the readers will spot what they need. Definitely a fun run all the way, with the exception of some adverse weather, and one I would cheerfully repeat if only for the dramatic differences and contrasts in scenery. This is the sort of tour one would like to make in a motor home, and take two weeks to leisurely complete. With fishing poles, or some oils and an easel, it could conceivably take quite a bit longer.

17. *Assuming everyone has seen pictures of the Imperial Valley in California, comprised of hundreds of square miles of flat farmland, I passed over taking pictures of the Nampa-Caldwell Valley. Instead, I wanted to show the scenery of the Indian Valley territory. It's the former home of Chief Joseph and the Nez Perce indian tribe and now haven for Morris' Antique Autos and Parts.*

DAN'S GARAGE

1

By Doc Howell

Though the combined population total of the Tri-City area of Pasco, Kennewick and Richland, Wash. only reaches 100,000, the area it serves is probably more than double that total. It does in fact, serve the entire southeast corner of Washington, and the northeast corner of Oregon as well. If something is popular there, it is equally as popular, and as much in demand, in the fringe areas as well. So it is with muscle cars of the '60s and early '70s, and GM cars in particular, in this area. For whatever reason, neither Ford or Mopar muscle cars made much of a dent on this area. GTOs, Chevelles, Olds 4-4-2s, Camaros and Firebirds, and the warmer versions of the personal luxury middleweights such as the Grand Prix, GS Rivieras and Toronados were the dominators not only in the marketplace, but also on sanctioned and unsanctioned competition events around the area.

Actively selling both Buick and Pontiac muscle during this period, I surmise the age and interest of the sales person at the time played a certain role in the numbers. I happened to be the youngest sales person working this milieu at the time, and my sales manager was also a bit of a squirrel at heart, so we moved cars and he turned the zone upside down making certain they were there for me to sell. And he turned a blind eye to my nocturnal Fri.-Sat. night endeavors on make shift drag strips, which often left the redline wide ovals on many GTOs more than a few 32nds shy of tread. But it got results.

2

After the GTO era, the Camaros, and Firebirds, and the lighter Chevelles with the bigger engines came to the fore, so given the interest and activity, it comes as no great surprise to me that someone like Dan Stafford, the owner of Dan's Garage in Kennewick, can focus entirely on these vehicles at his enterprise. In this area, it just happens to be a big niche market.

Though there is a very large agricultural side to the local economy, by far the largest is Uncle Sam, via the Department of Energy, courtesy of the

Hanford project, as it was labeled back in the '40s. Then, Pasco and Kennwick were virtually whistle stop farm communities, and Richland was but a germ of an idea. Then the Government, in their infinite wisdom, fired up the reactors, seemed to move a good portion of Tennessee's and Arkansas' population here with a substantial hunk of military, and an assortment of hardware. Though payroll checks might have read General Electric, Westinghouse, Batelle, or another of the numerous subcontractors to the project, there was no question

1. *Dan's Garage is surrounded by his premium restorables, which are kept inside the fence for obvious reasons.*

2. *Here are more of the restorable cars behind the shop building, and even a couple in the driveway waiting to get in.*

3. *More driveable and restorable cars almost plug the driveway leading to the salvage yard at Dan's Garage.*

4. *Inside the yard gate, there are a couple of rows of the better restorable Chevelle and Camaro muscle cars.*

5. *South fence provides a backdrop for the many extra nice front clips he currently has in stock.*

6. *Over the roofs of several Camaros and Firebirds are piles of excellent bumpers for GM cars.*

3

4

5

6

7. *Fenders adopt an erect position out of consideration for limited space.*

8. *This building houses Dan's toys and projects, and at present harbors a couple of Camaro convertibles.*

7

8

who was really picking up the tab. It used to be a standing joke among the auto salesman about how many of these people reacted to job security, and relative affluence. New shoes and a pickup last month, a Cadillac for Pa and Goats (GTOs) for the kids; it can't get any better than this. In many respects it was true. The move west, housing, medical etc., were all "on the house," leaving many with considerable disposable income. Now, it is rare to even find any vestige of the military barracks housing anymore. When razed, an enterprising wag with a sense of humor bought up all of the used plumbing fixtures from this government housing, secured a lot on what was known as "Auto Row," and erected a large sign which proclaimed, "Honest Carr-Used John Dealer." May not have endeared him to his neighbors with the white belts and blue suede shoes, but it made him famous (or is that infamous) in the area. Perhaps incidental information, but the economics explain why the abundance of sporty and muscle vehicles in the area.

10

9

9. Just don't see many of these any more, but the '63 Pontiac LeMans with the 326 V-8 was a respectable performer and credited with spawning the orginal GTO.

10. If you've been parking your Chevelle by sound, you could probably use one of these choice bumpers.

11. This SS 396 could very easily be revived.

12. This Rottweiler means business and the sign on the old van body lets you know it. I checked with Dan ahead of time to see how long his chain was.

13. GTO and LeMans corner on the southwest end of the lot. A couple of '65s are lurking behind the white '68 on the bottom.

14. From '63 to '73, more than a few Pontiac Grand Prixs idle in the shade.

11

12

13

14

15. *This Goat's restoration was started once, and it is all in primer, but apparently someone tired of the project.*

16. *Monte Carlos, Bel Airs, Impalas—this double decking will probably be a thing of the past once Dan gets the lot reorganized and some of the cars in the rear crushed and shipped out.*

17. *A few more Grand Prixs hiding behind the Jimmy, and a couple of nice '48-'53 pickup cabs in the rear.*

18. *Becoming more popular every day, these '70 Grand Prix hardtops in decent shape are getting harder to find.*

15

16

17

18

A car addict from his teens, Dan cut his teeth on many of these second-hand cars, and being a capable hand with a wrench and torch, made his living repairing, patching and modifying them for street and track. Plying the trade resulted in a stockpile of body and mechanical parts and before long he was functioning as both a shop and a used parts source.

Along the way came the realization that he'd always wanted to own a wrecking yard. His opportunity to capitalize on his forte came about when the operator of the yard next to him elected to throw in the towel, and Dan made the acquisition. Though small in acreage, the yard is dense in content and would require at least five acres to allocate a space for each, were they placed to provide access lanes between them. About three dozen restorable vehicles are kept on hand, and aren't parted out. The larger building on the north end of the yard houses Dan's "projects" as well as some choice parts. At present, a '69 Camaro convertible is his object of affection. From the traffic during the couple

19

of hours I was there, it's obvious that "spare or project" time around here is a rather sparse commodity. Since both he and his associate are walking/talking Hollander Cross Reference guides to GM vehicles, the phone is always busy responding to inquiries. He hopes he'll have more mail order business, and thin out some of his surplus stock, as well as scrapping some, in order to better organize his operation. Hours are generally 8-6 weekdays and often Saturday mornings. The lot is located in downtown Kennewick's industrial area, on Bruneau Avenue, which parallels Columbia Boulevard. Once on Columbia Boulevard, locate Washington Avenue, turn west for about half a block, then left (South) on Bruneau, just short of the railroad tracks which run between the big

20

21

22

beer and grape juice warehouses, and Dan's is about two blocks south on the right hand side. In parting, I take another wistful look at the very solid little '63 Tempest LeMans with the 326 engine, and speculate what it would cost to put it back on the road. I surmise it won't be long before someone better prepared to accept the challenge harbors the same thoughts, and it disappears for about six months to make a debut at some " Show & Shine" meeting.

**Dan's Garage,
Dan Stafford: owner,
508 E. Bruneau Avenue,
Kennewick, Wash. 99336
509-586-2579**

---

19. *More than a few of the popular '68-'72 pickups are on hand.*

20. *If you need more than just a nice bumper for your Chevelle, check up on the second floor.*

21. *A row of '60s and '70s El Caminos are tucked away toward the rear of the lot.*

22. *And even more El Caminos, which were very popular with performance enthusiasts in this area.*

23. *Just about any Powerglide, TH350 or 400 you might need.*

23

IRA'S SALES & SERVICE

By Doc Howell

Ira's, located about a mile south of the center of Madras, Ore., is on the left and can be missed easily if you aren't making an effort to locate it. A derelict vintage car body serves as a base for a four by five-foot orange and black sign, that advises you the yard is located a quarter mile down Merritt Lane. The sign is set back a distance from the highway and the fertile ground has the bunch grass growing as tall as the vehicle that holds the sign, and concealing this distinguishing landmark. Drive down the lane and over the hump that conceals the yard from the highway, and you'll know you've arrived. The biggest difference you note about his operation is the singular lack of any "project" cars, colorful hobby stockers or restored collectibles in evidence. If any of the employees are into the hobby, then they obviously keep their rigs at home.

Once a wheat ranch, this acreage was converted by Ira to be a money making vehicle salvage yard. Given the foibles and fluctuations of the grain farming business, he's undoubtedly farther ahead and doesn't have to get up as early in the morning or eat dust on a tractor all day.

Not focusing primarily on old cars does not mean he's unreasonable with regard to his prices at all, but simply that selling used parts is his priority, whether it's the axle from a Freightliner or the hood off an '87 Honda. Not immune to the collector or restorer as evidenced by the large group of older

3. *This surprisingly solid '39 GMC COE five tonner is headed for Bakersfield, Calif., and perhaps a future as a show truck, or perhaps a car carrier for another show vehicle.*

4

5

4. *Looking southeast across the expanse of Ira's lot, you can readily see I have a bit of a hike ahead of me.*

5. *Good solid body on this '56 Century four-door hardtop, and also the early Ford Ranchero in front of it.*

6. *With a Plymouth in front, Olds to the south, and tailgated by a Kaiser Manhattan, this Willys Aero has a surprisingly good body, and is but one of several here.*

pickups and cars tucked into the southwest corner of the yard, he's pragmatic about what sort of volume it requires to keep the doors open. Waiting for the one person who might want the glass and trunk lid off one of the Edsel hardtops, or the hood ornament off the '33 Hudson Terraplane, wouldn't keep the doors open very long. With a finite supply of vintage vehicles left around, yards dedicated to special interest vehicles are few and far between and fading from the landscape.

Ira gets calls from all over the country and ships in response to them. The big five-ton '39 GMC cab over engine truck out back is slated for a new owner in Bakersfield, Calif., who obviously has some upgrading and customizing in mind, since the order called for pulling the original engine out and leaving it behind. In nice shape, I wouldn't be the least bit surprised to see it a year or two

6

7

8

9

7. *Here's a '62 Corvair convertible, I hope a certain collector/dealer back east happens to spot this one.*

8. *Much sought after by street rodders, this Corvair rampside pickup is easier to spot than the early '60s Buick Special hiding in the grass.*

9. *A lot of work, but for those who won't settle for less than a Buick Woodie wagon, there's plenty here left to work with.*

10. *No rust and the engine is there, though sitting on the floorboards, but this BMW Isetta seems to be all there and just waiting for the right person.*

11. *Just one of several rows of vintage pickups.*

10

11

13

12. *This '53 Mercury Monterey has more than just a good solid hood going for it.*

13. *The little Rambler is a bit overshadowed by these two Packards.*

14. *This '40 Olds keeps watch over its younger '52 sister. Both four doors, they have a lot going for them.*

15. *This '55 and the last year of the Willys, at least north of the border, along with the '52 is but two of the many at Ira's.*

12

14

15

16. *I've known a few collectors and restorers who'd buy all of this Kaiser just to get the sun visor.*

17. *This hood ornament and a few other minor pieces, along with the trailer it was on, were all that survived a fatal accident involving the collector bringing this '35 Terraplane back from the Seattle area.*

18. *This '53 Chrysler looks a bit dated next to its finned '60 DeSoto Adventurer four door companion.*

19. *Another Packard with a lot of very nice sheetmetal. Surprising number of these post WW II models in the area.*

20. *Two '58 Pacers and surely enough good material to finish up the hardtop.*

16

17

18

19

20

21. *Except for someone getting to the tail feathers first, this '56 DeSoto Firesweep hardtop still has much to provide.*

22. *This early '60s Studebaker pickup looked as if it was capable of being driven away.*

23. *Car spotters delight, a whole row of Kaisers lurking behind this '55 Chevy.*

24. *This '64 Buick Skylark hardtop has a pretty decent body for someone.*

25. *This Packard has a Corvair Corsa coupe for a neighbor.*

26. *There were several of these little Rancheros and early '50s trucks offering skin grafts and organ transplants.*

21

22

23

24

25

26

27

28

29

27. *This '60 Ford T-Bird has more than just a nice hood and trunk lid to offer.*

28. *Now if you really want an exclusive rarity as a project, there were only 159 of these '58 Packard wagons built compared to 588 of the Packard Hawks!*

29. *Not a '56 Ford Crown Victoria, but if your front end doesn't look as nice as this rust free one, better call Ira quick.*

30. *When is the last time you saw a '51 Ford Victoria hardtop. This one has plenty left to share or could even stand up for a complete restoration.*

30

31. *A very straight '53 Chevy pickup cab and I'm sure Ira has a box around that will fit. The Cadillac in the background has some great pieces to share as well.*

32. *Nice place to start, this '55 Plymouth Belvedere, if you're a Mopar fan.*

31

32

rom now participating in a parade, all gussied up with a candy-apple red paint job, chrome stacks rumbling from a 396 or 454 engine.

Naturally, it will have a 500 watt stereo and matching fuzzy dice. It was rather surprising to find as many "orphans" such as the Kaiser Manhattans, Studebakers, Corvairs, Packards and Edsels in this part of the state. Past explorations have shown their concentration was generally around the more metropolitan areas where dealers were located. But where in the book does it say that there are territorial priorities where a car quits or gets hammered in an accident?

Ira maintains two heavy duty wreckers in addition to the smaller ones, and probably garners most of the area towing on the eighteen wheelers. If a trailer box is over the hill, it makes a handy storage building for engines, transmissions, and all sorts of parts storage, and the yard man working on the GMC indicated they could use some more when they start rearranging the inventory. The store stocks new and late model parts, and does custom work on many of the areas farm trucks in their well equipped shop.

Busy and interesting place, and a definite resource.

1

BRAD'S AUTO & TRUCK PARTS

Part 1

By Doc Howell

If the "greenies" ever stop nit-picking and pass out some compliments rather than criticism, I suggest they begin with Brad Carrell's operation here in Redmond, Ore. Located about two miles south of the downtown area, just watch for the only traffic light and take a left. Neat, clean and modern steel buildings immediately distinguish his operation from most salvage yards. The showroom is spotless and the premium items, such as bucket seats, grilles, etc., are on display here. The "waiting room" area by the front windows is unique, with two very comfortable settees custom tailored from rear clips of a '57 Chevy and a '59 Cadillac. Check out the wall hanging and try to remember the last time you saw a Cobra front end displayed this way.

The day-to-day business at Carrell's is enough to keep a crew of a dozen or more busy, including Carrell's two sons and a daughter.

It's a high-tech operation. Inventory is all computerized and the business uses a satellite hot line for locating parts and responding to customers. The back room is overseen by Ron Carter, who has been with Brad and Sharon for over eleven years, and back when this store

2

3

1. *First view of Brad's from the highway looks more like a new parts store, unless you note the rack of clips faintly visible to the right rear of the main building.*

2. *A closer view after crossing the railroad tracks. Unique model T "planters" are just waiting for their Rhododendron transplants. Neatness isn't by accident, Brad's has received several national awards.*

3. *Every car nut should have at least one piece of furniture like these around the house.*

4. *No, this isn't a specially prepared portion of the grounds inside, it all looks this way.*

5. *Even lowly fuel tanks have a special rack all to themselves.*

6. *Special racks contain fenders, glass and bumpers. The only thing on the ground is dirt.*

4

5

6

7

7. *Even the old landmark "teepee" sawdust burner from the mill which formerly occupied this property is put to good use as a circlular clip rack.*

was still an idea. His area is tidier than the back rooms of many new parts stores and everything is tagged and allocated a special spot in the designated racks. It's not unusual for Carter to be ankle deep in CV joints and half shafts, sorting and checking against inventory sheets.

In the yard itself, the organization is readily apparent. Aisles, much like a supermarket or library, are all clearly labeled. "Christmas trees" of axles stand at the end of each aisle.

The sawdust burner, a landmark and carryover from a decade ago when this was the site of a sawmill, serves as a centerpiece for a circular rack containing front and rear clips. Another big rack full of car and truck clips stands behind the "stripper" or dismantling shop.

Next to it is what can best be called a "used car factory." Here, late model vehicles which aren't too severely damaged are remanufactured to critical specifications using prime inventory material and finished to defy detection where they may have been damaged.

I had time to examine several of these "rebuilds." If I was in the market for the type displayed, I would have no qualms about purchasing one at Brad's less than current used car lot prices.

On the west end and to the rear of the main building are rows of racks with bumpers, doors, fenders, hoods, glass, radiators and mechanical parts, all tagged and neatly stored and sheltered from the elements. From a cursory glance, I would surmise that the opera-

tion, given time and motivation, could quite conceivably produce a fleet of a dozen completed late model pickups or cars from this inventory.

Unlike most salvage or wrecking yards, there is no acreage full of cars waiting to be selectively picked over for two or three parts. When a vehicle is towed in a decision is made. Either it's rebuilt right

away, or all useable parts are pulled, inventoried, racked and the balance sent to the smelter in short order. Even the majority of the big yards around the country stockpile acres of vehicles and pull parts on order as you either wait or come back tomorrow. If it is on the computerized inventory, it takes only a few minutes for a yard service man to trot

8

9

8. *A rack of doors from '72 to current models. Each carefully marked and tagged.*

9. *Lettered "Xmas Trees" all contain rear axles at the end of each row, and the letters act as guides for the yard personnel in rapid delivery of parts to the office or gate.*

10. *Eastern Oregon is "pickup country" and Brad focuses on having a plentiful supply of parts to keep them going. Cattle still have the right of way in Oregon, and more than a few front clips have replaced those that lost an argument with a Hereford or Angus on a back road.*

10

out to the yard and have it back on the counter, or waiting on a forklift at the gate. This yard specializes in parts from '80 to '93 models. It particularly focuses on light trucks, but does have considerable quantities of great sheet metal parts for both, from about '73 to '80 models.

Anything prior to those years, would have to come from the "Carrell's Collectibles" inventory, whose only connection to this yard is the owner and his family. With this sort of harmony and teamwork, it's easy to see why Brad isn't anxious to have the phone ringing off the hook with inquiries regarding the inventory at "Carrell's Collectibles" which I will endeavor to treat as a separate entity, per Brad's request.

One thing for certain, if you need a later model part, pick up the phone, call and you'll be assured of an answer in minutes rather than the usual, "let me have someone go check," response.

"Carrell's Collectibles" or "Brad's Boneyard" are my labels attached to the owner's separate collection, that he chooses to separate from his main sal-

**Brad's Auto & Truck Parts,
Brad & Sharon Carrell: owners,
2618 S. Highway 97,
Redmond, Ore. 97756
503-923-2723
Fax 503-923-3113
Hours: 8 am-5 pm Weekdays
10 am-2 pm Saturdays**

vage yard business.

It is not located near the main yard. In fact, it isn't even visible from the roads around the community. Many parts, parts vehicles, and eminently restorable vehicles in residence here are for sale or swap, but only by mail. Brad Carrell, his wife Sharon, and the whole family are enthusiasts and hobbyists, and the premises reflect their mutual interests. One building houses the body and paint shop, which is busy completing a solid Chevelle SS convertible and a '55 Chevy convertible. Other buildings contain numerous special projects and performance vehicles, including a unique red

'57 Bel-Air "hot tub," destined for a patio site which is already equipped with automotive seats and a bar made from an Edsel. Many of the vehicles are for sale or trade even though completed. A few, like his father's 409 Impala, are not. Nestled elsewhere, in a rock and juniper basin, is an isolated storage area of several acres, covered with numerous special interest vehicles, which should make any collector or restorer antsy.

Doesn't take a genius to determine his love for Pontiacs first, and performance vehicles next. Some are slated for restoration, some for parts, and several models, which appear capable of driving away, are "horse-trading" material. Brad spends a lot of time on the road looking for additions to his assortment and at present is more interested in acquiring than he is selling or swapping. But thinning out certain vehicles and parts is simply part of the hobby. His right hand man with the hobby material is Ron Carter, who graciously provided the tour, and wears two hats; one at the main store, and the other here doing off frame restorations. He takes the "keep

11

11. *Hoods and more hoods.*

12. *Another view of the pickup "clip" with boxes this time. Note how many late models are evident.*

12

ers" from the ground up, to where they are ready for paint and interior, and turns them over to Tom Conners, a pro with the spray gun, judging from the vehicles present. A ballpark guess would put the number of vehicles here somewhere around 150. It's conceivable he may have a dozen or two scattered around the country he has yet to bring home from his travels.

Until he's ready, and that may be a little while yet, this yard is primarily hobby oriented until he retires and leaves the operation of the yard downtown to his family. Then he can pursue his first love of tinkering and horsetrading full-time, along with his other leisure activities. If you see something in the photos that you don't think you can survive without, either a complete car or

parts thereof, *please don't call* Brad's. Rather, write to the address below and you will receive a prompt response either by phone or return mail.

BRAD'S AUTO & TRUCK PARTS
Part 2
(CARRELL'S COLLECTIBLES)

By Doc Howell

1. *Obviously Brad is not one of those people who adheres to the old adage that you should leave all business at the office. This deck at home just being completed just "happens" to have a '55 Chevy settee, overlooking a lower deck being prepared to receive a novel hot tub.*

2. *The northeast corner of the large deck has a unique wet bar most will recognize, even if he did scrape the Nixon sticker off the bumper. The vintage Magnolia pump obviously contains Mint Julip mix.*

1

Carrell's Collectibles or Brad's Boneyard, are both my labels, for lack of any formal title. They are out of deference to the owner of Brad's Auto & Truck Parts in Redmond, Oregon, who wanted readers to know that there was a difference between his main business and his collection/hobby, the latter of which is not located at the main yard. In fact, it isn't even visible from roads around the community.

Nestled in a rocky basin rimmed with sagebrush and juniper trees near his residence is a very enviable assortment of 175 to 200 vintage vehicles, only a very minor portion of which would be considered "parts vehicles." The majority of the cars are in good to fair condition, eminently restorable and rust free. With a jump-start and some priming, they could undoubtedly drive onto a trailer, if not down the highway.

Brad's residence, outside of Redmond, is landscaped with some unique automotive memorabilia. You'll have to admit, there aren't too many people who have Edsel wet bars, '55 Chevy seats, and a '57 Chevy convertible hot tub. All of the buildings in the immediate vicinity of the house, including the body and paint shop as well as the various storage buildings, have restored vintage gas pumps or islands leaving little doubt as to the family's interest and activities.dy and paint shop was busy working on a

2   3

5

6

7

3. Okay, now you've seen it all. Rear clip love seats are one thing, but a '57 Chevy hot tub?

4. Just more very neat decor, this old Gilmore pump has a sign that dates it a bit since Regular is listed at nine cents per gallon.

5. If you think this '60 Bonneville is nice, you should see some of the others inside the buildings.

6. Just a sneak preview of what lies in store at his isolated "goody" acreage. Count the Pontiacs visible and overlook the Mopar in the foreground. I have it on good authority it is on its way out.

7. Two nice '60 Impalas await their turn at bat.

8. A '58 Impala, '68 Chevelle Super Sport and '56 Buick Century were all performance cars in their day.

8

9

10

9. *Still being finished, in light grey primer that is more reflective than I figured, is this 429 Boss. Immediately aft is Brad's father's old "lead sled," if you want to call a '63 Impala with a 409 and original 29,000 miles, such a term. This Pantera is red, and another not pictured is a white GT with black trim. Behind the Pantera is a bright green Cougar Eliminator.*

10. *Sometimes Brad gets so busy, he doesn't know whether he's coming or going, so he made certain he had the right rig to take with him. How about the Siamese twin Chevy pickup behind the '61 Impala convertible.*

11

12

13

very desirable Chevelle SS convertible, a '55 Chevy convertible and a Lincoln Town Car. Outside the shop was a row of convertibles and hardtops waiting their turn for some refurbishing. The storage buildings contain numerous collector cars, some for sale or trade and some, like his father's 409 Impala hardtop, are in the "forget it" category. It is evident that Brad has three preferences; performance, Pontiacs, and convertibles. I would guess if all were lumped into one choice, it would probably be a '58 Bonneville convertible, with tri-power, and four on the floor.

11. *This area is well used by the various movie companies, so it stands to reason that at least one "movie star" would be around. This restorable black '59 Cadillac convertible was used in a locally filmed picture, and had a couple of novel "custom" features. First, a scene called for one of the stars to be held captive in the trunk. Not enamored of being shut in confined spaces, sans any light, it has a cord and light bulb rigged up under the trunk lid. In addition, this time presumably for insurance reasons, a small one or two quart "gas tank" is rigged up on top of the right front fender well. It must have been a once around the block shoot!*

14

12. *Ron and I decided opening one door would be ample to stimulate the reader. All four might induce shock, Brad's personal "body shop," contains enough lust provoking vehicles, that limited exposure was recommended. That little bit of red on the left is a nice '58 Impala, a '59 Chevy convertible, behind that a '63 Galaxie, and the Pontiacs speak for themselves.*

13. *A little TLC is still needed on this '60 Chevy ragtop.*

14. *Neither the '68 Pontiac nor the Edsel convertible were really one of my favorites, but they both will be in mint condition when finished. Personally, I took a shine to the Ford wrecker.*

15

15 *Another view of the "cache" and again Pontiac outnumbers them all.*

16. *No fill up here, I'm assured they were restored for decoration.*

16

17

18

17. *A little change of pace with two Oldsmobiles. You don't have to look far for a parts car.*

18. *An "orphan" '37 Studebaker looking a bit timeworn, next to a '55 Packard Clipper. I have a hunch Mark will be getting a letter from a fan on the Studebaker coupe and another one I spotted.*

19. *Both the El Camino and the '58 Safari are much sought after restorables.*

20. *This row will also get some fan mail.*

21. *Mostly parts cars back in this section, but the '49 Mercury is better than some I've seen ticketed for complete restoration.*

19

20

21

22

23

22. *Unlikely duo, a '58 Ford Fairlane and a '60 Pontiac, at least they're both two-door hardtops and share a healthy shade tree.*

23. *Just when you think you have a handle on the inventory, up pops a surprise like these Cadillacs, and a suicide door Continental.*

24. *Honest! This '40 Ford pickup used to belong to a house painter—the birds up here simply do not get that big!*

25. *Two more hard to find Pontiac convertibles.*

26. *Somehow, a '60 T-Bird slipped in here with these '50s GM cars.*

24

25

26

27

27. *Ron Carter, the Carrell family's prime restorer, points out another pair of strange faces in this yard, an older Jaguar sedan, and a '58 Lincoln Continental.*

28. *Obviously, the '49 Studebaker Commander convertible in the middle of this row simply doesn't fit.*

29. *You simply don't see '58 Bonneville hardtops around much any more.*

28

29

30

31

32

30. *A nice '60 Cadillac coupe lurks beside the shop.*

31. *Olds Starfires aren't exactly commonplace around the country either.*

32. *If I remember correctly, Ron said this custom homogenized street rod pickup was powered by a 350 Chevy, but other projects and activities took priority. Wouldn't take much to finish this for a "one of a kind ride."*

33. *If you thought the double ended Chevy pickup was a gas. Try this one on, former State Police HO Mustang was crunched and restored, with all of the regulation antennas and black and white sticker designating the emergency CB channels, it was too much for the crew to resist. The door sign is regulation size and color, but required some translating. I'd love to cruise by the barracks in the Capitol city with this puppy, but Ron said most of the troopers seem to shed their sense of humor during basic training, and it is almost guaranteed to earn a citation. Now how can that be?*

33

34

35

34. *A '58 Impala is on the way with a parts rig behind.*

35. *A decent and straight '63 Impala with Cadillacs and Pontiacs hiding in the brush.*

36. *Super straight '59 Bonneville from the time wide track got its start.*

37. *Not certain, but I think Ron said this hard-to-find model had been sold or traded.*

38. *This '65 Super Sport coupe and adjoining '63 Supersport convertible are getting closer to the restoration shop.*

36

37

38

39

40

His right hand man of nearly eleven years is Ron Carter, who graciously took time to lead the tour. Ron wears two hats, one at the main store, and the other doing ground-up restorations here at the "ranch." When they are ready to be painted, he turns them over to Tom Conners, a veritable wizard with a spray gun, judging from the completed "keepers" in evidence.

Many of the vehicles in the photos are to be restored, while others are to be sold or "horse traded" to improve his private collection. He is looking for restorable models of the '61 Ford Sunliner, '58 Bonneville or Chieftain convertible, '55 or '56 Ford convertible, '57 Chevy and '60 Chevy convertible. So if you're lukewarm about the one you have and would prefer one of those in the pictures, I suggest you write Brad a letter and see what the two of you can come up with.

Brad likes to travel around the country spotting and acquiring cars and knows many of the out-of-the-way sites that have been covered exclusively for "Cars & Parts" magazine. His ultimate goal is to retire soon and let his daughter and son take over the business downtown so he can pursue his first love of tinkering, acquiring, and trading collector vehicles.

HOPKINS ANTIQUE AUTOS & PARTS

By Doc Howell

Every once in a while, you meet someone in your travels to whom you instantly take a shine. They are natural and unaffected, always have something pleasant to say, wear an infectious grin, and just seem to bubble over with humor and good will. Having just driven over 300 plus miles through a snow storm, a hail storm, weathered some waits and several good spinal jolts from highway construction between Prineville, Ore., and the Idaho border on Highway 26, I certainly needed something to improve my outlook and disposition. Les Hopkins, owner of Hopkins Antique Autos and Parts in Middleton, Idaho provided the enthusiasm and humor that made me do a 180 degree turn-around. Judging from the customers at hand, he certainly wasn't going to starve for the lack of publicity an article in *Cars & Parts* would provide. So perhaps it was just two down

1

2

103   AMERICAN SALVAGE YARD TREASURES

3

4

1. *Les Hopkins standing outside his office and "barn." Note the sign over Hopkin's left shoulder.*

2. *These sheds, about 300 yards of them, are stuffed with '30s and '40s parts of every conceivable description.*

3. *All of the better folding hoods are located in one handy spot.*

4. *This view is from immediately behind the "barn" and I'd guess it is a full half mile from the northwest corner here, to the southwest corner over by the treeline.*

5. *This is the "bird's eye" view west from on top the venerable fork lift .*

5

6

7

home old boys swapping yarns and the time of day without any pretexts or fanfare to set the mood. We toured the "barn" as he calls the main building. I was intrigued by the display case of old Moto-Meters, and the very reasonable prices he was asking. In the next room hundreds of door and window cranks of every conceivable make and vintage festooned the ceiling and walls. Upstairs in the loft a new series of racks and shelves are in the process of being organized for window crank mechanisms, tail lights and lenses, vent windows, and other parts needing shelter. The north end of the loft was conspicuously empty and an inquisitive look prompted a response from Les. He said he used to have it full of NOS bearings, tie rod ends and such, that he'd picked up from dealers 15 years or so ago. He'd sold all of it to Joe Diorio in Portland, who operates Old Car Parts on Powell Blvd. in Portland. "Shucks, I'd been eating purty good off them for years and he made me a fair offer for the whole litter, so I done sold them to him. Besides, he's a good customer." In fact, he happened to call again when Les and I were about to step out and shoot his picture.

The yard covers about seven acres and is as flat as a pool table. As I was crawling up onto the chassis of a '30s vintage Ford heavy truck to get a couple of overall shots of the 700 plus vehicles, he hollered, "Hang on, I got an idea that will save a lot of climbin' around."

A few minutes later, he chugged around the corner in a vintage forklift that would have looked right at home out in the middle of all the cars. He tossed in a couple of sheets of well used 3/8-inch plywood across the tines to

6. Another "aerial" view, this time northwest toward the barn, "hubcap" shed, and other outbuildings, with some of the '30s and '40s cars in the foreground.

7. This is the east view in the middle of the yard from 35 feet in the air.

8. Down on the ground, a closer view of two rows of '30s vintage humpbacks, flatbacks, and about any other shape you'd want.

9. You'll notice the big question mark behind the chalked "Whippet" description. I couldn't find any reference material to improve upon the question mark.

9

10. More '30s and '40s bodies, and the surface rust is minor.

11. Rows and rows of doors for '40s and '50s on one end, '30s on the other end.

12. One of about three rows of '30s with some '40s edging their way in.

13. A '64 Dodge Polara convertible, and most of it seemed to be there.

10

11

12

13

serve as a platform. I hopped on and out into the field we went. I didn't notice at first, but this was one of those triple level jobs that really gets up in the air, and here I am over 30 feet above the ground with wind gusts of 40 knots, threatening to have me and the plywood airborne any minute. Once I had a leg cocked around one of the uprights and

the other size 12 shoe planted in the center of the boards, I took time to survey the yard and the surrounding farm land. Great view, good light, now lets see if I can coordinate the shutter release with the intermittent gusts. What you see is what you get. It's decidedly a better view than from ground roosts. After several shots, it was down to earth again

and a lengthy mosey through the yard. The earliest model I saw was the cab of a 1918 T, and I recognized it immediately after reading the chalk marks on the side door. After I covered the area and had gotten back to Les, I commented that he must have scoured the whole countryside for 100 miles to gather this many old timers. He said, "try 250!"

14

15

14. *East end of the field has a number of '50s and '60s cars that really haven't been pirated too much for parts yet.*

15. *Two rows of '20s and '30s. Model As, Dodges, Hudson, Durant, Essex, and a few that will send me thumbing through my directories.*

16. *More '50s and '60s with a lot of good parts.*

17. *Some '40s and '50s and the '54 Roadmaster has a lot of nice trim and sheetmetal left.*

18. *One of the panels was about a '46 and the one to the rear of it appeared to be about a '38 or '40 model.*

19. *Just one section of the '39 to '48 Fords and Mercurys.*

20. *Here the '30s and '50s meet back to back, but an occasional '40 model weaseled in somehow.*

21. *A Terraplane, a few Hudsons, '48 Dodge, and some Fords looking north off the forklift perch.*

16

17

18

19

After farming all his life, he decided he wanted a little hedge against inflation, something to fiddle around with when he retired and wasn't fishin'. So back in '72 he started buying old cars and parts of dated NOS parts from dealers. Now he finds he doesn't have as much time for fishing as he'd like. His two sons, Don and Bob are on hand full time now as well.

20

A lot of work has gone into organizing and stripping many of the vehicles. Along one fence are dash panels ranging from early Ts through Hudson, Studebaker and, up to what appeared to be a '48 Dodge. On another rack there were scores of window frames from '20s to '40s models of every type. There were headlamps, hubcaps, doors, running boards, engines, driveshafts, a virtual grab bag of vintage parts.

For the most part, he just lets his customers wander at will and scrounge for themselves. One fellow described what sort of tail light lenses he needed for his '50s vintage Ford, so Les just scratched his head and told him to wander over to a section he pointed to, and told him to see if what he wanted wasn't over yonder. Twenty minutes later the man was back with the pair and a big grin. Les charged him $20. and the size of the grin just doubled; small wonder!

There are a few very restorable complete cars along the tree line at the edge of the pasture.

As I was about to depart, two fellows from Seattle were trying to organize their newly acquired load of '37 Ford coupe parts on their dinky trailer for the long haul home. All for $400. Cost them more than that in gas and hamburgers to get over here and back.

I would have spent more time rummaging through everything simply out of curiosity, but it was close to dinnertime and I didn't want to monopolize his time any longer.

The address I will be listing is correct for mail, but if you go wandering around Caldwell, Idaho looking for this place, you'll get lost. Take I-84 headed towards Ontario, Ore., and about three miles out you'll see an off ramp for Middleton. Take that exit and immediately take a left where the sign says Old

21

22

22. *A whole fence row of dash panels from a Ford T up to a '46 Dodge.*

23. *The pickup cab section and vintages for '28 to '48 .*

24. *Can't find a window frame for a model up to late '49, I bet the one you're looking for is in this collection.*

23

24

25

26

25. *This showcase of vintage moto-meters and hood ornaments is quite impressive. Prices seemed quite reasonable and after viewing the contents, and some of the vintages, I can appreciate the padlock.*

26. *Just out back, you can browse through the hood department.*

27. *Hubcaps, trademarked axle caps, vintage parking lamps, and all sorts of items decorate the walls.*

28. *A row of Nash bathtubs behind the hubcap shed.*

27

28

29. *Air cleaners, motors, heater panels, and a whole shed full of more hard to find items.*

30. *A row of Hudsons I missed in the first pass.*

31. *Just a portion of the hubcap shed, and strangely, a pair of front fenders for a '58 Cadillac.*

32. *Nashes, Plymouths and a couple of Zephyrs nearby.*

29

30

31

32

33

34

33. *Another overview shot of the Nashes and Hudsons; just an idea of how many are out in this eight acre pasture.*

34. *A longshot view of the hupcap covered walls in the sheds east of the barn.*

35. *The ear-to-ear grins on these fellows from Seattle indicate they made a great buy. They bought a trailer load of '37 Ford coupe parts for $400. They were in the midst of loading their tiny trailer for the long drive home.*

35

Highway 30. A big sign on the left about three miles down the road lets you know you've reached Hopkins Antique Car Parts and Xmas Tree Farm?

" Yup, feller needs something to do in the winter." Open 8 to 6 daily, except Sunday and Monday, or when Les goes fishin', and the boys aren't covering like they should. This was a real treat thanks to Les' warm hospitality.

**Hopkins Antique Autos & Parts
(and Xmas Trees),
24833 Highway 30,
Caldwell, Idaho 83605
208-459-2877**

1

INDIAN VALLEY

By Doc Howell

Actually, the title I used is the location, but as easy as it is to overlook on a map, or spot on Highway 95 between Cambridge and Council, Idaho, I didn't think it would hurt to repeat the name a few times. Being just one part of old Chief Joseph's Nez Perce tribe's favorite hunting and camping areas, it's not surprising this irenic little valley bears the name it does. It's just one of many such, you'll see between here and the Canadian border. Back in the Lewis and Clark days, this was exclusively their territory.

This time it's the Morris' "Antique and Classic Cars & Parts site I'm hunting for, so I take it slow when I'm thirteen miles North of Cambridge, looking for the "Alpine" cafe. Spotting it, I continue another quarter mile where I note a small green arrow sign that reads, "Indian Valley Road. About three miles down this road, I came to a turn of the century old white building on the right which says "Indian Valley Store." On the east side of the building is the road I think I want, judging from the directions I received in town. After what seems like five miles of gravel road, I see the glitter of early morning sun off numerous windows and metal. Now the road bends left and another quarter mile brings me to a lane which has an old military armored scout car as a landmark or guardian. I arrive a little earlier than I anticipated and indicated on the phone the evening

2

3

1. *The Hitt Mountain ski area provides a snow capped backdrop to Lynn Morris' cache of antique and collector cars, in this isolated grassy pasture in Indian Valley.*

2. *This '33 Nash serves as a prop for several '20s vintage pickup and passenger car doors.*

3. *An assortment of vintage wire, steel, and wood spoked artillery wheels are stacked in the northeast corner of Lynn's pasture.*

4

5

6

4. *Later model hubcaps reflect the early morning sun, and provide a contrast to the vintage '20s and '30s radiator shells racked beside this small parts storage shed.*

5. *A row of late '40s and early '50s Nashes whose "bathtub" nickname stuck until the styling was modified with this '52 model at the end of the row.*

6. *This row of older trucks, includes a '58 Dodge, a '47 Chevy, and a '37 GMC truck.*

7. *What looks like it was once a vintage woodie wagon of unknown make, keeps company with a couple of solid old vintage sedans of the '20s.*

7

8. *I suspect this mid-'50s model Dodge, "Job Rated," truck was actually utilized in hauling the '37 Nash coupe to where they both repose.*

9. *Both the '41 Chevy sedan and the '53 Packard sedan seem to be very solid old cars.*

10. *A variety of Chevrolets, leading off with this '65 Corvair, hold down this piece of the yard.*

8

9

11. *A row of Hudsons reflects Lynn's interest in non "Big Three" autos.*

12. *What could be more appropriate than a group of Chiefs retiring in Indian Valley.*

13. *Not much left of this old C cab Autocar truck, but you never know who might need what, when it comes to restoring old vehicles.*

14. *Nash, Packard, and Willys make up an assortment in this lineup.*

15. *Here a row of Buicks from '41 through '55 appear to be chewing their way through the knee high grass.*

10

11

12

13

14

15

before, I have several minutes to wander around the immediate vicinity of the house stretching while waiting for the owner, Lynn Morris to make an appearance. The soft rolling green grassy hills that form a ring around Lynn's home and pasture almost give the appearance of mossy sand dunes. Clear, crisp, clean air, and as quiet as a tomb. Suddenly the quiet is pierced by a pair of meadowlarks trilling at each other. They sounded as if they were nearly underfoot. A scan with the 300mm lens, with a doubler, reveals that both are nearly a quarter mile away. Beautiful! They

16

16. *A long line of late '40s and early '50s Chevrolets.*

17.-20. *Nearly all Chrysler products, these pictures best reflect Lynn's preference for Mopars. Surprisingly, I didn't note any with rust-through body panels.*

21. *These '61 Buick hardtops seem to be a much desired car for those GM restorers in the "Bubbletop" era. The 401 engine was a noted performer in its day.*

22. *This '68 Chrysler 300 coupe seems pretty solid and in better condition than most.*

23. *From the early '53 right up the line, none of these cars seem to require a great amount of work to hit the road again.*

17

18

19

20

21

22

23

24

24. *No group would be complete without some Cadillacs, and here's a whole row starting with a hoodless '60.*

25.-28. *They are all Studebakers of varying years. The Conestoga wagon in number 26 is a rare car, and no explanation was given to why the '38 sedan in number 28 is quarantined.*

29. *This "teenager" still has a lot to work with, despite a few bullet holes.*

30. *The '36 DeSoto in the middle is restorable and needs an interior, but the '56 Dodge pickup was really in A-1 shape. Unfortunately, from what Lynn indicated, the Mopar engine was swapped for a Chevy.*

25

26

27

reminded me of youthful mornings on the ranch in eastern Oregon. A door bangs and here comes Lynn accompanied by a pair of dogs. His soft voice and unassuming air, he somehow fits the locale and environment to a T. Lynn advised me he has been with the Forest Service for twenty-five years or more and somehow it seems appropriate. He's been a car addict since he was 14 or 15. Having "always had a few around," he started gathering older vehicles in earnest about fifteen years ago. Again, as a hedge towards retirement and something to occupy his time

28

29

30

31

32

31. *This '62 Chrysler 300 didn't start out as a four-door convertible, but undoubtedly was stimulated by some Lincolns of its era.*

32. *Lynn's pride and joy, a '29 Dodge coupe. Good mechanical condition, the owner has driven it often over the years. It could use a trip to the beauty parlor, and Lynn assures me with a pull start, it would make it under its own steam.*

hat he enjoyed doing. Other than some business cards which he passes out about twice a year, when he hauls a load of parts to swap meets, Lynn doesn't really advertise or promote his yard. It's mostly by word of mouth, and I was fortunate enough to be listening when the old boy who runs the yard in Vale, Ore., was talking.

In the shed behind the house sits a '29 Dodge coupe which looked very solid, and which Lynn advised me was running last year, and would probably pull start now if I wished to see it run. Lynn said he'd driven it for quite a few years and was quite partial to Dodge in particular and Chrysler in general.

So, the four of us, which included the two dogs, set off to wade out into his pasture, and take photos of his inventory of restorable and parts vehicles. Since the grass was knee high and soaking wet with a heavy morning dew, "wade" is the appropriate term.

Though he may be partial to Chrysler vehicles, he also seems to have an affinity for orphan cars as well as many GMs: Hudsons, Nashes, Kaisers, Studebakers, and a few real oldies that might well have been Willys-Knights, Essex or Hupmobiles. There really weren't that many Ford vehicles in evidence other than some vintage pickups.

There were lots of old artillery and wire spoke wheels, fenders, and several old larger trucks whose names I have forgotten; but one I recognize as an Autocar. In response to my question, Lynn said at last count he had nearly 700 vehicles on hand and he wasn't through yet. Says he continues buying up whatever he can find, so long as it's within his budget. What few small outbuildings were in evidence, were crammed with parts, and some, like the rack full of engine heads, date back to the late '20s.

In the course of conversation, I mentioned some of the places I'd been, and who I'd seen in the past four days, and he commented that one of the parties whom I was covering in another article had been over more than once and purchased several complete cars. I knew this particular collector liked to personally go out and "beat the brush," but wasn't aware of just how extensive, and far ranging his foraging expeditions really were. Like most of the unpublicized places, a few of the collectors and restorers know where, but the average "road-hunter" out scrounging for vehicles or parts simply is not going to trip over them. Asking at the local gas station or auto dealer isn't going to help much either. This is one of those places, Lynn seems to be a rather quiet and retiring person, not prone to announcing to everyone within earshot what his hobby is or how many vehicles he has. Like many others I've met, he probably becomes more active around a swap meet environment with people he knows from other trips. Then again, how cheerful and communicative can you be when some stranger gets you out of the house at 7a.m. to wade through grass that has you soaked to the hips in minutes? It took the heater till Grangeville to dry my pants and shoes.

Since he works full time, Lynn requires a phone call for an appointment.

SALVAGE YARD TOUR:

HOT AUGUST NIGHTS TOUR

Phase IV

By Doc Howell

Any major apprehensions I had been harboring about starting out on a 2,300 mile trip, covering heretofore unpublicized salvage yards, to and from Hot August Nights in Reno, Nev., with a freshly installed, modified 440 Magnum engine, were largely dispelled after meeting a couple from Canada, who were homeward bound, and made my tour look like a run to the corner store.

In fact, that's exactly what I'd been doing, only in this case it was a parts store, and I was filling the "whale's" cavernous trunk with fan belts and all sorts of eclectic "things," I just might need enroute. On my way back, I fell in behind a pristine '55 Ford panel van, with fresh baby blue paint and Ontario plates. As it turned onto "my" street, and proceeded to pull into a local steak house, I couldn't miss the professionally done dark blue script lettering on the side panels with the legend, "Middle Aged Crazy." Assuming here was a couple also on their way to Reno, I followed them in and introduced myself. Worthy of a "spotter" photo, I inquired of their destination. "Home." They had been in Reno nearly a week ago, and were unaware of the Hot August Nights event coming up.

Norm and Pat Cryderman hail from Orellia, Ontario, Canada, and had purchased the van not too long ago in Indiana. Since the existing engine

expired on the way home, Norm got busy and installed an HO 302 Mustang engine, twin I-Beam suspension, and all sorts of nice little touches, including a bunk bed which saw ample service during their tour. As of August second, their tour had covered Alaska, the Yukon Territory, part of Mexico, and 30 States here, for a total of 9,882 miles. With at least 1,200 to 1,500 miles to go, they certainly covered some ground in their vintage custom. If you have problems with your street rod or vintage rig up in eastern Canada, I'd sure give Norm a call for advice, given the professional job he's done on this rig, and in view of his trouble free "road test."

Not that my modifications to the "whale" were so exotic, but the demo-derby crew I help sponsor, and yours truly, spent Sunday yanking the tired 440 out and dropping in the Magnum. The internals were reduced to 8.5:1 to cope with what the petroleum companies are palming off for gas, hardened valve seats, sodium valves, Offenhauser 360 degree single plane manifold, topped with one of the new Carter/Edelbrock aluminum four-barrel carburetors. A dual snorkel air cleaner, and an Edelbrock VaraJection system were hooked up. We installed Bosch plugs through Accel wiring and coil, and the tried and true Mopar Orange Box. The Mallory distributor would have to await my return. Next came a dual turbo exhaust, and a new 727 with a shift kit and no EGR stuff other

1. *Norm & Pat Cryderman from Ontario, Canada, with their very nice '55 Ford panel van, on the last leg of a 10,000-plus-mile trek, stopping in Coeur d' Alene to try out a hunk of steak.*

2. *Upper Klamath Lake in southern Oregon is usually covered with pelicans, but none were in evidence on this trip.*

3. *Captain Jack's stronghold in Newell, Calif., where the Modoc Indian chief of the southern Oregon tribe, made the U.S. Calvary go back and read the strategy books all over again.*

1

2

3

han the vapor can. A quick trip to Spokane emissions center saw green light readings—it passed with flying colors. In fact, one of the testers was so skeptical, he ran the NOX three times with little or no differential. Satisfied, it was time to go home and get the "whale" loaded for the trip.

I launched at four a.m., Tuesday the third, and my itinerary called for covering one salvage yard in Klamath Falls, Ore., 609 miles down the road. My route retraced a previous tour as far as Bend, Ore., so I needn't be redundant regarding the terrain and scenery. By the time I reached Bend, I noted the temperature gauge was running warmer than normal, and stopped to pick up some magazines while I had Insty-Lube change the oil and filter. The completed engine had been sitting under wraps for a few months and I wished to give it every benefit of the doubt. The fan belts popped off when I started it and cracked the neck of the overflow bottle, so a quick patch was done on that along with really snugging up the double belts.

By the time I reached Klamath Falls, it was run-

ning excessively warm again, so I let it cool down while I covered Klamath Auto Wrecking, owned and operated by Bill Hulbert since 1980. In business since '55, it is probably southern Oregon's oldest salvage yard. Of the four to five yards in the area, his is the only one with any inventory of interest to restorers and hobbyists. All of the others succumbed to the lure of the scrap steel prices of yore, and let the crusher run amok in their yards. At that, Bill's inventory is limited to mid '50s and early '60s, and for the most part GM's and Chevys, which lets you know where his interests lie.

Completing the yard coverage, I hastened down to Sure-Save Auto before they closed, and had Randy's mechanic yank the thermostat. Good thing. Either yours truly or one of his helpers had kinked the gasket, which kept the thermostat cocked open. A new one went in properly along with a wire coil reinforced top hose. That evening, it got a back flush in a friend's driveway. I had a nice dinner with an old friend and was confident at breakfast time that the heating glitches had

4

5

4. *This gorge under the Bridge at Twin Falls, Idaho is the one that Evel Knievel had second thoughts about jumping a number of years ago. I can't imagine why.*

5. *Largest A & W drive-in around the country, and a second home for many during Hot August Nights in Reno.*

6. *Stand here on Virginia Street, under the millions of lights, on any night of Hot August Nights, and you'll see around 5,000 vehicles cruise past.*

6

been cured. To cover all bets, I made a call to the Chrysler dealer in Reno and ordered a replacement overflow bottle which was to arrive via air from Portland the next day.

After breakfast, it was on to Newell, Calif., and Withers Auto Wrecking. The yard covers 10 acres on the west side of the highway south of Newell. For the unfamiliar, Newell is about 10 miles south of Tulelake, Calif., where some great duck and goose hunting prevails. Newell has some historical significance that many are unfamiliar with unless

7

8

9

7. *No, not giants, nor is that a customized Austin or Bantam. The owner actually hand built this diminutive 1939 Chevy two door from the original McCoy, and everything appears to be correct and to scale. I was trying to figure what the engine was and Belinda Grisez from* Cars & Parts *was trying to figure out how it would fit in her tote bag.*

8. *Convention center site for the Silver Auction and Show Car display was packed with choice vehicles: originals, restored cars, street rods, customs and a special one-owner Ford Collection.*

9. *At the Reno-Sparks Fairgrounds where the acreage was covered with vendors and their wares, what else would you figure the owner of this nice Eldorado would be selling other than Cadillac parts.*

10. *This keen-eyed shopper just found the Holley Carb he has been looking for among the Chevy parts.*

10

11. *Early Saturday morning there were more than just a few nice cars and trucks gathered at the fairgrounds swap meet and car corral.*

12. *Indoors at the fairgrounds, vendors abounded on the mezzanine, and the center floor of the arena was getting ready for the "Workingman's Auction," where the vehicles were limited with a price lid of $6,000. We didn't get close, but a '60s vintage T-Bird and several others appeared worthy of being close to that money.*

11

12

13. *Ken New, left, gets to meet Mitch Silver, who spearheads all of the Silver Auctions, which bear his name. Mitch was seen earlier in a corner making obeisance to some spiritual entity for this event being indoors this year, rather than under a tent outside in the 90-plus-degree Reno heat.*

13

into early American History. It was the last hold-out of one of the wily and rebellious Modoc Indian chieftains, Captain Jack. Here, in one of the buttes, a few miles south of the highway, now dubbed "Captain Jack's Stonghold," he and a handful of followers proceeded to make donkeys out of a rather large contingent of US Calvary. In later years, the government, in its infinite wisdom, built an internment camp here to house quite a number of the Japanese citizens of this country during WW II.

An early arrival finds Jess Withers eager to guide me on a tour of the yard. An eclectic assortment of vehicles dating back to the early '30s and more than a few decent military vehicles, which I assume were from the local area, including not only a decent white halftrack, but a tracked Bren gun carrier. A vintage International truck under cover looked very good, as well as many of the '50s and '60s vehicles present.

Next on the agenda was Alturas and Susanville. Inquiries there divulged that the lots that existed

14

15

16

14. *A different view of the auction cars glistening under the bright lights at the Convention Center.*

15. *The stands were packed with spectators at the auction. There was a 75 plus percent sales result, with a net of over $3.5 million, after three days and over 400 vehicles!*

16. *Ken New, Art Director for* Cars & Parts Magazine, *angles for a good shot of the '55 Corvette that Chevrolet gave Zora Arkus Duntov, for his contribution to this famous model. This was before the overhead lights gave us good shooting weather.*

back in the mid '70s, when I worked in this area, had incurred the wrath of the DEQ, due to oil spillage during engine removals, and were out of business for all practical purposes. Bucking road construction, and with one eye on the temperature gauge, it was time to gas up in Standish, and get on over the hill to Reno and get checked in.

The next morning I was at a radiator shop not too far from the Hilton, having a block check done, which revealed no combustion leaks, relieving me no end. I was assured the fan clutch was A-OK, and spent the next few days caught up in the whirlwind of activities Hot August Nights offers. As I'm known for being windy, I could

17

17. *Just one of the star cars at the show adjacent to the auction. Now how many Bel Air hardtops could one buy with this investment?*

18. *Well, after viewing this late model Cadillac at the Car Show display, maybe there is hope for some of the '80 and '90 model cars—at least as far as customs go.*

18

probably fill a book, but since a goodly number of the staff of this publication were present covering it, I will leave coverage up to them. Suffice to say that every circus in the country combined with some big ones of yore, wouldn't compare to the color and number of activities. Whatever your interest in automobiles, plan to go to next year's event.

Though it is probably pointless to comment, I

can't resist mentioning that the city fathers would do well to levy a windfall profits tax on the hotels, motels, and selected vendors, and use the proceeds to improve the streets, and lend the National Automobile Museum (nee Harrah's) a hand in retiring the construction bonds. It seems the alternative, if donations and assistance aren't forthcoming, is to auction off the cars and accessories worth over $30 million, retire the bond obligation, and funnel the excess into the general fund. That would be a disaster and we all know how general funds have a tendency to vaporize when politicians have their own pet projects. Anyway, it would be a toss up to decide who was griping the loudest; the guys having to pay $3 for a beer, or the owners of the customs, street rods, and low riders, cursing a blue streak at the condition of the streets. It wasn't uncommon to see a roadster or coupe beside the road with someone sticking their head underneath. The local Midas shop must have had a field day.

East of Sparks, I located Mustang Auto Wrecking, owned and operated by Dan Bowers. Contrary to the name, he specializes in vintage Mopars and Cadillacs. The Mustang name, or "handle" around here, is attached to anything near Exit 23 on Highway I-80, in the general area of the notorious Mustang Ranch where the world's oldest profession is not only legal, but flourishes. Being curious, I shot a couple of night pictures of this establishment which is lit up like Casino Row downtown. The resemblance didn't end there either—it was late Friday night and the number of cars in the parking lot would have rivaled any of those belonging to the casinos. Traffic on the road in and out was only sightly less than Virginia Street during the Cruise. Every third vehicle seemed to be a taxi, and weekends must be the driver's bonus payday.

But to digress, Dan Bowers has about six acres of assorted vintage vehicles, and has his own on-site crusher. According to him, a large percentage of his business is by mail/freight, and he ships a lot of parts to outfits in Wisconsin and Pennsylvania, who in turn ship them to Europe. Since there is no moisture, there isn't any rust, which makes his sheetmetal parts very desirable. On Hot August Nights weekends, he packs his vintage Chrysler 300 and heads for the hills. He says, "the people flocking in here drive me crazy."

This year he might have gotten a break had he stayed home, since some "wacko" stole a van in San Francisco, rolled it over up by Elko, and the State Patrol had the highway blocked off for nearly twelve hours. Not that the wreck was all that spectacular, it was just that this aspiring crack manufacturer not only had a load of highly flammable solvents and stuff on board, he also had two fused bombs he'd made up from ammonium nitrate. After apprehended, he said he was on the way to northern Idaho, and all I can say is "thank you Nevada," we certainly don't need any more antisocial eccentrics up here. Maybe some of the more hardy Reno bound people opted for the 250 mile detour through Wells, Ely, Eureka, and Fallon, but I suspect that given the empty slots at the swap meet the next morning, more than a few turned tail and went home.

From Mustang, it is a long haul across the hot, barren, alkali flats to Winnemucca. The road was straight and smooth and you'd think it would be the ideal place to stick your foot in the pump and

19. *Not Death Valley, just some of the 100 plus miles of alkali scenery between Reno and Winnemucca. Now you see why more than just a few tote spare fan belts, and a few gallons of water!*

20. *Between Wells and Jackpot, Nevada, I must admit the scenery was vastly improved. See if you can spot the Pronghorn Antelope that prompted this shot.*

make express time. However, given the number of Highway Patrolmen who were busy pulling people over, I'm sure this stretch of monotonous highway generates a lot of revenue for the State of Nevada. It's nice to know they're out there though, since a breakdown here, a long way from nowhere, could be a problem. I stopped midpoint to add some water as a precautionary measure, and didn't see a car in either direction. The hood was barely up when one of the troopers pulled in behind me and gave me an inquiring look. I waved an A-OK. Don't ask me where he came from, but from there on, I viewed every clump of bushes with suspicion, and double checked my detector and cruise control several times.

Winnemucca has been plucked clean of restorable older cars and parts cars, and the whole community appears fresh and new. Open-pit gold mining with the leaching process has really been a shot in the arm for this old town. One of the nicest parts of the trip was finding the old and rather haggard appearing Winnemucca Hotel, which houses a Basque bar and dining room. Everyone eats family style—I can assure you it was excellent, a treat and a bargain. The platters go around and there seems to be no end to them. I thought dinner was over, and after loosening my belt for the second time, and wiping my chin, here came heaping platters full of T-bone steaks that

were at least 3/4 inch thick and not less than 12 to 14 oz. each. Since these people relish their food, I let my belt out another notch, and joined them. "All you can eat for $12"—it doesn't get any better than this! Don't miss it if you're in the area. It was a pleasant surprise after the tariffs in Reno.

The next morning a cruise of Elko proved fruitless so far as salvage yards were concerned. There was, however, a small operation north of Wells that appeared to have some nice pieces, at least from my binoculars. Unfortunately, there was no sign indicating it was a commercial venture or open to the public, so I continued on toward Twin Falls. A short stop was made in Jackpot to load on board a case of cards which I dole out to various charities like the VA Hospital. Some of these casinos go through decks like we would napkins when the highrollers get into a game. They might holler for a new deck every third or fourth hand and the club managers are happy to see the barely used decks go for a good cause.

In Twin Falls, it seems everyone has upgraded to being concerned about vehicles only 10 years old or newer. The one yard that does have some older parts, Idaho Equipment and Salvage, isn't looking for any more vintage acquisitions, and when what's on hand is gone, the well will be dry.

21. *Well, I don't remember anything on the travel brochures about the country between Twin Falls and Boise, Idaho being touted as scenic, but at the same time, they didn't mention the Kamikaze Jackrabbits either.*

On to Wendell, Idaho and what may be the biggest vintage salvage yard in the country. Desert Sky, located just outside of Wendell on state Highway 46, has 180 acres of property, approximately 100 of which is covered with every imaginable car from around '46 to '73. Of these, about 1,200 or so are intact and restorable. Not only do they do a land office business locally, but Glenn Mott, the head of sales, tells me they ship an abundance out every day. Definitely high on any restorers number one list, they are anything but static or inactive. Monday, the owner was up in Stanley, Idaho negotiating for another 150 assorted vehicles. If you check your map, you'll find Wendell about 14 miles west of Twin Falls, just north of Highway I-84. Circle it on your map!

From Wendell, the next stop was Glenns Ferry. I had learned an old boy who used to have quite an assortment of old GM and Mopars in his yard had passed away. However, his son no longer pursued the activity.

From there, I headed towards Mount Home, Idaho. Just west of there, off the freeway and onto old Highway 30, is located Highway 30 Auto Salvage. On the north side of the highway and down in what used to be a gravel pit, the owner has about five acres of various vehicles. He is obviously partial to GM vehicles, Pontiac wagons in particular, if the row of early '60s is any indication. This seems to be a favorite source for many of the tinkerers from the airbase nearby. When the young A and P mechanics get tired of tinkering with F-15's, here is where they come for bits and pieces for their project cars.

After Desert Sky in Wendell, anything further would really be anticlimactic. Having covered the western end of southern Idaho on another tour, it now remains a matter of mulling over where I've been and what I've seen and photographed. Some, like the picture of the gorge at Twin Falls where Evel Knievel didn't do his leap for fame, and some of the shots of the alkali flats and the after dark shots of the Mustang Ranch etc., may be reproduced in articles, or may just repose in my own archives. I can propose, but others dispose. Right now, it is a long haul up Highway 95 from Boise to home, and I've already done this stretch for another tour, so I can tuck my shooters away and enjoy the beautiful scenery up this stretch of the Nez Perce Trail of Tears. Actually a great trip despite some teething problems with the old Chrysler's cooling system, but somehow she must have sensed my displeasure, and responded like a young gazelle when punched. Whether due to the manifold or carb change, or tweaks to the transmission, she is somehow getting about 60 percent better mileage and I can assure you, I've got the ticket from a county mountie proving that this was no sedentary cruise. I won't mention where, but at one point the speedo registered 100 miles per hour at 3150 rpm, and out of curiosity, I ran the tach on up to just under 3350 rpm, and was curious what that may have been. Any math geniuses out there who are good interpolating? On second thought, maybe it is just as well I don't know.

KLAMATH AUTO WRECKERS

By Doc Howell

Being a tinkerer and an old car nut at heart, I become instinctively wary anytime I get around an operation where the owner isn't of the same inclination. In this case, shoppers needn't worry about Bill Hurlbert, who is a dyed-in-the-wool addict, with more than a few restorations under his belt. The red custom '60 Chevy pickup bears testimony to his interest and efforts. With a '50 Olds coupe up on blocks in the shop undergoing an off-frame restoration, he is also well acquainted with what scavenging around for that exact part is all about. And, if my second-hand information is correct, he is also a supporter of the very active hobby-stock racing group at the local paved speedway.

Bill acquired the yard from the former owner in 1980, but the business was established here in 1955, making it one of the oldest in Oregon. Like many others in salvage yards, he succumbed to the siren's lure of high scrap steel prices at a time when '40s, '50s and '60s were plentiful, and let crushers run amok in his yard as well, but a tour around the yard reveals those days are gone forever.

The entire center portion of the yard, and some fringe areas are devoted to cars of the late '50s and early to mid '60s. No question that he leans toward GMs in general and Chevy specifically, but other GM marques as well as some Ford and Mopar are also evident. There is also an abundance of parts for the vintage four wheelers in this area, who consider them as their first vehicle and a car as the second vehicle.

1

2

3

1. *If you're anywhere along South 6th Street in Klamath Falls, Ore., and looking for Klamath Auto Wrecking, it's not too hard to spot Bill Hurlbert's Corvair "beacon" atop the roof. The customized red '60 Chevy pickup, parked in front of the garage door, is but one of his restoration projects.*

2. *This very decent '56 Buick Special hardtop wouldn't take all that much effort to fit right in at the Reno Cruise or any other show and shine event.*

3. *I'm not quite sure how the Lincoln clip fits in this lineup, but I suspect the Olds front end in the lower middle already has a designated home, with the '50 coupe being restored inside.*

4. *A learner from past mistakes, overusing the crusher, Bill has this solid '64 Pontiac Tempest LeMans clearly marked "no parts-no strip."*

4

5

6

5. *Under all the debris beats the faint heartbeat of a solid '60 Chevy El Camino, which you certainly don't see much of anymore. The sibling '61 Impala four-door resting alongside has lots of clean sheetmetal and trim to spare.*

6. *There are a lot of brew pubs and nostalgia enterprises using panel vans, which started out life in much worse condition than this one.*

7. *Just one of the rows of rust-free late '50s and '60s monopolizing the whole center section of Klamath Auto's acreage.*

7

8. *Bill slipped a Ford and Buick Skylark into this row of '60s, but it is the three, count 'em, '57 Chevy wagons that should be your focus of attention.*

9. *In 4X4 country, good International Scouts and Jeep parts are almost as prized as '55 to '57 Chevy parts. This is the place to find them.*

10. *I'm surprised, given the proximity to Bend, Ore., that this '60 Ventura Pontiac wasn't spirited away to Brad Carrell's stash up there, but maybe he doesn't know about it. It is definitely well worth someone's attention.*

8

9

10

11

12

11. *Same thing applies to this '60 Bonneville four-door hardtop, which seems poised to escape the confines of the yard, and get back to cruisin' a wide track trail.*

12. *Tacky, but solid, this '63 Impala has several more like her along with some '64s in Bill's inventory.*

13. *Another '63 in a side view, shows how well the southern Oregon climate preserves good sheet metal and trim.*

north and east of here, in the area of central and eastern Oregon generally called the "High Desert." It is a climate highly conducive to preserving good sheetmetal and trim items. Such being the case, the operation does ship numerous parts to disadvantaged areas back east, who compound their climate induced attrition by salting their highways. Yuck! Anyway, if you don't see what you need in the photos, give Bill a ring, and odds are, if he doesn't have it on hand, he'll know where to find it.

13

Klamath Auto Wreckers,
3315 Washburn Way,
Klamath Falls, Ore. 97603
503-882-1677
1-800-452-3301
(Ore., Nev., Calif. only)
Hours: 8-5 Monday-Friday
9-1 Saturday

By Doc Howell

Y ou definitely need to be an early riser to catch Jess Withers, and avail yourself of a tour of this 10 acre yard located just south of Newell, Calif., across the state line from Klamath Falls on Highway 139. Oregon Highway 39 changes to California 139 as you cross the state line and drive through the waterfowl refuge area at Tulelake, Calif.

Withers Auto Wrecking is located approximately 10 miles south of Tulelake and about two miles south of the Handi-Market and souvenir shop, which is apparently Newell's prime business, along with all of the potato packing and storage sheds. On the west side of the highway, it is easy to spot, due to the series of faded red bungalow buildings, which years ago, provided crew living quarters for a mining operation. Out front, in lieu of a sign, sits a '37 IHC pickup, a '30 or '31 Model A truck, and a solid old '35 Chevy truck, which obviously had either some selective customers or "do-it-yourself" after-hours interlopers.

Jess lives on the premises in the low white building set back behind rows of vehicles, and is available only from seven to nine a.m. "most days," and the same time on Saturdays, "sometimes." The assortment inside dates from early '30s up to a few early '70s models, and runs the gamut from passenger through commercial to military rigs. A good solid M15A halftrack is behind the house and apparently a later owner used it as a flatbed truck. Under a small pole-barn - type roof is a tracked Bren gun carrier much like a WW II M29C Studebaker Weasel, right next to a surprisingly well

1

2

WITHERS AUTO
WRECKING

1. *This '37 Dodge 1 1/2 ton is just as solid and rust free as it appears. The rarely seen fastback, circa '49-'52, Plymouth behind it was in even better condition.*

2. *Front view of the operation as seen between the highway and the old miner housing shows, three vintage trucks, from right to left; '35 Chevy, '31 Model A and '37 IHC. These are still solid but obviously either parts hunters have been at work or they are subject to scavengers after dark.*

3

3. *This yard is full of surprises, and the decent condition of the '65 T-Bird Landau and the '69 Plymouth beside it gives the viewer at least a taste of the solid, rust-free condition of the majority.*

4. *This print gives a better idea of sheetmetal and trim condition on these cars. This '63 Dodge Dart is but one example. Sorry, I already checked and it isn't a 413 with dual quads, or it would have been on a trailer following me to Reno.*

4

5

5. *A really straight body and good trim on this '57 Ford Fairlane two door hardtop. The surface rust appears manageable on this much-sought-after model.*

6. *The engine and hood are both there with this '62 Buick Skylark. Decent ones with the 215-cid aluminum engines are hard to find.*

6

preserved '29 IHC truck. There are several rows of GM middleweights, all with excellent sheetmetal and trim due to the dry climate and minimal rainfall, whose grilles, bumpers, and trim are excellent in condition. A good solid '53 Plymouth Belvedere appears to have been just driven in and parked. For that matter, a large percentage of these vehicles seem to be in a condition that suggests they arrived under their own steam.

What was intriguing was the endless variety, with no particular emphasis on any given make, model or year. Nor are they necessarily stored in anything other than random fashion, in order of arrival. According to Jess, they prefer to sell complete units, and for that matter, they would like to sell the entire 10 acres and inventory. Since there aren't

7

8

7. This '61 Dodge Phoenix hardtop is solid. It's a very popular model in some Mopar collector circles.

8. This '58 Edsel rubbing elbows with the late '30s IHC pickup, needs a lot of TLC on the hood, but is otherwise in very decent shape.

9. Excellent trim and front end on this '60 Chevy would make it a bargain parts car for someone.

9

10

10. *The '55 Olds was quite decent, but it was the unique Bren gun carrier with its' headlight peeking up in front of the pickup box that intrigued me.*

11. *The '60 Ford Ranch wagon tucked in the middle is becoming an extremely rare find anymore. The dry climate here preserved this one from the fate of most.*

12. *The straight, nearly rust free sheetmetal and trim items that are evident in this line-up of mixed '50s middleweights, are rapidly vanishing commodities.*

11

12

13

13. *Two more examples of really straight restorables available. Supposedly, the nailhead V-8 in the Buick is in good condition.*

14. *Another '60 Chevy Impala, in four-door hardtop form, with everything there. The appearance of sheetmetal and trim speak for themselves.*

15. *This '46 Dodge was really solid, but the box and the contemporary picket fence bumper guard arrangement, would both have to go!*

14

16

16. *There were several of these mid '50s Pontiacs here, and it is remarkable how the chrome plated parts have avoided pitting, like most of the early post-Korean-War era trim items.*

17. *This GMC military rig is one of several in excellent condition here in the yard. This one has a rare configuration that I'm neither familiar with nor find any reference to in my military books.*

17

any other yards except farther north in Klamath Falls, and the DEQ crippled those between here and Reno, this could be the bargain of the year, depending upon price. For that, you'd have to contact Tom Withers via phone at 818-894-9464. Keep trying as he has other interests and is sometimes difficult to locate. Given its' somewhat off-the-beaten path location, ownership isn't likely to change hands overnight. If some auto addict out there somewhere is considering retirement where the climate is great, waterfowl hunting is superb, one number one baker potato from the locals is a full meal, a large city less than an hour away, and the glitz and glamor of Reno are two hours away, better grab the phone.

For now, prices on the inventory are negotiable and Jess is the dickering type.

Withers Auto Wrecking,
138AAA Rt. 2,
Tulelake, Calif. 96134
916-664-2204

Mustang Auto Wreckers is located on Highway I-80 a few miles east of Sparks, Nevada. Take exit 23, pass under the freeway and you are there. It is readily visible from the freeway, and lies on the north side, to avoid confusion with A-Auto Wrecking on the other side of Mustang Ranch Road. It covers about seven acres in this area of arid rolling hills. A crusher stands at the east end of the yard. The name might be misleading if you happen to be looking for parts for your Falcon based Lee Iacocca pony car. The owner, Dan Bowers, specializes in vintage Cadillac and Mopar cars and parts. The "Mustang" name is derived from this location's proximity to the famous Mustang Ranch, which is across the freeway and down in the

1

MUSTANG AUTO WRECKERS

gulch alongside the Truckee River. You may not see "Mustang" on your Rand McNally Road Atlas, but rest assured, it is not only on the local maps but the Highway Department has prominent signs on display to assure you.

Dan does a lot of business overseas through some outlets in Wisconsin and Pennsylvania, who re-ship to owners who want grade A rust free sheet metal. As may be discerned from the photos, even the easily removed surface rust we're all familiar with, is a hard commodity to find on any of these cars. Besides, who ever heard of salting desert roads anyway?

A Mopar enthusiast himself, Dan's personal pet is a vintage Chrysler 300 and it gets some extra exercise during Hot August Nights weekend. He says the "people drive him nuts" (asking for Mustang parts no doubt), so he packs his camping gear and heads for the hills. With the Sierra Nevada range on Reno's western doorstep, and Lake Tahoe less than an hour away, who could blame him? He's not really anti-social, but I got the impression that the horde that descends on the Reno area during this week's events is equated somewhere along the lines of the historical sacking of Rome.

According to Dan, he's "just making a living at something he enjoys" and having his own on-site crusher probably helps matters. With his interest in the vehicles, it is a safe bet that whatever gets fed to the beast is either beyond salvation or not much in demand. At the current price of nine to ten dollars per ton for scrap, it takes more than a few to pay for the diesel.

2

3

1. *The Mustang Auto Wreckers specialize in Cadillac and Mopar parts, not pony cars.*

2. *What year and ratio do you want? Do you want it with or without locker gears?*

3. *You'll need to bring your own microscope to find any rust on this '59 Ford front door or the inverted hood on the ground. Rust heck, tough to find any water around here.*

4. *A long shot from the crusher over a third of the yard. I suspect the herd of Omnis and Horizons have a close view of their ultimate fate.*

5. *I heard a suspicious buzzing from beneath the rear end of the Imperial. Since I was not wearing my boondockers and did not have a good forked stick handy, I felt the view from here was excellent.*

6. *Over in the Eldorado and van section, you can readily see there are plenty to select.*

7. *You must have some imagination. At first, from farther away, it looked as if this Cadillac Brougham had a set of bed springs on it. This close to the Mustang Ranch, I had all sorts of ribald scenarios formulating before I got up to it! No, it isn't attached and no, I really don't know what it is since it doesn't appear to be a luggage rack for an airport limo, but the Cadillac is in better shape than the rack.*

5

6

7

8

8. *Either way, sand them, paint them and hang them, or hang them first and refinish them. These doors just don't need a whole lot of help.*

9. *The paint may be sun faded, but all three of these Mopars appeared as though they could have been driven away.*

10. *Given their vulnerability to rust back in the mid-'50s, most '56 Plymouths like this one were history many years ago. I'm surprised it is still intact, given the ever increasing interest in Chrysler products.*

11. *I had already shot this one before I discovered it belongs to John at the used oil recycling center next door. There weren't all that many of these early panel vans around with the V-8s. Whether it is for sale or not might depend upon a call to Dan.*

9

12. *I sold a lot of these '66 De Villes back then, and have always been partial to them, particularly the Eldo convertible. They may be boxy, but they were solid and were real cruisers. With some of the parts here, and some TLC on the rear quarter, this one could well be on the road again.*

13. *These white Mopars in a pile remind me of some chase and crunch movies that were shot in this area, and who knows, maybe they starred briefly in a Burt Reynolds or Clint Eastwood film. Around Reno, anything is possible.*

14. *Looking relatively unscathed, perhaps these two police rigs have some special significance. Notice how far away they're parked from the Cadillacs and Mopars.*

15. *I know of one person up in central Washington redoing an S model 'Cuda who could sure benefit from this one, and I'm sure there are numerous other hobbyists that could too. The same goes for the Chevy II sitting along beside it.*

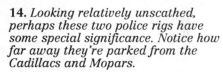

12

13

15

14

DESERT SKY AUTO SALVAGE

By Doc Howell

Knowledgeable collectors and restorers, along with other wrecking yard operators, simply refer to this yard as "Desert Sky." It's located just outside of Wendell, Idaho. So where's Wendell? Dig out the road atlas and find Twin Falls in south central Idaho, just above the Nevada line. Got it? Now, take your pencil and track I-84 about 3/4 inch west, and find where State Highway 46 cuts across the Interstate. Once there, you can't miss Wendell. And, once you go to Wendell, you can't miss Desert Sky either. With 180 acres, nearly 100 of which are covered with more than 5,000 vintage vehicles, dating from '46 to '76, you'd need a trip to the optometrist if you couldn't spot it.

This operation started about 30 years ago, and the owner, Larry Harns, is still acquiring cars and trucks. In fact, on the day I visited Desert Sky, he was up in Stanley, Idaho, near Sun Valley, negotiating on another 150 vehicles to add to what has to be one of the biggest collections in the country. Larry's sales manager, Glenn Mott, figures at least 1,200-1,400 of the cars on hand are good restoration projects and the balance are excellent rust-free parts vehicles.

Having restored over a dozen vehicles of his own, Larry is a dedicated hobbyist. I imagine if you called him looking for the little triangular widget that braces the power antenna on a '53 Belchfire 8, he'd know exactly what you're talking about. He would then translate that to Glenn who could inform you how many were available and in what condition.

With the crops of "generic" vehicles sans character and personality produced in the last decade and a half, there are all too few salvage yards

1. *A sample of the 5,000 plus cars at Desert Sky. There are more than a few popular mid-size models like this solid Ford.*

2. *Since Desert Sky sometimes buys 50 to 150 cars at a time, the inventory isn't necessarily organized by make, as shown by the T-Bird, the '60s pickup with the utility box and the VW.*

3. *A helicopter would have been perfect, but even a spotting scope would help, given how big the yard really is! Despite the size, Larry or Glenn can tell you what's there and give you a good idea of where it is located.*

4. *The Z car does a fair job of trying to stare down the GTO convertible.*

5. *Pickup and wagon "nuts" will swear they've died and gone to heaven*

at this point in the yard. There are pickups, anywhere from a '28 Dodge, to a '38 Chevy, to several '55 to '56 Fords.

6. *The '64 Impala needs some rear quarter work, but both the '65 Comet wagon and Suburban looked as if they'd hit the road again, as do nearly 1,000 others in the yard.*

7. *I saw an ad not too long ago where someone wanted a good solid '57 Ford hood. Here is just one of about a half dozen or so.*

8

9

8. *The unpitted chrome on the '60 Chrysler New Yorker would make someone very happy, since these are tough models to find.*

9. *Rows of hardtops! I definitely should have brought the 500MM lens and a tripod. A box lunch and a thermos wouldn't have hurt, either.*

10. *I'm not sure how the Studebaker pickup ended up with all the Mopars, but there's a collector in Moscow, Idaho who should give them a call on this one.*

10

11

11. *If you are a fan of the '49 to '51 Fords, original or street rod, this is a must place to visit.*

12. *I have a hunch the guys from the Flathead Valley Racing Association and the Duke's Street Rodders from Spokane will be paying a visit down here when they get a peek at how many street rod '20s and '30s vehicles are available.*

13. *The Barracuda looks like an orphan in the midst of the '30s and '40s parts cars.*

14. *This solid '41 Chevy two door sedan is a prime example of how well sheetmetal parts hold up in the high-desert climate.*

12

13

14

15

16

15. *Needing a front end, this '55 Chevy won't have to look very far to take its pick.*

16. *This view gives you an idea of just how expansive 100 acres of cars really are.*

17. *Check the body panels on this '70 Buick.*

18. *A '56 Dodge keeps the '53 Chevy and '38 Chevy pickup company on this knoll.*

19. *Home, home on the range. Don't forget to wear your Nikes or Reeboks.*

20. *Another view from the tail end of the 1941 Chevy four door. Let me know how many '30s, '40s and '50s you can identify from one spot.*

17

18

19

20

21

22

21. *Rambler American, Edsel, Buick, T-Bird, no discrimination here.*

22. *I couldn't resist the excellent condition of this Edsel Citation and the Buick a little farther down the row.*

23. *"Dearborn Row" in Wendell, Idaho, includes (from right to left) a well preserved '67 Mercury Comet, a '52 Ford Sedan, and a '73 Torino.*

24

24. *You don't see many of the big '50s Lincolns or Continentals any more, (far left) but I guarantee there are even fewer '38 Ford pickups!*

25. *Sandwiched between two '57 Mercurys is a nice '59 Lincoln and the remains of a '65 Ford ragtop.*

25

whose primary interest is keyed to the hobbyist and restorer. It makes one wonder what the upcoming generations are going to be tinkering with — Nissan or Toyota pickups? Anyway, there is an abundance of late-model salvage yards that are all computerized with sanitary conditions to satisfy the greenies. It's a real treat to see someone committed to keeping a good segment of our automotive heritage alive and running. As a drag racing friend of mine from Twin Falls commented, "If Desert Sky doesn't have it, it ain't around here."

Local traffic is brisk and the phone is on the go constantly, with calls from all over the country. It is a rare day when Glenn doesn't have a load for the UPS driver. If you've got the itch, the "know how" and the dollars, there are plenty of

'50s convertibles, hardtops, GTOs, 4-4-2s and other prized collectibles scattered all over the premises. Getting whole cars and parts from this source can save a step in the restoration project, since you won't have to invest in heavy-duty sand or bead blasting to have decent metal with which to work.

If you're from out of the area, you can readily fly into either Boise or Twin Falls and rent a truck or car and trailer from any one of several vendors. If you don't spend everything at Desert Sky, you just might enjoy taking a little side tour up to Ketchum and Sun Valley, about an hour's drive away. If you time it right, you might just hit the Silver Collector Car Auction which takes place in early September. There isn't a swap meet with the auction, but it wouldn't

be the first time someone happened to haul a project by during one of these events, sold it at a good profit and had to go back for another one.

Don't miss Desert Sky. If need be, pack a good lunch and bring your camera. The day isn't long enough to absorb it all in one lap around the grounds.

Desert Sky,
Larry Harns: owner,
Glenn Mott: sales,
2742 State Highway 46,
Wendell, ID 83355
Phone 208-536-6606

HIGHWAY 30 AUTO WRECKING

1

By Doc Howell

If you happen to be in the general area of Mount Home, Idaho and need a part to keep going, then I suggest getting off the freeway, go into town and take the old Highway 30 West. A couple miles from the city center, you'll spot the sign on the north side of the highway. On second thought, you keep your eyes on the road and let Jr. look for it, because traffic is pretty steady and the yard is down in what appears to be a former gravel pit and can be easily missed. Below highway eye level and covering about eight acres, Highway 30 Auto Wrecking has a potpourri of parts vehicles dating from the '40s to early '70s, with the bulk appearing to be of GM origin. In fact, if the owner has any partiality, I'd venture a guess it is for Pontiacs, given the abundance present, and particularly wagons of the early '60s. There are many more vans and wagons than one usually encounters in a smaller yard, and I can only attribute that to the proximity of Mount Home Air Force Base and the ever changing roster of military personnel who favor these cargo carriers when moving from one base to another.

In years past, this was always "the

2

place" to go for the base personnel, who, when not tinkering with Uncle Sam's hardware, were busy on restoration projects of their own. In the past, the base could field quite an entourage of show vehicles and rods for local events, and, I surmise, they are still around in one form or another. One thing I learned a long time ago was not to challenge any of these rigs to an impromptu drag race. Not that you're likely to encounter a GE turbo-jet lurk-

1. *The yard seen from the edge of what appears to be a former gravel quarry encompasses six to seven acres. A discerning eye will note an obvious preference for GM cars, though there is generally a fair representation of all marques.*

2. *Station wagons and vans are more prevalent here than in most areas, and these early to mid '60s Pontiacs are but one example. Given the migratory nature of Air Force personnel who must tote family and all the essentials from base to base, the practicality of these haulers fits the need.*

3. *Boxed in temporarily, this VW Campwagon is surprisingly intact and in good condition aside from missing some motive power under the tail end. Something like this would certainly have been handy during Hot August Nights.*

4. *Some solid sheetmetal rremains on this '68 Continental coupe with a sister parts car next to it. Thirsty but strong, these cars could tow a freight train with maximum comfort.*

5. *This vintage Chevy panel offers a good solid base to start a street rod, custom or nostalgia rig.*

3

4

5

ing under the hood of an otherwise innocuous but sharp vehicle, but given the talents of some of the best A and P mechanics, you can be assured they are geared to go. The only clue you may have is seeing the DOD Gate Pass decal glued to the front bumper.

All the cars present, except for a few out-of-state licensed ones, were clear of rust and tin worm holes as is the norm for cars of this climate and area. Chrome and trim is bright, and sans salted roads, one needn't fear having the floor pan drop out from under you.

Highway 30 Auto Wrecking,
Cort Braithwaite: owner,
960 Sunset Strip,
Highway 30 W,
Mount Home, Idaho 83647
Phone 208-587-4429
Hours 9-5 M-F and 9-1 on Saturday

By Doc Howell

Were it not for a break in service, it is very possible Jim Hines of Mount Home, Idaho, would be the proprietor of Idaho's oldest salvage and parts yards for vintage cars. He started back in 1959, as a means of paying his way through college, and had a three year head start on the next oldest yard I know about. However, Viet Nam rudely interrupted both of his endeavors. When he returned, he opted to devote full time to his business interests, rather than pursue his academic ambitions at the College of Idaho. Given his interest in old cars and knack for restorations, as seen in his Metropolitans, it appears to have been a good choice. So, for the record, he lists '72 as his date of "full time" operation in the vintage car and parts business.

Located on the north side of Mount Home, an Air Force Base community, the lot covers approximately 15 acres

1

VINTAGE AUTOMOTIVE

and contains over a thousand vehicles. In fact, as of the second week after Hot August Nights, the yard held exactly 1,050 cars. Of that number, he considers about three dozen well worth complete restoration, adding that each should have a back-up parts vehicle. Unlike many I've encountered in the salvage yard business, Jim emphasizes the need of restoring the powertrain, brakes, suspension and chassis and stocks a very substantial supply of NOS parts for mixed vintage marques. Whenever dealers were ready to divest themselves of dated or "obsolete" new parts inventories, Jim was generally there with a check to relieve them of their unwanted supply. Unlike many yards whose emphasis is on selling entire vehicles, which he will of course do, his primary interest is providing new, near new, refurbished, or refurbished used parts. Fortunately, the benevolent southern Idaho climate works in his favor by being very kind to chrome, trim and sheet metal parts. His phone stays busy with callers from other areas who have first hand or word of mouth information about his inventory.

The yard is well organized insofar as keeping like marques together. And, like so many in older salvage yards, Jim invites you to browse. If you fall in the novice category, he also does restoration work. So, if you happen to want to make a street rod out of the '15 Dodge over in the Mopar section, and really don't know where to start, you might

2

3

4

5

6

7

1. *An overview of Vintage Automotive's acres of parts and restorable vehicles clearly shows the diverse inventory. It doesn't take a sharp eye to spot the hard to find '57 Mercury hardtop wagon.*

2. *This '61 Ford Starliner, and the '49 Ford keeping it company, both have some good parts left to help some hobbyist or restorer.*

3. *This '63 Olds '98 hardtop wouldn't be the least out of place cruising Reno's glitter gulch after some TLC.*

4. *Packard fans all seem to agree that of all the post-war models, the carry-over '46 and '47 Clippers are the most desirable. Someone obviously had that in mind while cherrypicking some parts off this one, but the "basis" for a good restoration remains.*

5. *The ever popular '65 Pontiac Tempests, LeMans and GTOs never have trouble finding a home. This one is simply too good to end up as a parts car.*

6. *This REO, right, is a very good candidate for some street rodder to build into a car hauler. Imagine the stir it would cause decked out in hot pink and graphics!*

7. *If you like '56 Studebakers, here is a very decent example. Note the Crosley station wagon and the Nash Ambassador to the rear.*

8. *Vintage's Studebaker row includes, among others, a '49 model, right, and a '50 model. They have been picked over, it appears.*

9. *This 1951 is one of the early Imperial two door hardtops with the 331 Hemi. It should find a home after some exposure.*

10. *Given the strong following of '62 and '63 widetracking Pontiacs, it's somewhat surprising that these two '63 models aren't up on blocks somewhere getting new life.*

11. *A good variety of material awaits those of the porthole and fins persuasion; a '57 Buick, left, and a '59 model, right.*

8

9

10

11

12

heed whatever advice he has to offer. Check one of his Metros if you need assurance about his credentials or his know how.

His inventory ranges from the '20s (and sometimes earlier) up to the '60s, and there are definitely several I'm sure you haven't seen around for some time.

Affable and helpful, he is often called upon for advice and a helping hand by the locals, because of his interest in seeing older vehicles preserved.

So whether you see something in the photos that intrigues you or not, it wouldn't hurt to give him a ring and inquire about other cars he has or parts for your project. As long as it isn't half a car, he is very accommodating about shipping smaller items.

13

14

12. *A rock band in search of a unique "ride," need look no further than this '61 Olds limousine. It definitely has character.*

13. *An elite model of its day, this '51 Packard 400 would make someone a great road car. The hefty 327 cubic inch straight eight was a workhorse.*

14. *The remains of a Studebaker coupe resides by a '51 Oldsmobile sedan.*

15. *Both the '50 Olds and a '51 Hudson have a lot of decent parts to contribute to someone's restoration efforts.*

16. *Minor surface rust, that can be easily removed, is evident on this '50 Buick. Imagine how this inventory would disappear if it were in Michigan or Wisconsin!*

15

16

SALVAGE YARD TOUR:
ALL AROUND AMERICA
Phase V

By Eric Brockman

The last of our "adventures in salvage yard-ing" isn't really a "tour" in the same sense as the previous tours.

We didn't load the entire *Cars & Parts* staff into my '60 Lincoln (although we and a small army could fit in the "Titanic") and go galavanting around the U.S. and Canada looking at decrepit old cars. We may be some of the luckiest "working stiffs" around, but we're not that lucky. These yards represent a roundup of various outings by *Cars & Parts* staff members and freelance writers over the past year or so. Many of the excursions were actually side-trips while attending car shows and auctions.

Being the new guy on the block at *Cars & Parts,* I haven't photographed any yards yet, but I'm no stranger to salvage yards. I have haunted several southwestern Ohio yards numerous times in search of elusive bounty, and I am eagerly await-ing the return of warm weather in order to resume treasure hunting. The rest of the crew did a bang-up job braving heat, insects, floods, ticks, junkyard dogs, tornadoes and various assorted other obstacles to capture some of the best "junk" any car enthusiast could ever hope to find.

The first stop on our zig-zag jaunt across the continent takes us to Martin Salvage in Windsor, Colo. This has to be the only salvage yard in the country with one of those coin-operated telescopes you see at tourist attractions. It's mounted on a tower near the front of the yard, and lets cus-tomers check out the stock. And there's plenty of stock to see, including a '50 Kaiser Traveler and one of the more bizarre-looking custom '58 Chevys to come down the pike. While most of the vehicles are parts cars, a few restorables lurk among the rougher occupants.

Taking a sharp turn from there, we head into the Great White North to Elliott Auto Parts in Newtonville, Ontario, Canada. These guys have a thing for military vehicles, and the yard includes armored personnel carriers, olive drab trucks and even a tank or two. It's hard to miss that big armored car parked out front. Plenty of prewar cars also dot the northern landscape at Elliott's.

Another hard turn south takes us to an absolute-ly unbelievable treasure trove in the hills of Jamestown, Tenn. J.C. Lane's been collecting the old stuff for many years, amassing an impressive collection of pre-war and post-war cars at Lane Auto Salvage. The jaw-dropper comes when you look at the pictures: many of these cars are com-plete—down to tires, windows and hubcaps — and look restorable. Check out the prewar Nash and

Model A pickup! Get your pen and paper out, though, because you'll have to write to J.C. Lane to get your hands on these machines.

A short run up into New England finds our attention on Mt. Tobe Auto Parts, Plymouth, Conn., a second-generation family business that has withstood the test of time and remained a source of choice parts. The emphasis here is on post-war models, ranging from the '40s to the '60s.

Heading back closer to our Ohio home base, the ever-daring Dean Shipley braved the mosquitoes and overgrowth to get a glimpse of a Garrettsville, Ohio yard that has nearly disintegrated. The interesting collection of vehicles constituting Sibal's Salvage Yard is so badly decayed that very few useful items remain. Since our visit, we've learned that many of the cars have been sent to the crusher. Some were so badly decayed, they broke in half when fork lifts attempted to remove them.

Pointing ourselves west, Randy Moser takes the helm, with the first stop being E&J Used Auto Parts in Rock Island, Ill. The midwestern operation covers 30 acres and contains 3,500 vehicles. This yard has a little of everything, with more than a decent helping of '60s-vintage derelicts — some not all that derelict — judging by the pictures.

The next stop on our crusade, B&M Auto Wrecking in Tempe, Ariz., is run by a Chicago native who finally had his fill of pulling parts in the snow and freezing temperatures. He realized Arizona in January was much more comfortable than January in Chicago and relocated his business to the Southwest.

However, while our man Randy was there, tornadoes, rare for that part of the country, tore through the Phoenix/Tempe area. Who would have thought looking at old cars could be so dangerous? Most salvage yard operators make a living selling late-model parts, and owner Bobby Zanon is no exception. But a few late '60s and early '70s refugees find their way into his yard.

Kelsey Auto Salvage takes us back to the Midwest to Iowa Falls, Iowa, where what appeared to be one lightning-fast junkyard dog, turned out instead to be several nearly identical pooches. This yard started out as a "hobby" in the early '70s, but quickly escalated into a full-time venture. After stopping to take a doggie head count, strolling through the yard revealed a mouth-watering selection of post-war vehicles ranging from a '47 Dodge pickup to a '79 Spirit-based AMX. Unusual finds along the way included

a '53 Willys Aero Falcon (when was the last time you saw one of those?) an Edsel and a couple of Packards. Due to its higher-ground location, Kelsey Auto Salvage was spared from the Midwestern flooding of '93. These gems may still be in residence.

Yet another U-turn takes us to the usually-arid Southwest again, to track down a yard that almost got "rained out." While traveling in the area of Black Canyon City, Ariz., Dean Shipley found himself in the shadow of the "Devil's Thumb," which isn't as bad of a place to be as it sounds. Locating this local landmark puts you near Black Canyon Old Parts Company, a salvage yard that felt the wrath of Mother Nature last winter. Raging flood waters destroyed several hundred cars: many were mangled, buried, filled with sand and rocks, or completely swept away. The yard's owners are busy crushing the victims and restocking with more rust-free iron that is definitely worth the trip. And Dean recommends a stop at the "Four B's" for breakfast while you're in the area.

Another western trip later in the year found Dean having a run-in with the "moving freckles" (aka ticks) at Hauf Auto Salvage in Stillwater, Okla. A third-generation family business, Hauf's had one of the more unusual finds we've come across, a restorable Skoda Felicia convertible from Czechoslovakia. A few prewar cars and trucks are available, but the majority of the inventory falls in the post-war category.

Cars & Parts editor Bob Stevens rounds out the tour with a pair of Campbellsville, Ky. yards that are virtually down the street from each other. R.C. Van Cleave & Son Used Cars & Trucks deals mostly in complete, restorable cars. An abundance of prewar and post-war vehicles are in residence. Prewar luxury cars were well represented by a '37 Lincoln coupe, a '40 Lincoln-Zephyr three-window coupe, and a couple of '40 Cadillacs.

Nolley Auto Sales is smaller, but has some rare and desirable stuff. How about a '57 Chevy convertible or one of several Fords with the retractable hardtop? Way back in a corner, there was even the rear clip of a first-generation Corvette. But don't think this stuff comes cheap, just because it's in a salvage yard.

Here, in a nutshell, is what awaits on the following pages. Fasten your seat belts and dial in the way-back machine. I'll fire up the "Titanic," and, to paraphrase the film critics slightly, we'll see you at the salvage yards!

MARTIN SALVAGE

Photos by
the author

By John Lee

Getting run out of town may have been the best thing to happen to Mervin Martin. In 1951, he established Martin Supply and Salvage Yard in the little northern Colorado town of Milliken. But 10 years later, with the town raising an outcry about the "unsightly" property, Martin bought a piece of ground and moved his operation out into the country where only cottontails would be bothered.

The location could hardly be better — halfway between Greeley and Loveland, right on U.S. Hwy. 34, the main route to popular Rocky Mountain National Park and the tourist town of Estes Park. Years later, Interstate 25 between Cheyenne and Denver came though just 4½ miles west of Martin's.

Brothers Chuck and Carrol Martin and their sister, Shirley Gardner, literally grew up in the "junkyard." They now run the business started by their father, who remains active in it. The operation is predominantly older cars and parts. It didn't start out that way,

1-2. *The tower and telescope were intended for tourists to view the mountains a few miles to the west, but can also help scout out a target in the recycling yard at Martin Supply and Salvage in Windsor, Colo.*

161   AMERICAN SALVAGE YARD TREASURES

3. A price tag of $1,000 was on this '61 Mercury Comet S-22 coupe with a six-cylinder, bucket seats and console.

4-5. Martin's had recently acquired this '58 Chevy Impala, customized in the early 1960s and stored for years. It was running a 283 V-8.

6. A '51 Chevy sedan delivery, '56 Packard Clipper and '49 Pontiac coupe are in this mass of '40s and '50s iron.

3

4

5

6

7

8

9

10

but as the years slipped by, the original stock Mervin Martin built up became antique, and the demand for it continued to grow.

Out on the high plains, in the shadow of the Rockies, rainfall is sparse and trees are few, so steel lasts a long time. Upholstery goes to pot and paint oxidizes, but there are plenty of bodies and parts back to the 1930s and 1940s still solid enough to restore.

Ford products date back to Model A days. We saw both coupe and Murray sedan bodies. There were restorable '38, '41, and '42 coupes. A complete '40 Mercury fordor sedan was parked toward the front, where the Martins keep complete, restorable vehicles for sale.

Some others, like a '51 Ford, '53 Mercury and a '56 Ford Park Lane station wagons, appeared to be a toss-up between restoration and parts cars. It depends on how much work and money you're willing to expend. There are also a '62 Ford convertible with some rust and missing its top and engine, a good '54 Ford Mainline tudor with extra trim, remnants of late 1950s Rancheros and sedan deliveries and assorted early 1960s Falcons.

Chevy lovers can also find a lot of nice projects and parts at Martin's, except the neo-classic '55-57 models. One that caught our eye (station wagon lovers that we are) was a '58 Yeoman two-door, partially dismantled but still saveable. A '60 Biscayne two-door was complete from the cowl back.

Restorable Chevys from the 1950s and 1960s are still fairly plentiful, and this yard has a lot of the parts needed to restore them.

Chrysler products are not as plentiful here as Fords and Chevys. We did see a '65 Barracuda with a slant six, a '52 Plymouth Belvedere hardtop with a usable body, a '47 coupe, and several other Plymouths and Dodges from the 1950s.

11

12

13

7. *1955 Packard was nearly complete and appeared to be a recent arrival.*

8. *All glass except the windshield is intact, as is the slant six, in this '65 Barracuda.*

9. *Someone made an interesting sedan delivery conversion out of this '66 Falcon four-door wagon.*

10. *The elder Martin has traveled to Australia and developed contacts who have helped him import unusual vehicles like this '50 Ford Ute.*

11. *A '38 Ford coupe has become a resting place for a top removed from a '41 business coupe.*

12. *A good grille and pair of headlights remain on this '67 Comet Capri.*

13. *Here's a rare pair of haulers; A '50 Kaiser Traveler without engine and a 1960s Studebaker Lark Wagonaire.*

14. *A '53 Packard Clipper four-door occupies a spot alongside a '49 Cadillac four-door sedan.*

15. *This '54 Mercury station wagon is pretty rough, but has some interesting parts, such as a roof rack.*

16. *There are extra parts in the back of this '40 Mercury sedan. It's complete with flathead and radiator and in basically good condition.*

17. *A '42 Buick and an early '50s Chrysler are stacked like toppled dominos.*

18. *This '54 Ford sedan appears to be a Mainline with Crestline trim, plus some Western Auto add-ons. It has a V-8, minimal rust and a $1,000 price tag.*

19. *A '46 Ford pickup body and bed are solid.*

14

15

16

17

18

19

20

21

22

23

20. *The engine and front seat are the main components missing from this '57 Studebaker Commander.*

21. *Doors for many different 1930s and 1940s models are in this stack.*

22. *This 1959 Bonneville hardtop hadn't been in the yard long, but had already been relieved of several parts.*

23. *There are mostly Fords and Mercs from the late 1930s to the late 1950s in this area.*

24. *This trio would probably make one good car with some marketable spares left over. The two '57 Ford Rancheros had engines, the Courier didn't.*

A '55 Packard Patrician four-door appeared to be a late arrival; it still had its trim and taillights. Some Kaiser lover should be interested in the '50 Traveler, even without an engine. Next to it is an early 1960s Studebaker Lark sliding-roof station wagon.

The selection of Cadillacs includes a '66 convertible, '68 coupe and '57-58 four-door hardtops. We saw the remains of a '59 Pontiac Bonneville two-door hardtop, a '52 Olds 88 four-door sedan, a '49 Pontiac coupe and a restorable '63 Olds F-85 coupe without an engine. There are also hundreds of pickups and other trucks.

24

25

26

27

28

29

30

31

25. *A '50 Ford (ex)woodie and a '56 Merc Monterey hardtop have parts to offer.*

26. *This 1962 Ford Galaxie 500 XL convertible needs a top and engine; the '50 Chevy delivery, a seat.*

27. *The rear fenders are inside this minimal-rust '41 Ford business coupe body and chassis. Behind it are a pair of early 1960s Falcon Rancheros.*

28. *Need a hubcap?*

29. *This 1959 Pontiac Catalina hardtop was offered as a complete and restorable unit.*

30. *This is the better side of a '58 Chevy Yeoman station wagon.*

31. *Ford's answer to the Chevy Nomad was the Parklane. This '56 model was missing the four-barrel carb from the T-bird engine, but had A/C and extra parts.*

When cars and trucks have been pretty well stripped, the Martins remove the remaining parts. Sheet metal pieces like doors, fenders, hoods and trunk lids are stacked in rows. There's a huge hubcap pile that could take a week's vacation to go through.

Thousands of mechanical and small parts are shelved inside several old van bodies placed along one side of the yard. "We save everything," said Chuck. Although they have a crusher operation going on the grounds, it's mostly for later model iron.

If a Rocky Mountain vacation is in your future, plan an extra two or three days and bring your parts list to Martin Salvage. We visited with one couple who bought a whole '54 Chevy station wagon and were busy torching off all the body panels, floor, bumpers, doors, etc., and loading them into their truck. They were going to take all they could carry back to Texas to complete a restoration project.

About the yard
Martin Supply & Salvage Yard is located at 8405 U.S. Hwy. 34, Windsor, Colo. 80550. For more information about the yard, call 303-686-2460.

1. *The Elliotts are avid military collectors and the yard contains a number of old tanks and personnel carriers, plus a huge inventory of olive-green panel trucks.*

2. *Protected from the elements, a 1932 DeSoto with four suicide doors awaits sale as a complete unit.*

3. *A 1928 Reo dual-wheeled truck is almost complete, and Don Elliott claims that it still runs.*

ELLIOTT AUTO PARTS

By Jil McIntosh

A lot of yards have been around a lot of years, and Elliott Auto Parts in Newtonville, Ontario, Canada is no exception. The first cars were towed in way back in 1928, and it just grew from there.

Founded by Bruce Elliott, it is still in the family, with daily operations now overseen by his sons, Don and George. Located some 50 miles east of Toronto, the yard, has become a mecca for restorers searching for old and rare parts.

Elliott Auto Parts advertises that it has parts from 1925 and up, many stored away from the elements in barns. Cars of that vintage are still in the yard as well, shaded by the trees that have grown up around them in the last 60 years. Many cars are highly desirable convertibles and roadsters, but Don Elliott cautions readers, "This

4. *Two '41 Plymouths represent a small portion of the yard's large inventory of Chrysler products.*

5. *Much of the stainless, and a fairly presentable grille, are waiting to be gleaned from a '52 or '53 Nash Ambassador Custom.*

6. *A four-door 1938 Studebaker Commander is still pretty solid.*

7. *The hood is long gone, but many parts, including engine accessories, are still available on this '38 Oldsmobile.*

8. *The chrome trim that identifies this as a '48 Pontiac is intact, although the tinworm has been busy on the fenders.*

4

5

6

8

7

is Canada, and naturally, rust is a problem here.''

Even so, a cursory peek at these older residents (well guarded by mosquitoes in the summer months!) showed that some pieces are still salvageable.

Cars from the '40s and '50s are much more abundant and in better shape. Elliott's was a favorite casting-off site for local businesses and a huge number of commercial vehicles, panel vans and trucks sit in neat rows waiting to give up their treasures. Restorable vehicles are sold as complete units, and many of these are protected from the elements in steel sheds on dry floors.

9. *A 1953 Chevrolet panel van is one of many such vans on the lot, which contains a huge supply of commercial cast-offs from local businesses.*

10. *Both the rare double-tank gas pump and the Isetta are for sale. The pump is one of several available from Elliott's.*

11. *A fairly complete and solid '38 Ford rests outside one of the well-stocked parts barns.*

12. *A '39 DeSoto looks like a solid restoration project. The streetcar in the background is an old "Red Rocket" from the Toronto Transit Commission.*

9

10

11

12

13

13. *The restorer looking for a real challenge should know that the yard's double-decker bus is definitely for sale.*

14. *A 1966 Marlin has a shady spot under the trees.*

15. *The yard has a surprising number of convertibles, including this 1947 Cadillac.*

16. *Considerably worse for wear, a 1957 Chevrolet two-door wagon still has a lot of chrome trim, including the taillight bezels.*

17. *A '37 Pontiac and an early '50s Studebaker pickup with a solid, straight grille sit in one of the yard's long, straight lines.*

18. *A civilian Ford cab-over is flanked by a military truck and a tank.*

19. *The yard has been in operation since 1928, and many current residents have been here that long. There are a lot of '20s and '30s cars, and many of them still have a number of salvageable parts.*

20. *The "sweetheart dip" rear window identifies a 1952 Kaiser.*

14

15

16

17

18

19

20

The yard is of special interest to military enthusiasts. The Elliotts are avid military buffs themselves, and their personal collection contains at least one of everything from wheeled guns to huge amphibious vehicles. The yard also has several old tanks, as well as a large number of supply wagons, trucks and panel vans, most still wearing their original shade of olive green.

Elliott's does not ship, and customers must visit in person, preferably after calling to see if the desired parts are available. The yard is not open to browsers, but visitors will be taken through and Elliott's will remove parts from the cars.

About the yard

Elliott Auto Parts is located at 4752 Highway 2, near Newtonville, Ontario. Take Highway 401 to exit 448 (Newtonville Road) and travel north to Highway 2. Turn east and go one mile to Elliott Auto Parts. The yard is open weekdays 8 a.m. to 6 p.m. and Saturday 9 a.m. to 1 p.m. The phone number is 416-786-2255.

1

Photos by Ken New

1. *Owner J.C. Lane displays one of the "keepers" of the yard, a '29 Ford roadster.*

2-3. *Hubcaps, trim, license plates and hordes of other parts adorn the walls of the buildings at Lane Auto Salvage.*

4. *A real cruising vessel, this '60 Buick two-door is now relegated to fighting off the weeds.*

5. *Even amidst the brush and weeds, it's hard to mistake the taillights of an Imperial. It's hard to mistake a late '50s or early '60s Imperial from any angle. The styling was, uh, unique. A number of good trim pieces are still intact on this '62 Crown Imperial.*

6. *A '46 Hudson Super Six sedan looks to be fairly complete.*

7-8. *Beep! Beep! This "Little Nash Rambler" station wagon won't be racing the weathered Caddy sedan anymore.*

9. *Need any Oldsmobile trim? This '49 two-door still has most of its brightwork.*

10. *Like many of the other cars pictured here, the early '50s Chevy wagon looks surprisingly complete and solid.*

LANE AUTO SALVAGE

By Eric Brockman

Take a moment, close your eyes, and visualize a "salvage yard." Most people would picture derelict cars with no wheels, buried to their axles in mud, windows and headlights long-since broken by vandals, and many major body and drivetrain components spirited away by hungry parts hunters.

Now glance through the photos with this story, and try not to drool on the pages.

No, not every car at Lane Auto Salvage, located near Jamestown, Tenn., is complete. Plenty with broken windshields and headlights can be found, as well. But there are a lot of unmolested gems in the rough sitting in these Tennessee fields. And we're not talking about late-model iron here, either. There are an amazing number of complete, albeit rough, fat-fendered machines from the '40s, as well as many '50s and '60s cars.

J.C. Lane started the business over 30 years ago, and a lot of the automo-

2

3

tive residents look like the original inhabitants of the yard. A '41 Nash still wears a Tennessee license plate from 1962.

Lane owns 42 acres, of which 30 are occupied by roughly 2,500 cars. Out of that number, Lane had 75 complete cars at the time of our visit. Sure, that's only a small percentage of the total number of cars, but that's certainly a lot to find in a salvage yard. Quite a few even still wear hubcaps.

Many treasures hide in the weeds and underbrush at Lane's. The southern climate has been a little kinder to some of the tired old machines. Prewar iron is not a common sight at junkyards these days. However, included on the roster of fairly complete and solid cars, to name just a few are: '39 Plymouth two-door sedan, a '40 Olds rough, the aforementioned '41 Nash, a very solid-looking '41 Buick sedan and a '41 Chevy coupe.

The neatest of the prewar lot was a Model A Ford pickup with its radiator

4

5

6

7

8

9

10

11. *Off the highways for quite some time, a '41 Nash Ambassador still wears its '62 Tennessee license plate. Even so, it looks ready to return to duty. What's left of the trim appears to have been painted over at some time.*

12. *This '49 Chrysler looks like a good candidate for a restoration, even though the trim appears to be pretty badly weathered. Even the glass seems to be intact, which is unusual for a salvage yard car.*

13. *Although a lot of its trim looks badly weathered, a '40 Oldsmobile offers plenty of straight, solid body parts for someone's restoration.*

11

12

13

14

15

16

17

and shell, and headlight assembly still there and in good shape. The front fenders also looked pretty cherry. When was the last time you saw those items, in fairly decent shape, in a salvage yard?

Late '40s and early '50s machines are plentiful and cover a wide array of makes. Chevys, Olds', Pontiacs, Fords, Chryslers, Dodges and even a couple of Hudsons and a Rambler wagon reside at Lane's. Unusual finds such as a '56 Lincoln and a '59 Cadillac were also present.

Anyone looking for a challenging restoration, but not one that is a complete basket case, should take the time to get in touch with J.C. Lane.

14. *A '46 Ford offers more solid body parts, while the '53 Poncho two-door hardtop looks like another fairly complete and solid machine.*

15. *This '41 Buick sedan is another of the "all there" pre-war cars at Lane's. It still has some decent chrome and trim pieces.*

16. *What appears to be a '47 Chevy Fleetline still has its front and rear fender trim. Like many of the older cars here, time and the elements have done a good job of stripping the paint off the car.*

17. *Here's some rare Mopar muscle, a '66 Dodge Polara convertible. Note the 440 badge. As a restoration project, however, it's a bit too far gone.*

18. *This '56 Vicky still has emblems, grille, windshield and good side trim. In fact, someone looking for a challenge could probably rescue this one.*

19. *Model A Ford truck's interior is shot, but look at those front fenders, headlight assembly, and radiator. The projectile taillights next to it belong to a mid '50s Oldsmobile.*

20. *All by itself, this step-down Hudson could still yield a number of usable items to the industrious parts scrounger.*

21. *Another easily recognizable specimen is this "bat wing" '59 Chevy Impala.*

22. *Perhaps this old '50 Ford is the Thunder Road Ford a Cars & Parts reader asked about in the August '93 issue. Nah! Then again, it looks like it's been there for quite some time ...*

23. *A '54 Merc still sports its two-tone paint job. It's missing a taillight lens, but not much else. Just look at that back window glass.*

18

19

20

21

22

23

1

MT. TOBE

2

By Dennis David

In 1940, Pat Perillo Sr. started a salvage yard. His intent was to supply motorists with the means to keep their cars on the road. His yard became a boon to motorists attempting to keep their machines on the road through the lean years (no cars made) of World War II.

The war came and went, but Mt. Tobe Auto Parts proved to be a lasting enterprise. Pat Sr. ran the yard for 50 years until his death in 1990. His son, Pat Jr., now oversees the 15-acre yard that is home to many cars and trucks of all years, makes and models.

Nestled in the foothills of Northwestern Connecticut, the yard is literally locked in time. Pat Sr. was a devoted hobbyist and the collection at Mt. Tobe proves it. Virtually every car that entered the yard is still there. "Dad never crushed a single car," said Pat Perillo Jr.

Though the yard itself has no particular order, the cars are thoughtfully inventoried in Pat Jr.'s mind. He knows where every car is, as well as its condition and when it arrived at Mt. Tobe.

Photos by
Steven Bendzuinas

1. *A Metropolitan rides high over a section of Mt. Tobe with a variety of unidentified vehicles at its wheel wells.*

2. *After years in the woods, this '60 Thunderbird is showing its age. Remaining sheet metal appears straight.*

3. *With its top raised, the '54 Cadillac convertible appears to be waving goodbye as it returns to earth.*

3

4

5

6

7

AUTO PARTS

4. *The air cleaner on the fender indicates some work has been done under the hood, but the remainder of this '59 Plymouth four-door appears intact.*

5. *The windshields have been wasted on both the '63 Corvair and the '58 Chevrolet Brookside wagon. The latter has already has some trim peeled off.*

6. *Though reasonably intact, this bottom-of-the-line '55 Pontiac Chieftain is not the most desirable restoration project, but it is a two-door hardtop.*

7. *A '60 Studebaker Lark appears to have some brightwork to offer.*

8. *Yard owner Pat Perillo, Jr., left, and his son, Justin, pose by a '41 Lincoln that Pat, Sr. restored. It is not for sale.*

8

10

11

9

A walk through Mt. Tobe is a stroll down memory lane. The old car fan is greeted at the entrance by the remains of a 1941 GMC bus that serves as the yard's office. The eldest resident of the yard is a 1931 Model A Ford pickup truck.

The '40s are represented by DeSoto, Nash, Packard and Studebaker, as well as Chevy, Ford and Mopar. The '50s roll call includes at least a half dozen Oldsmobile convertibles, '55 and '56 Chevys and several Cadillacs.

The '60s are evident by a number of Chevy and Ford convertibles and a legion of station wagons. There are some newer cars in the yard, but the bulk of Mt. Tobe's business is in vintage and antique parts.

The yard is located in Plymouth, Conn., on South Road. Oddly enough to get there, you travel north to get to South. Take Route 8 north out of Waterbury to exit 39, turn right, go one-half mile and turn right onto South Rd. Proceed four miles. You'll see it on your left.

The yard is open 8 a.m. to 5 p.m., Saturdays only. Visits are by appointment only. Parts seekers can call 203-753-0332 and leave a message on the recorder. Perillo follows up phone calls all day Saturday. The prospective buyer is informed of the availability and condition of the parts at that time.

Mt. Tobe also fills mail orders through UPS. Written inquiries are welcome: Mt. Tobe Auto Parts, R.F.D. 1, Plymouth, Conn. 06782. A video of the yard is also available.

If Pat Sr.'s intent was to help keep old cars on the road, the yard has surely succeeded. Now in the capable hands of Pat Jr., Mt. Tobe will likely provide hobbyists with rare parts from its extensive inventory for years to come. And that's fine with Pat Jr.

"Dad would have wanted it that way," he said.

12

13

14

9. *Though the top has deteriorated, the rest of this '53 Pontiac convertible shows potential.*

10. *A complete but rusty '55 Ford Thunderbird rear end awaits atop an unidentified panel truck.*

11. *A Brockway truck, circa 1950, formerly hauled ice cream. Now it just gathers leaves.*

12. *This '53 Chevrolet, one of several, has some good Bel Air trim to offer.*

13. *Time has ravaged the uncared for convertible top of this '64 Buick Electra 225. Thus, the interior is also wasted. But it's still a convertible!*

14. *A very solid-looking '65 Ford Thunderbird, interior and all, appears to need some serious freshening to make it roadworthy again.*

15. *It will be an uphill pull for the restorer who wishes to tackle this '54 Chevrolet Bel Air.*

16. *The top of this rough '62 Mercury convertible is just about to shoot through. When it does ...*

17. *By '58, the Chevy Bel Air was no longer the top of the line. This four-door model can supply a windshield, but not much else.*

15

16

17

18

About the yard
Mt. Tobe Auto Parts is located on Mt. Tobe Rd. near Plymouth, Conn. The mailing address is: Mt. Tobe Auto Parts, R.F.D. 1, Plymouth, Conn. 06782. The phone number: 203-753-0332.

19

20

18. *A '41 Nash four-door sedan, though it has been around a while, could still make a decent restoration project.*

19. *A '65 Mustang convertible still has the 289 two-barrel engine, but the carb is missing. The top bows may still be good.*

20. *Birch, birch, birch! Three of them have this '47 DeSoto Club Coupe imprisoned.*

21. *A '51 Plymouth Concord business coupe looks fairly complete.*

22. *Though the "bridge work" in this '58 Buick Roadmaster appears to need some realignment, other trim, glass and interior parts can be lifted without subsequent "dental work."*

23. *A '48 Pontiac coupe has retained its engine over the many years of residence at Mt. Tobe.*

24. *An Imperial, circa '57/'58, has some good windows and trim, but the sheet metal has "cancer."*

21

22

23

24

SIBAL'S SALVAGE YARD

1

2

By Dean Shipley

Every now and then a yard comes to our attention for which we feel a certain sadness. We feel that way (as should hobbyists who love salvage yards — that's why you bought this book) because the contents of the yard have decayed so much, it almost ceases to be able to provide usable parts for restorers. For Frank Sibal's of Garrettsville, Ohio, we feel that sadness.

It was a hot, humid June day in Northeast Ohio when we visited Sibal's aka Frank's, on Shanks Down Road in Garrettsville, near Warren. It is literally out in the sticks several miles and more than several turns from the "main drag," US 422, that runs by The Gables tavern.

If you didn't know how to get there or were a total stranger to the area as this reporter was, you'd never know Frank's existed. The yard itself is shielded from view from the narrow road by thick barriers of foliage. Unchecked by any cutting blade, it grew wildly in the yard, as well.

The inventory of the yard, which shares space with the mature trees, saplings, tall weeds and fallen leaves

3

4

5

6

Photos by Dean Shipley
and Mike Whaley

1. Frank Sibal's salvage
yard near Garrettsville,
Ohio, sits "way out in
the country" in
Northeast Ohio. It has
been there since 1948.

2-4. Frank's has
numerous Mopars from
the '50s in his yard that
appear to be grouped
together. Photos 2 and 3
are two views of a '50
Plymouth two-door
wagon that is sinking
into the ground. A '51
Plymouth wagon has
permanent residence
next to a '49 Buick. All
are rough, but the '51
may yield some reusable
trim.

5. A '49 Buick is the odd
man out in a row of
Mopars: a '53 Plymouth
(left), and a '51
Plymouth wagon and '57
Chrysler (to the right).
All are in poor condition.

6. A '49 Dodge
Meadowbrook is barely
discernible as fallen
leaves and growing
weeds do their best to
camouflage the car.
Some stainless trim may
be good, but little else.

7. *A small fleet of Dodge postal service vans at one time might have made interesting vehicles for restoration. But rust rules and has rendered them to relic status.*

8. *A sad end for a once lovely '61 Pontiac Catalina convertible. It appears to have broken in half.*

9-10. *Early '60s Rambler Americans; a wagon (photo 9) and a convertible (photo 10) have taken their places in the yard. The glass in the wagon may be salvageable, but the ragtop between the birches is less than a shadow of its former self.*

8

9

10

was begun in the late '40s. Frank Sibal, who worked at Dan's Auto Wrecking at 93rd and St. Catherine Streets in Cleveland up through 1940 bought the tract in 1948 after deer hunting in the neighborhood. He wanted "his own place." From that time, up until several years ago, he added regularly to the yard's inventory.

The latest residents are those from the mid-60s. Many cars and trucks hail from the '50s, with a complement of vehicles from the '40s, '30s and one or two from the late '20s.

Before you start to salivate too heavily, though, here's a word of warning and it's "a four letter word." Rust. Yes, rust, the arch enemy of any restorer. The relentless foe that doggedly pursues every vehicle, particularly in these parts of the country. Rust is tough enough to stave off when a

11

13

12

14

11-12. *Two views of a '58 Studebaker Golden Hawk. The gilt on its "feathers" has been replaced by rust. The yard takes on quite a different look in autumn (photo 11) than it does in summer (photo 12).*

13. *A '47 Chevrolet has an interesting green plastic visor that could be salvaged, and perhaps some trim. Alas, the rest has gone to rust.*

14. *This '51 Mercury still holds on to some intact glass, but the lower body shows evidence of rust from beneath.*

car is being cared for, let alone when it is exposed to the harsh elements of Northeastern Ohio.

When cars and trucks travel the roads there, particularly in the winter, their metal underbellies are frequently showered with salt water, the by-product of snow removal. The briny mist covers the frame, fenders, rocker panels, and quarter panels. It incites the metal's decay almost on contact. Once the oxidation process has started, it is difficult to stop. Many of Frank's "residents" have experienced such exposure.

Add to that the years of laying in the woods. Sap falling from the trees gradually eats away paint. Unprotected metal oxidizes as rain pelts the automobiles. Heavy foliage holds that moisture beneath the leafy canopy above that shields the wood's floor from drying sunlight. And then in the autumn, when the trees release their leaves, they fall on the cars and gather. The leaves retain any moisture that falls in the late fall, winter, and spring, and in

and in summer. Years of leaves have collected on the cars. Add to that mixture the humid air that surrounds the cars. The moist environment continues the nefarious work begun when the cars were still on the road.

So sheet metal and chrome parts have suffered greatly. Some fenders, checked for condition by this reporter, were found to be separating from their underside reinforcing brackets. Other parts — doors, rocker panels, rear quarter panels — have also succumbed to rust's insidious advance.

Frank Sibal himself admits his cars are "too old, too rusty." Such being the case, he is slowly sending them to the crusher. Sibal said some of the cars are so rusty they break in half in the loading process. He has no NOS parts.

We visited the yard in the summer, the absolute worst time (except maybe for a winter snowstorm). Not only is the foliage high, but also the insect population. Deer flies and mosquitoes don't take kindly to human intruders and descend with a vengeance. Boots

protected us from the mud, but we had no long sleeve shirts (hey, it was SUMMER) and worst of all no insect repellent.

If you go, we wish you good luck. If, during your visit, you feel a sadness for the many interesting vehicles that have "terminal rust," you are not alone. We share the same.

Sibal requested his phone number not be published. He is 72 and has asthma. He said a barrage of phone calls would only bring him headaches and the callers frustration.

About the yard
Frank Sibal's salvage yard is located at 10635 Shanks Down Road, Garrettsville, Ohio 44234. Hours are 9 a.m. to 5 p.m., Monday through Saturday, 9 a.m. to 4 p.m. on Sunday. Sibal requests no phone calls, please.

E & J USED AUTO PARTS
ROCK ISLAND REQUIEM

By Randy Moser

If you ask Larry Tschappat how he got into the salvage yard business, he'll look you straight in the eye and answer, "I was a real SOB." Tschappat is really a great guy. The SOB stands for "son of the boss."

His father opened the salvage yard back in 1951, adding used parts to the repertoire in 1966. Larry literally grew up around the operation. A Vietnam veteran and a graduate of Augustana College (B.A. in Business) and the University of Iowa (M.A. in Fine Arts), he moved away to manage a Santa Barbara, Calif. yard during the early '70s. He returned to take over his family's business four years later.

At one time, this Mississippi River basin land used to be an orchard truck farm. When sand was needed for building the nearby expressway a few years ago, an adjacent landfill was re-

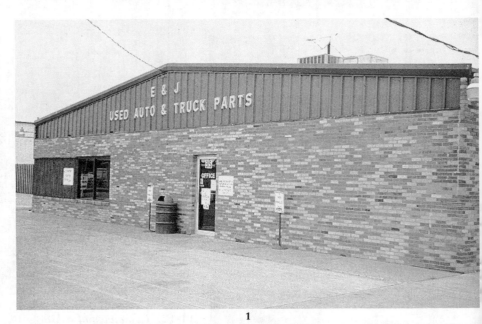

1

2

Photos by the author

1. *Located at 315 31st Avenue in Rock Island, Ill., E & J Used Auto and Truck Parts has been a family-run business for the past 42 years. Every car in the yard is inventoried in the office by individual marque.*

2. *Stretching out over 30 acres of Mississippi River basin, E & J has over 3,500 American and foreign cars and trucks from the '30s on up.*

3

4

5

6

7

3. This '68 Cougar was one of the more complete cars in the yard; indeed it could be driven away. The white-over-maroon pony car had a 302 and automatic transmission.

4. A little rough around the edges, but this '63 Cadillac two-door was pretty well intact. The roll of toilet paper on the dash is no extra charge.

5. Another complete car which had been taken off to the side was this '64 Buick Electra sedan. Loaded with working options, this car probably went quickly.

6. These Dodge Royal sedans were quite popular back in 1955, when over 100,000 of them were sold. This one has automatic transmission and a still-intact interior.

7. Most of E & J's cars still have glass, wheels, tires and trim, like this '62 Studebaker Lark two-door sedan.

8. You'd better hurry and get to this '56 Ford before the tinworm beats you to it. Other than the front end, the salmon-colored four-door Victoria was pretty straight, with lots of sheet metal and trim to donate.

8

9. *This was not the best Comet in the yard, but it was a '65 convertible with top bows intact. The motor's gone but the automatic tranny is still there.*

10. *There's not much left of this '71 Impala convertible. Top bows, engine, windshield and front clip are long gone.*

11. *This '66 Bonneville four-door with automatic has sustained a major hit on the passenger side.*

9

10

11

12

13

12. *Despite the Midwest location, Mustangs were not prevalent at the E & J yard. This red '69 automatic had a decent interior and some good trim pieces.*

13. *This white Monterey caught our eye as we traveled through the rows of metal carnage. The sharp two-door hardtop would be an excellent parts car.*

14. *Several nice Falcons graced the Illinois yard, including this complete red '63 four-door with automatic.*

14

15

16

17

15. *Another nice Dearborn product was this aqua '64 Mercury Montclair four door. With a little paint and body work, this Iowa car could be on the road again.*

16. *It looks like someone really wanted that Barracuda emblem on the front fender well. There are still lots of good parts left on this '67 coupe, though.*

17. *When we opened the suicide doors on this '69 Thunderbird, we were surprised to find a fully loaded and intact interior. Other than the engine, this is a prime donor candidate.*

18. *There are some bruises on this cute little '63 Comet sedan, but otherwise it appears complete.*

19. *Just under 5,000 of these big Buick LeSabre convertibles were produced in 1966. This one's had a rough go of it, but might offer some good parts yet.*

18

19

20. *It's not often that you see a "Pack Rat" in a salvage yard. From the looks of it, this Packard 400 hardtop has been here for some time.*

21. *This '51 Kaiser two-door hardtop still looks graceful, even at this late stage in its life.*

22. *With Hudson nearing the end of its run, very few Hornets were produced in 1956. One interesting feature on this car is the rare factory antenna.*

23. *There were many Corvairs at E & J. We found this red '62 model near the end of one of the rows.*

20

21

22

23

24

25

24. *The pickins are getting slim on this mid-'70s AMC Javelin, which was last licensed in 1979.*

25. *There are also some pretty interesting haulers in the western Illinois yard. This late-'40s Ford four speed was relatively straight and complete.*

26. *There's plenty left of this '69 Dodge Charger to either restore or pick apart.*

27. *Representing the Blue Oval's first totally new postwar automobile, this slab-sided '49 Ford is starting to lose ground to the yard's foliage.*

26

27

28

28. *These '63 Futura twins, one blue and the other cream-colored, keep each other company during the lonely times on the lot. Both have been well-kept and appear ready to go.*

29. *A '46 Chevy four-speed pickup has some dings in the grille and a surprisingly good interior.*

30. *Rust is starting to get the best of this '57 Buick Special hardtop. The engine and wheels had been removed already.*

29

30

31. *This copper-colored '66 Galaxie 500 still has its 352-cid engine and automatic tranny. There are numerous excellent parts left on this one.*

32. *There's hardly a dent in this '78 Plymouth Volare, disguised as one of the last Road Runners. Even the paint job has held up on this car.*

33. *The passenger-side front door is lying on the front seat of this '50 Chevy sedan. Exterior panels are very straight and could be borrowed.*

34. *A '55 DeSoto Fireflite has been hit in the side and rear, but the hood is straight and the automatic transmission remains.*

35

36

35. *Lots of Mopars, including this nice '64 Dodge four-door, call E & J home. This one had excellent glass, sheetmetal and trim.*

36. *Though "sightless" and without power, this '60 T-bird had relatively rust-free sheet metal.*

37. *Peeking out from behind some brush, a postwar Dodge four-door gleams in the afternoon sun. Its engine has already been plucked, and the '47 Dodge seems willing to surrender more so that another brother can live again.*

37

38

39

located, providing expansion room for E & J.

Now spanning 30 acres and approximately 3,500 used vehicles, the business is growing by leaps and bounds, according to Tschappat. E & J's 12 full-time employees bring in an average of 10 to 20 cars per week to the yard's extensive inventory.

All cars are cataloged by individual marque on separate pages listing equipment specs and options. As parts are removed, notations are made until the vehicle is totally parted out and removed for the crusher. The system has worked well for the growing Illinois business.

So join us for a truncated pictorial tour of E & J Auto and Truck Parts, in Rock Island, Ill.

38. *There are plenty of pre-war parts cars at E & J, like this '41 Ford two-door sedan. Most have been picked over, but are not yet totally stripped.*

39. *It looks like the vultures have already visited this '69 Plymouth Barracuda.*

40. *Owner Larry Tschappat grew up at this Rock Island, Ill. salvage yard, as the son of the first proprietor. He managed a yard in California before returning to take over his father's operation in the mid-'70s.*

40

About the yard

E & J Used Auto and Truck Parts is located at 315 31st Street in Rock Island, Ill., part of the Quad Cities area. Owner Larry Tschappat welcomes visitors in the 30-acre yard, but they must be supervised. Business hours are 8 a.m. - 4:30 p.m. Monday through Friday, and 8 a.m. - 1 p.m. on Saturday. The yard includes 3,500 domestic and foreign cars dating back to 1937. Mail order service is available. Write to P.O. Box 6007, Rock Island, IL 61204-6007; or phone 1-309-788-7686 or 1-800-728-7686 (outside the Quad City

B&M AUTO WRECKING

BOBBY ZANNON'S PLACE IN THE SUN

By Randy Moser

Through the years, the warm, dry Arizona climate has drawn hordes of transplanted individuals from the colder East and Midwest regions of the U.S. Bobby Zanon, owner of B&M Auto Wrecking, Inc., makes no bones about his reason for relocating from Chicago some 13 years ago.

"One winter's day when I tripped over some transmission parts buried under two feet of snow, I just decided there had to be a better way to make a living," he explained recently. "That's when I decided to come out here."

Having grown up among "old car guys" in Chicago, Zanon couldn't bear to get out of the business altogether. So he opened his own yard in the southeastern Phoenix suburb of Tempe, not far from the Arizona State University campus. The yard is home to some 850 vehicles on five acres near the Salt River basin.

B&M specializes in clean used parts from American and foreign vehicles dating from 1965-85. "That's what sells well in this area. Good pieces up to 30

1

2

Photos by the author

1. *Located in Tempe, the same southeast Phoenix suburb as Arizona State University, B&M Auto Wrecking is home to several hundred parts cars. Most of the older cars have been parted out and sent to the crusher.*

2. *This white Nova is minus its steering wheel and front clip, but sheet metal and interior parts are salvageable. A small amount of surface rust is beginning to etch its way through the paint.*

3. *A first-generation Cougar has already donated its doors, interior and engine, but taillights and rear glass remain.*

4. *If you're refurbishing a '67 Mustang, this one still has some great sheetmetal.*

3

4

5

5. *B&M owner Bobby Zanon keeps plenty of hubcaps available for his customers. He also has a good supply of original glass, hoods and drivetrains.*

6. *This blue, mid-'70s Impala four-door sedan was in excellent condition, other than the flat tires.*

7. *Though a good portion of it is already gone, what's left of this '70 Cadillac Sedan de Ville four-door hardtop appears salvageable.*

6

7

years old can still be beautiful out here in this climate. It doesn't pay to keep the older cars around too long, though," he explained. "The real demand is for the later model parts. We still keep quite a few of the '60s cars around, but once a car is pretty well stripped, it gets

crushed, no matter how old it is."

B&M retains a staff of six which removes all parts for customers. The yard does most of its business with local patrons, who are advised to leave their credit cards at home. Currently, no shipping service is available.

As for regrets, Bobby Zanon has had few in his 13 years out West. "It was one of the best moves that I've made in my career," he claims. "You can sell auto parts anywhere, and you don't have to be miserable while you're doing it. It's just a lot nicer out here than back home.

8

9

10

8. *It might look like it's ready to ascend in flight, but this '68 Thunderbird is "grounded," sans engine and drivetrain.*

9. *As you might expect, pickups are popular items out west, and parts are in hot demand. This late '60s to early '70s Ford Ranger has donated doors, wheels and axles.*

10. *There normally isn't much demand for '68 Falcon Futuras around Arizona, but this '68 two-door sedan shows evidence that someone has been picking on it. The engine has been pulled.*

11. *This junkyard mongrel was behind a short fence, but one look into his eyes lets you know to use the long lens for his portrait.*

11

12. *This is why so many of B&M's vehicles appear in the yard without door panels; many are extracted as they enter the yard, since the operation sells more parts than entire cars.*

13. *Arizonans seem to prefer American products, and this '67 Volvo 122S was one of the few foreign numbers that we saw in the yard. Both the exterior and interior of this four-speed sedan were sound and the engine had not yet been removed.*

14. *This '70 Ford Ranchero has been picked over, but if you're looking for some trim parts, it might be just what the doctor ordered.*

12

13

14

15

15. *Big cars are "in" and this yellow '69 LTD two-door would make a nice ride. Equipped with power steering, power brakes and automatic transmission, the big Ford was still pretty much intact.*

"Actually, I rarely think about Chicago anymore," he says with a grin. "Except during the winter when a snowstorm hits and I'm out here in the sunshine."

About the yard
B&M Auto Wrecking, Inc. is located at 225 North McClintock Road, in Tempe, Ariz., a southern Phoenix suburb. The five-acre yard is managed by Bobby Zanon. Business hours are 8 a.m. to 5 p.m. Monday through Friday, and 8 a.m. to 12 p.m. Saturday. Visitors are not allowed in the yard, and all parts are pulled by the B&M staff. Contact B&M at 602-968-1111.

KELSEY AUTO SALVAGE

IOWA'S HEARTLAND HAVEN

By Randy Moser

Way up in the beautiful rolling farmlands of north central Iowa, you expect to see acre after acre of amber fields of grain and grazing livestock. That's why it almost stops you in your tracks when you approach Iowa Falls from the southeast.

For the cash "crop" at Kelsey's is row after row of old cars and appliances, with the only living things roaming the pastures being customers and a few small junkyard dogs.

Kelsey Auto Salvage started out as just an interest to Dean Kelsey, but quickly escalated into a full-time "hobby" in 1974. A natural mechanic, the affable co-proprietor owned a motorcycle shop at the time.

"People would ask if they could park their old cars on our property here and it just sort of happened," he explained. "I found out that I liked to be out in the open, and this business is one of the few that allowed me that freedom. It's not like milking cows . . . you can work at your own pace at this job."

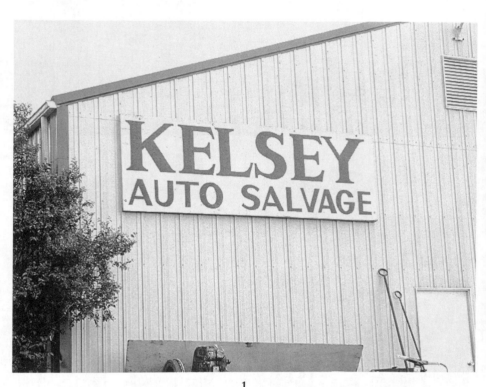

1

2

Photos by the author

1. Located next to his family residence in north central Iowa, Kelsey Auto Salvage has become a full-time "hobby" for owner Dean Kelsey. The 15-acre site is home to some 250 cars, appliances and other miscellaneous items.

2. If you're looking for Volkswagens, Kelsey's is a good place to start. These three mid-to-late '60s examples were still in good shape, along with several others, including three VW buses.

3. This nifty old '56 Packard Clipper sedan has been hit on the passenger side, but the rest of the body still seemed quite solid.

4. Despite what it might look like, neither this Edsel nor the yard was affected by the terrible Iowa floods of '93. This very solid, aqua-colored '59 model was placed on its side to expose the suspension and framework.

5. Sitting atop a pile of refuse, this '72-'73 vintage Plymouth Gold Duster seemed pretty well intact, with the exception of its missing "eyes." It had straight bumpers, sheetmetal and lots of interior pieces.

3

4   5

6. *Despite missing its engine, this green '64 Ford Fairlane sedan seems to have escaped the parts pickers. It was probably a pretty nice ride for some family back in the mid-'60s.*

7. *This 1950 Plymouth Special Deluxe four-door has obviously been parked for quite some time, yet remains remarkably intact and free of major rust. The black beauty was equipped with a three-speed column shift.*

6

7

8

8. *An unusual sight was this well preserved 1962 Studebaker Lark four-door wagon. The little orange wagon seemed to have all the major pieces intact, including its original 170-cid six under the hood.*

9. *There is also plenty to delight truck aficionados at Kelsey Auto Salvage, including the remains of this 1947 Dodge WC series half-ton pickup. As you can see, there are still some excellent grille and trim pieces remaining on this first-generation postwar hauler.*

10. *This happy little fella, along with two other look-alike cousins, serve as the official junkyard dogs, carefully guarding the contents of the Kelsey yard.*

11. *About 3,000 of these Willys Aero Falcon four-door sedans were built during 1953, the only year of their brief existence. This one is still fairly straight, and could easily donate some vital "organs."*

12. *This '56 Buick Century four-door sedan is starting to show the ravages of time, as the engine and rear bumper have been plucked and quite a bit of rust is starting to show. The blue Buick still retains nice taillight assemblies, trim pieces and interior goodies, however.*

9

10

11

12

13

14

13. *No respectable salvage yard is without a Corvair, and Kelsey's had this red '63 example. Still pretty well intact, the rear-engine machine showed little indication that it had been in any significant accidents. Probably just another Ralph Nader victim.*

14. *This is Iowa Hawkeye country, and the Hawk symbol is ubiquitous. This one appeared on the upper rear panel of a discarded van.*

15. *The second year of a three-year styling cycle, this brown '53 Lincoln Cosmopolitan looked almost nice enough to drive away. Note our little friend guarding the front bumper.*

16. *This '49 Packard has taken a major hit in the front end, but the rest of the body is still quite straight. A good rear bumper, taillights and steering wheel are certainly salvageable.*

15

16

17

18

17. *On a bluff overlooking the rolling northern Iowa scenery sits another early '70s Plymouth Duster. This one hasn't fared quite as well as the earlier mentioned example, but glass, chrome trim and some accessories were still available.*

18. *The interior is still good on this white '65 Plymouth Valiant, but rust is starting to claim the edges of its exterior.*

19. *Ford produced its club wagons through the early- to middle-'60s. This one, on a Falcon frame, needs some glass, but otherwise looks ready to haul again.*

20. *This '79 AMX showed little signs of external damage, with glass, interior and trim parts available.*

19

20

Dean and his son, Chuck, run the 15-acre operation, which accepts appliances, scrap iron and various other loads of salvage, in addition to used motor vehicles. When we visited, inventory included railroad ties, soft drink machines, and supermarket shelves. Kelsey claimed that his car and truck supply was down a bit over previous years, though still exceeding some 250 interesting vehicles.

"It's just an interesting business," Kelsey said, recounting some of his past experiences with customers. "It's interesting to discover what comes in with the loads. One time I found an entire box of authentic German beer steins inside one of the cars. For the most part, I really enjoy working with people."

Browsers are welcome at Kelsey Auto Salvage from 8 a.m. to 5 p.m. Tuesday through Friday, and 9 a.m. to 12 p.m. on Saturdays. Dean or Chuck will pull needed parts or will sell the entire vehicle, whichever the customer needs. Mail order service is also available

---

About the yard

Kelsey Auto Salvage is located on 00 Avenue southeast of Iowa Falls, in north central Iowa. Take Rocksylvania Avenue and turn right on 00 Avenue; the yard will be two miles away. Owners Dean and Chuck Kelsey allow customers to browse the 15-acre site unsupervised during the normal business hours of 8 a.m. to 5 p.m. Tuesday through Friday and 8 a.m. to 12 p.m. Saturday. Mail orders are acccpted. The mailing address is Rt. 2, Iowa Falls, IA 50126; the phone number is 515-648-3066.

BLACK CANYON OLD PARTS CO.

ARIZONA'S GOLD

By Dean Shipley

Beneath a nameless Arizona butte that the residents of Black Canyon City have nicknamed "the Devil's Thumb," lies a salvage yard that Mother Nature tried to wipe out in one swift aquatic assault. She did a bang-up job, but she can't have it quite yet. The old car guys aren't quite done with it.

In January of '93, Mama Na' (pronounced nay) sloshed the north central region of Arizona with 5.22 inches of rain (4.55 inches more than the normal rainfall). That's a ton of precipitation for any area to absorb, let alone a normally arid region. The sparse, scruffy vegetation of the region, which is accustomed to surviving on little more than water vapor, couldn't grab and hold onto much of that precious and rare liquid. As a result much of it ran off.

The runoff from the nearby New River Mountains collected in the Squaw Creek. The creek, which is dry most of the year, bulged and blasted down out of the mountains and onto the flats, suspending tons of sand and gravel, and rolling granite boulders in its watery bulk. This irresistible force rushed furiously to the Agua Fria River, into which it empties.

Located on the southern bank of the Squaw Creek is the Black Canyon Old Parts Co. — the "immovable object" in our equation. This is not to say BCOP does not move parts. Quite to the contrary. The company sells parts and cars all over the world. But you get my drift; you get an idea of what happened.

The mountain-fed torrents of water smashed into Squaw Creek's southern banks, dissolved them, and roared through hundreds of cars at BCOP. Some

1

2

Photos by the author
1. *"The Devil's Thumb" stands above Black Canyon Old Parts Co., Black Canyon City, Ariz. Squaw Creek cut a new channel through the salvage yard in Jan. '93 and destroyed hundreds of cars, as illustrated by the '71 Dodge Charger in the drink at left. The '46 Ford was left high and dry, however.*

3

4

5

2. *The sign outside the office says it all.*

3. *That's not a '58 Buick Special convertible. It's a two-door hardtop model with the top cut off. Despite the alteration, the car still has some good brightwork available. It runs and drives.*

4-5. *Rick Ludlow, one of BCOP's partners, poses with the "company car," a '54 Cadillac hearse parked near the front door. Technically, it's not for sale. But, if someone wants it badly enough ...*

6. *Visible here is some of the devastation rendered by a furious Squaw Creek in January 1993. The trunk lid on the "square bird" was ripped open then filled with sand and rocks.*

6

7. *This '68 Buick Riviera could have its edges smoothed out and be made into a proper driver.*

8. *With a saguaro cactus in the background, this brace of '54 Chevrolet station wagons has solid sheet metal available, but most trim is gone.*

9. *A '67 Mercury Cougar, left, shares space with a '64 Cadillac Coupe de Ville. Ludlow has an abundance of these big Caddy cruisers.*

7

8

9

10

11

10. *This isn't the only '59 Chevrolet at Black Canyon Old Parts Co. Several more are there, including a convertible with a 348 V-8 engine and a pair of two-door hardtops.*

11. *Yes, the glass is gone, but some of that unique Super Sport trim is still available from this '64 Chevrolet Impala SS.*

12. *Looking for a Chevrolet El Camino? Not only is it Rick Ludlow's ride of choice, many of its brethren reside in the yard. He has models from '59, '60, and '64-'70.*

13. *It may not be the greatest right front fender for a '56 Chevrolet, but it certainly has potential.*

12

13

became boats and floated to the Agua Fria and on downstream. Other cars were flipped on their sides. Still others had closed trunks and hoods torn open and filled with sand and granite boulders. Car interiors were filled to the window sills with the stuff. The Squaw Creek gouged a new bed for itself right through the center of the yard before finding its way back to the Agua Fria.

The creek absolutely ruined hundreds of vehicles that bore numerous salvageable parts. It was a sad day for the old car parts business.

Partners Rick Ludlow and Ron McClure mourned the sight. But not for long. Ludlow, a former captain of ocean-going oil tankers, had previously seen water's potential for devastation. Though the flood dealt them a setback,

it was not going to wash them out.

With the flood behind them and Squaw Creek dry once again, BCOP, at this point, is well into its clean-up phase. Some of the cars destroyed in the flood were crushed; others await a similar fate. By the time it's done, some 300 cars will have been compacted. Some cars remain partially buried and may stay that way.

14. *This '60 Olds 88 has been jacked around some, but there's another one, a 98 two-door hardtop, that's much better, according to Ludlow.*

15. *Black Canyon's staff pulls parts, catalogs them and places them on pallets in neat order.*

16. *Though the top is a bit ragged and there's a crease or two in the sheet metal, this '65 Plymouth Fury III convertible is on its feet and restorable.*

17. *As many as six of these '66 Dodges reside in Black Canyon.*

14

15

16

17

18

19

18. *Though the left rear quarter is waving at us, the remainder of this '58 Chrysler Windsor looks pretty solid. Remember, sheet metal and chrome rarely rust in Arizona.*

19. *Seafood anyone? This '69 'Cuda comes served on a pilaf of sand and gravel, thanks to the flood of Squaw Creek.*

20. *The residue left behind by a raging, flooded Squaw Creek has to be hundreds of tons in weight. Now nearly buried by the sand, this '64 Plymouth was "high and dry" before the flood.*

20

21

22

23

21. *Squaw Creek did not quite nab this '57 Buick, but it came close.*

22. *A '63 Olds 98 four-door hardtop has a ding here and there, but is solid. There are two others on the lot.*

23. *A '60 Cadillac Coupe de Ville with lots of potential awaits restoration.*

24. *A blue '73 Dodge Challenger with a vinyl top and 340-cid V-8 engine could be made to cruise the streets again.*

24

25. *Shades of the "Rain Man:" a '49 Buick convertible needing restoration.*

26. *Yet another '49 Buick, a Super four-door sedan also has stablemates: two Supers and two Specials.*

25

26

But we're here to tell you BCOP has remained busy and has not neglected building an inventory of old cars for its customers. Thanks to a small-business loan, BCOP remains alive and well, according to Ludlow.

BCOP's crew of seven men is increasing the car inventory daily. The approximate car count is again bumping the 1,400 mark, the yard's "high water" mark prior to the flood. New additions to the inventory include:
• Three '66 Pontiac GTOs;
• Three '67 Pontiac GTOs;
• '70 Chevelle SS;
• '57 Chevy two-door hardtop;
• '54 Oldsmobile two-door hardtop;
• '58 Buick two-door hardtop;

• A variety of '56 Fords;
• Five '55 Ford parts cars;
• A restorable '60 Olds 98 two-door hardtop;
• The list could go on.

In addition to this inventory, BCOP has other vehicles, many of which are nearly complete, stored at another location.

Visitors to the area are invited to stop by. (It's very pleasant there in January—except when it's raining). Rick is the husky-voiced fellow with his blonde locks in a queue, a ready smile and a hearty handshake. Norm Wilson is the behind-the-counter man. He's a mature gentleman, who'll remind you of your favorite uncle. Nick-named "the old fart," Norm manages the office.

A visit to Black Canyon City is not complete without breakfast at The 4B's. The food is good, there's plenty of it and waitresses make sure your coffee cup is always full. We have it on good advice The Rock Springs also serves a good meal.

HAUF AUTO SALVAGE

FAMILY STYLE YARD IN STILLWATER, OKLA.

By Dean Shipley

As a wry smile moved over the face of Gene Hauf, he said, "Watch for the moving freckles." His caveat came just moments before the tour of his 25-acre salvage yard began. He was referring to ticks, those pesky insects that look indeed like mobile freckles on steroids. They are a fact of life in Oklahoma, and as such were no cause for alarm to Hauf.

Hauf advised the reporter to brush the ticks off after the tour and make a thorough self examination before stepping into the shower later that evening. He assured me they were not of the disease-carrying variety. (The reporter did indeed carry a tick back to Ohio with him, but with no apparent consequence. That accounted for him being a little "ticked" by the time he returned home.)

Ticks aside, the task at hand was taking a gander at the Auto Salvage Yard of old cars and trucks. (The trucks were covered in the winter 1993 issue of *Cars & Parts' Collectible Trucks* magazine.) The yard lays on the west side of Oklahoma State Route 177, four miles south of Stillwater, the

home of the Oklahoma State Cowboys. The yard has been in that location since 1946. It is a gently rolling plot that, once upon a time, had enough oil beneath it to warrant having a well drilled. It provided some income over the years, but has now played out. The well has been capped and Hauf said he'll miss the income it provided.

But Hauf was not born to be an oil baron. He's a born salvage man. "I was born in it (the salvage business)," Hauf said. His father had been working with his father, also a salvage man, who started his work as a "recyclist" in the '20s.

Though his sons, Rick and R.B., help their dad pull parts on their days off, Gene is the last of his family to make a career of the salvage business. Rick is a firefighter, while R.B. is a deputy sheriff. Their mother, Jo, Gene's wife of 33 years, works the office side of the business.

3

4   5

Photos by the author

1. Gene Hauf has continued a business initiated by his grandfather and sustained by his father.

2. Hauf's salvage business stands aside Route 177, several miles south of Stillwater, Okla. The acreage of the yard has shrunk in recent years, which makes it more manageable, according to Hauf.

3. Old Ford product lovers, start drooling. Here's a grouping from the '40s, with a youngster, a '51 model two-door sedan, on the far right. To the rear of the '42 Ford coupe in the foreground sits a '48 Lincoln that has been picked over.

4. A '52 Buick Super hardtop coupe has good glass and sheet metal, for the most part. The top has sustained a hit, though. A '52 Super four-door sedan sits to its left and has front end damage. To the right resides a '58 Buick.

5. A '49-'50 Jeepster has had some parts removed, but could still be resurrected in the hands of the right hobbyist.

6

7

8

6. *Oklahoma is Ford convertible country. Here are three from the '60s: a '64, right, a '62 model in "decent" shape and a '65 model. The latter has no engine, but otherwise is also in decent shape. The top bows are still there.*

7. *A '60 Chevrolet Impala two-door hardtop shows rust-out on the left front fender, but the car can certainly provide some other salvageable parts.*

8. *Though the engine is gone from this '56 Pontiac Star Chief hardtop, the body is good enough to support life through an engine transplant.*

9. *A '64 Impala Super Sport has had an apparent tough time of it, as it has "cancer" and has had some of the interior removed. Anyone want what's left? There are also several more '64s and a '63 as well.*

10. *A '42 Buick Sedanette has seen its engine and transmission depart. The right rear fender has sustained some damage and the grille bars show slight indentations. A clock is hiding in the glove box. The "fastback" could make an interesting ride though.*

11. *Though the interior is missing, the engine and transmission are still inside this '63 Pontiac Grand Prix.*

12. *Here's an unusual model, a '60 Chevrolet Bel Air two-door hardtop. It was built in Canada. It's nearly complete with a 283 V-8, automatic, and a radio, but also some rust.*

9

10

11

12

13. *This '65 Plymouth Barracuda still has the 318-cid V-8 under the hood, but a non-stock rear end under the glass.*

14. *A brace of '64 Ford Galaxie 500 hardtops still hold good glass and some fair sheetmetal.*

15. *A '38 Buick has given up its engine and miscellaneous parts to hobbyists, its glass to vandals. But some sheet metal or the remainder of the car could be salvaged. These fat-fendered babies have been known to make good street rods.*

16. *While we're talking Buicks, have a look at this '60 Invicta Custom convertible! It's a rare item, to be sure, and may be worthy of saving.*

17. *There's not much remaining to salvage of this Model 75 '57 Buick Roadmaster.*

18. *This '50 Pontiac station wagon still has its engine. But it also has a little rust on its rear fenders. Could be interesting, though.*

13

14

15

16

17

18

19   20

19. The right rear fender of this '47 Dodge four-door sedan has a few wrinkles in it, but the car is in decent shape. It has a "Fluid Drive" rear bumper. Hauf, right, talks to a friend who stopped by to visit.

20 In Hauf's shop sits a '61 Skoda Felicia, a Czech automobile. It has a four-cylinder sleeve engine that needs work. It also has a four-speed, column-shift transmission, independent rear suspension, keys and paperwork.

21. Looking very much like an orphan, this '58 Studebaker Commander is all alone in the world.

21

Hauf's reputation for supplying solid, salvageable vehicles and parts stretches across the U.S. and beyond. Customers have come from Europe to buy cars and trucks. Hauf said he will ship cars and/or parts anywhere, so long as the customer pays the freight.

The holdings of the yard truly run the gamut from the '30s through the '60s. The inventory of GM products and Ford are probably about equal. Mopar and orphan products are not as plentiful, but have representation.

Cars come in a variety of body styles and equipment, from convertibles to station wagons. Hauf said he has very few muscle cars. We noticed only the shell of a '66 Olds 442 in residence.

All of Hauf's inventory has been propped up on blocks to keep ground moisture from decaying the cars from underneath. Many of the cars show only surface rust. Oklahoma cars are not subjected to the ravages of salt, used elsewhere to treat winter's snow-covered roadways. "We don't get the rust like other parts of the country," Hauf said. However, some cars in his yard are "imports" from other areas of the country and have more than surface rust.

Some recent additions to Hauf's inventory include:
• a '56 Packard four-door sedan;
• a '53 Plymouth with a complete body and "smoking"engine;
• a '50 Chevrolet two-door sedan;
• a '52 Studebaker;
• a '64 Buick Skylark wagon;
• two 1 1/2-ton '46 Ford trucks;
• a '66 Mustang coupe, body only;
• several Metropolitans with numerous usable parts.

The Haufs exude a friendliness to their clients that apparently returns to them multiplied. Customers from far and wide return to them on a regular basis. That suits the Haufs just fine.

"The most fun is meeting the people from all over (the world)," Jo Hauf said.

Sounds like keeping the salvage yard business in the family is O-K by them.

R.C. VAN CLEAVE & SON USED CARS & TRUCKS

1

By Bob Stevens

There are salvage yards in every town of substance in the country, but only a precious few offer golden oldies from the prewar era, the '50s or the '60s. And their numbers are dwindling with each passing season. Even harder to find are yards that specialize not in parts but in vehicles that are still restorable, or at least offered as complete parts cars. Well, there are two such operations, and they're only a few miles apart in Campbellsville, Ky., a small town of some 9,000 about 50 miles north of the Tennessee border. The nearest city of any size would be Bowling Green, Ky., which is about 75 miles to the southwest.

The two operations, R.C. Van Cleave & Son Used Cars and Trucks, and Nolley Auto Sales, are only a few miles apart, but they're worlds apart in the kinds of cars they stock, and the way they're operated.

Step back to the '30s at Randall Van Cleave's

The specialty at R.C. Van Cleave's place is prewar tin, with the emphasis on the '30s. Operating from his home on a large plot of farm land just outside Campbellsville, Randall Van Cleave has grown and nurtured a remarkable crop of rare and desirable cars and trucks. And it's now harvest time.

A hobbyist for more years than he wants to admit, Van Cleave has bought, sold, traded, restored and parted out hundreds of cars and trucks. He has single-handedly saved many rare relics from the crusher, including some that have been restored and returned to the nation's fleet of antique vehicles. He has a special fondness for trucks, and seems to be a magnet for cars from the prewar and early postwar periods.

Strolling around the Van Cleave farm, one can find anything from a '30 Plymouth coupe to a '49 Lincoln. In between there are such treasures as a '35 Chevy sedan, '34 Plymouth coupe, '33 Dodge, '40 Chevy, '36 Buick, '37 Plymouth, '40 Cadillac coupe, '37 Lincoln V-12 coupe (now powered by a Cadillac engine), '42 Chevy, '57 Chevy wagon with a late model Corvette engine, '40 Lincoln coupe, a running and complete '48 Chrysler Windsor coupe with a parts car, '47 Lincoln Zephyr coupe, '46 Chevy sedan, and a '48 Mercury coupe.

Among the newer cars present are a '50 Olds 88 two-door, '57 Chevy wagon, running '62 Pontiac Catalina two-door hardtop, '68 Thunderbird, '61 Chevy Bel Air sedan, '63 Ford Falcon Futura, '53 Olds two-door, '56 Cadillac two-door hardtop, '60 T-Bird, '56 Lincoln Premier, '52 Merc two-door hardtop, '67 Ford, '52 Caddy two-door hardtop, etc.

There are a lot of trucks at Van Cleave's. Among them are a '33 Dodge, '52 Ford, '46 Ford, '37 Ford, '36 Dodge, '37 Chevy wrecker, etc. Gathered in one spot are three '37 Ford trucks, and Van Cleave is asking $1,500 for the trio. There's also a '33 Dodge truck with a DeSoto engine from the '50s, reflecting a clean, bolt-in installation. Another interesting find is a '34 Dodge pickup truck in thoroughly original condition, and still looking pretty decent.

Stacked around the yard are piles of hoods, some fenders, a few grilles, a bunch of vintage engines, some bumpers, etc. They date back to the '50s, '40s and '30s, and fit a variety of

2

Photos by the author

1. Located on farm land off an old country road just outside Campbellsville, Ky., R.C. Van Cleave & Son Used Cars & Trucks is marked by this small sign alongside the roadway. It's the only hint that vintage treasures are hidden behind the hills and trees of the Van Cleave family farm.

2. Randall Van Cleave (right) shows a '33 Ford pickup truck to a prospective buyer, Terry Kesselring, of Elsmere, Ky.

3. The grounds are well trimmed, so access to all units is easy.

4. A '40 Chevy two-door sedan awaits better times.

5. He doesn't look like much, but Blackie, a mixed breed stray who took up residence on the Van Cleave farm, can be rather vicious when one of the family isn't present. He's otherwise good natured, as is Red, another mixed breed who helps protect the family collection of antique cars and trucks.

6. Terry Kesselring, who owns a restoration shop, ponders the possibilities for this '36 Buick. The car needs a total restoration, or, better yet, would make a decent parts car. It is fairly complete, including an engine.

7. It's been street rodded, courtesy of a Chevy 350-cid V-8 with 350 Turbo tranny and Corvair front end, but this '30 Plymouth coupe is pretty much stock in appearance, save for the custom wheels and fat tires. This little number is priced at $4,000.

3

4

5

6

7

8. *Up on blocks, this '60 Thunderbird would need a set of wheels and tires before it could be hauled away.*

9. *Only some 1,550 three-window Lincoln Zephyr coupes were made in 1940, and one of the survivors is hiding under a roof attached to one of Van Cleave's storage buildings.*

10. *Cars are lined up neatly, which makes everything easy to find, and also makes it a lot easier than usual to retrieve a vehicle.*

11. *V-8 powered '40 Caddy coupe is pretty much complete, including its interior and dash, but in need of total restoration.*

12

12. *A good solid car, this '56 Lincoln Premier has only 70,000 original miles on its odometer. But it's been tucked away in a barn for a number of years, judging by the layers of dust that have accumulated on it.*

13. *This mostly complete '53 Olds 88 two-door sedan is ready to be rescued from the elements.*

14. *Not for sale, this '34 Plymouth coupe is a keeper. In fact, it belongs to Van Cleave's wife.*

15. *In pretty decent shape, this '35 Chevy four-door sedan is priced as a complete car for $5,000.*

13

14

15

16

17

16. *This '56 Cadillac two-door hardtop is restorable, but needs everything redone.*

17. *Partially restored, this '40 Cadillac coupe will hopefully be back on the road soon. Van Cleave has a couple of cars under restoration at any one time; some he keeps and others he resells.*

18. *There's a big cache of engines stowed away in one of the outbuildings. The three motors seen here are (from left) a Lincoln V-12, a '35 Chevy six, and a '37 Plymouth flathead six. All are looking to be reunited with a vehicle of the appropriate breeding.*

About the yard

R.C. Van Cleave & Son Used Cars & Trucks is located at 344 Salem Church Rd., Campbellsville, Ky. 42718, and the phone number is 502-465-2329. An appointment is necessary. Randall Van Cleave is the sole proprietor. Van Cleave prefers to sell whole units, either as restorable vehicles or parts cars, but some parts can be acquired individually off selected units.

18

19

20

21

22

19. *A bit weathered from outside storage, this '50 Olds 88 two-door sedan is ready for a second lease on life, or at least to make a final contribution as a parts car. In the background is a '62 Falcon that has been rear-ended.*

20. *Van Cleave has owned this '48 Mercury coupe since 1971, and it's as complete now as it was when it was driven into storage a few years ago. With a little persuasion, its original flathead would probably fire up.*

21. *Cadillac power now propels this striking '37 Lincoln V-12 coupe (at least it carried a V-12 when it left the factory more than half a century ago).*

22. *One of many trucks in the collection, this pickup is a '52 Ford.*

23. *Having traveled a total of less than 35,000 miles since rolling off the assembly line, this '50 Olds 88 two-door is just too nice to part with, so it's a "keeper," Van Cleave says emphatically.*

23

24

24. *A '36 Ford pickup is piled on top of a '46 Ford truck, while a newer Chevy truck rests in the foreground.*

25. *This '61 Chevy Bel Air two-door sedan looks like it was in pretty decent shape when it was parked here many moons ago.*

26. *Undergoing a complete restoration is a '52 Cadillac two-door hardtop. This one's fairly far along, and looking sharp.*

27. *In complete, running condition, this '29 Model A pickup truck would be a relatively easy restoration.*

28. *The dashboard of this '47 Mercury sedan still hosts an original radio and instruments.*

29. *Still in pretty solid shape, a finned '49 Cadillac two-door sedan looks ahead to better days in the hands of an ambitious restorer.*

25

26

27

28

29

30. *Stock '49 Lincoln four-door was driven home by Van Cleave, and with a little coaxing, could probably be driven home again by someone else. The original flathead V-8 is still at home under that big hood, and it's hooked up to the three-speed overdrive transmission that was installed at the factory.*

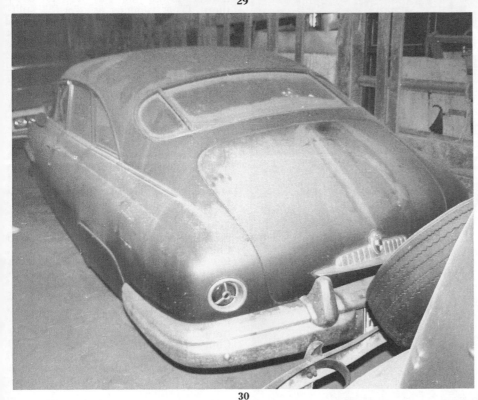

30

makes and models. Even though Van Cleave has been accumulating cars, parts and related items for only seven years, the collection has grown to immense size. His dad was an International dealer, so there are a few IH related items scattered about, as well as an International truck or two.

Van Cleave is a licensed car dealer himself, and had planned on restoring many of the cars in his yard in conjunction with his son-in-law, who was the "son" in "Van Cleave & Son," until his untimely death a few years back in a tragic automobile accident. The two had planned to restore the cars in the yard and re-sell them. Now, Van Cleave realizes that he has neither the time nor capacity to handle so many ambitious projects, so he's selling the majority of the yard's inhabitants. Most are offered only as complete cars, either for restoration or as a parts car. A few are keepers, including a couple now under restoration and a couple that his wife owns.

A visit with Randall Van Cleave is an interesting experience, as he knows the history behind many of the cars in his collection, and each has its own story. But if a tour of the yard fails to produce just the right car for this year's project, don't despair, because there's another vintage car dealer just across town.

NOLLEY AUTO SALES

The '50s come alive at Nolley Auto Sales

When was the last time you saw a retractable Ford hardtop in a junkyard? Or a '57 Chevy convertible? How about a 1956-57 Corvette body? Not recently, we'd suspect, because we tour dozens of yards every year and in the past five years or so, we have only unearthed three major discoveries (a '53 Buick Skylark convertible that was removed before our story even hit print, a '57 Chevy ragtop, and a '57 Ford Skyliner). Well, there exists a yard with the aforementioned treasures, and many more, in Campbellsville in southern Kentucky.

It's just a few minutes from Van Cleave's, but unlike that operation out in the country, this one is quartered in the city itself. Part of the operation is a going auto repair business, but the interesting facet of Nolley Auto Sales, Inc., is the yard that surrounds the shop. Lining the street out front are a dozen or more 1955-57 Chevys. Most of them are sedans, but there is at least one two-door hardtop, a four-door hardtop and, yes, a convertible. The latter is pretty sad, but presented as restorable (and it would be with much money and effort!). Back into the yard, one finds several mid-fifties Chevys that are stripped of many parts, but still offer a few items for the erstwhile parts hunter. There's yet another '57 ragtop, and its top has indeed been reduced to rags by the elements.

One big surprise in this yard is the rear end of a 1956-57 Corvette body. It's hard to see, being surrounded by other cars and a very thick collection of wildflowers and weeds, and even harder to get to, but it's definitely there. (That reminds us of a '63 split-window Corvette we found in a yard a couple of years ago, but there was even less left of that car than there is of this one!)

Walking farther down the infrequently traveled trail, we found more surprises, such as several Ford Skyliners from 1957-59. Yep, there were a number of Ford's famous retractable hardtops lining the path through this thickly wooded yard, which relies on the heavy growth to shield it from the adjacent residential area. All of the flip-top hardtops were in pretty sad shape, but at least a couple appeared restorable.

While the operation focuses on the '50s, there are plenty of cars from the '60s present, everything from SS 396 Chevys to Camaros and Mustangs. A few of the more interesting finds are a '67 Pontiac Grand Prix convertible, a '63 Buick Riviera, '55 Ford convertible, AMC Marlin, 1946-48 Chevy sedans, a mid-'60s Cadillac ambulance, a '65 Plymouth Satellite convertible, '68 Plymouth Sport Fury convertible,'64 Chevy Impala two-door hardtop, '69 Camaro coupe, '65 Mustang hardtop, and a few miscellaneous orphans. There are many Corvairs, both coupes and convertibles.

But the mainstay of Nolley's is the lineup of 1955-57 Chevys, there are a

1

2

3

4

5

1. *Nolley Auto Sales isn't hard to find, even for an out-of-town visitor who's never visited Campbellsville, Ky., before. Just ask where South Central Avenue is and head south out of town; no self-respecting car hobbyist could miss this lineup of old cars at the roadside, especially since they're all '57 Chevys.*

2. *One of the lot's premier inhabitants is this '57 Chevy convertible. It's restorable, and it's not cheap!*

3. *What was once a flashy and fast boulevard cruiser, this '66 Chevy Super Sport convertible still carries its original 396-cid V-8.*

4. *One of the rarest cars in the Nolley yard is this 1967 Pontiac Grand Prix convertible. It was the only year that the Grand Prix came in the softtop configuration, and just 5,856 were built.*

5. *Solid looking '69 Camaro coupe has been engulfed by nature. It appears to be fairly complete.*

6. *There are several Corvair convertibles at Nolley's, including both major body styles.*

7. *Stored on asphalt at the front of the yard, or at the back of the used car lot, depending on your perspective, this '63 Buick Riviera still shows the shapes and definitions that made it a styling sensation some 30 years ago. It was one of Bill Mitchell's favorite creations from his many years as the top designer for General Motors.*

6

7

8

8. *Certainly restorable, but needing virtually everything, this '65 Mustang hardtop comes with an original 289 engine, automatic, pony interior and a little of the original light blue paint still on its body.*

9. *Another gem is this '68 Plymouth Sport Fury convertible. It's basically intact and restorable, and will be sold only as a complete unit.*

10. *A rare and desirable Rally Sport, this '67 Camaro coupe has had a rough life, but it's ready for another shot at it.*

9

227

11. *Weathered '65 Ford convertible may be salvageable, but would serve better as a parts car.*

12. *This Plymouth Satellite convertible, a '67 model, is pretty badly ravaged, but a dedicated Mopar enthusiast with a lot of time and ambition could return the old girl to her former glory.*

13. *It would take a lot of motivation for even the most zealous Corvair restorer to haul this one out of the woods. It would make a halfway decent parts car, though. After all, it is a convertible.*

11

12

13

couple dozen of them, and the 1957-59 Ford Skyliner retractable hardtops, of which there are half a dozen or so. There are also several Pontiacs, Studebakers and other brands from the '50s.

It's like stepping back in time to a yard that was in operation in the late '60s. Actually, that's not too far off, as Charles Nolley, proprietor, has operated his used car dealership, service garage, and salvage yard since 1970. A few of the cars look like they've been there that long, too.

Spending a day, or a good part of it, touring Campbellsville, Ky., can produce a project car of nearly any description. Between the Van Cleave and Nolley operations, virtually every major era from the '20s through the '60s is covered and there are a lot of trucks as well as cars. Someone looking for a project car wouldn't go wrong starting his search in southern Kentucky.

About the yard

Charles Nolley is the man to see at Nolley Auto Sales, Inc., South Central Ave., Campbellsville, Ky. 42718, and he can be reached at 502-465-2306 at the shop, or 502-465-4413 at home. Walk-in traffic is okay, but it's best to call ahead. Nolley prefers to sell whole units, either as restorable vehicles or parts cars, but some parts can be acquired individually off selected units.

DIRECTORY OF SALVAGE YARDS

ARIZONA

Art Coffer Auto Dismantlers., Inc.: 3127 W. Broadway Rd., Phoenix, Ariz. 85041. Telephone 602-276-7377. Contact: Tom Taber. Open Monday through Friday 8 a.m. to 5 p.m., Saturday 8 a.m. to 2 p.m. Customers may browse yard with supervision. Specializes in Chrysler, Plymouth and Dodge from 1960 to 1991. No Ford or GM. Used cars and trucks. Founded in 1966. Approximately 500-600 vehicles in yard. In business 27 years.

B&M Auto Wrecking Inc.: 225 North McClintock Rd., Tempe, Ariz. Telephone 602-968-1111. Contact Bobby Zanon. Open Monday through Friday 8 a.m. to 5 p.m. Saturday 8 a.m. to 12 p.m. Visitors are not allowed in the yard, and all parts are pulled by the staff.

Black Canyon Old Parts Co.: 21055 E. Tara Springs Rd., Black Canyon City, Ariz. 85324. Telephone 602-374-5515. Monday through Friday 8 a.m. to 5 p.m. Saturday 8 a.m. to noon. Contact co-owners Ron McClure and Rick Ludlow.

Fort Auto Parts: P.O. Box 4528, Huachuca City, Ariz. 85616. Telephone 602-456-9082. Contact Milo Parizek. Open Monday through Friday 9 a.m. to 5 p.m. Saturday by appointment. Inventory list available. Mail-order service. Specializes in all makes and models 1923 to 1973. Approximately 600 vehicles in yard. In business 34 years.

Global Auto Parts Connection: P.O. Box 15548, Phoenix, Ariz. 86060. Telephone 602-376-1561 (24 hours) FAX 602-852-0442. Open by appointment only. Customers may browse supervised. Rust free Western used auto parts. GM 1949-79, specializing in Cadillacs. Can video cars for out of state and overseas customers. Locator service for all makes and models. Parts for most makes. Inventory list available for $3. Mail-order service. 200 car inventory.

Hoctor's Hidden Valley Auto Parts: 21046 N. Rio Bravo, Maricopa, Ariz. 85239. Telephone 602-568-2945, 252-2122, 252-6137, FAX 602-258-0951. Contact Jeff Hoctor. Monday through Friday 8 a.m. to 5 p.m., Saturday 9 a.m. to 3 p.m. Customers may browse yard unsupervised. About 8,000 newer, foreign and vintage cars, mainly 20 years old and older. Mail-order service, no lists but SASE required for mail requests. Radiator service & tire service. Parts shipment available. 7,500 inventory. Two other locations in Phoenix area. In business 31 years.

Speedway Automotive: 2300 West Broadway, Phoenix, Ariz. 85041. Telephone 602-276-0090. Contact Jerry or Phil. Open Monday through Friday 8:30 a.m. to 5:30 p.m., Saturday 9 a.m. to 3 p.m. Customers may browse yard supervised. Mail-order service. Specializes in 1961-87 Buicks. Approximately 400 vehicles in yard. New, NOS, reproduction parts for Buick. In business 16 years.

Wiseman's Auto Salvage: 900 West Cottonwood Lane, Casa Grande, Ariz. 85222. Telephone 602-836-7960. Contact Ron Wiseman. Open Monday through Saturday. Call for hours. 2,000 cars from '30s-'70s. Customers may browse yard supervised. Mail order; include SASE with query. Approximately 2,500 vehicles in yard. In business since early '60s.

ARKANSAS

Big Ben's Used Cars & Salvage: Highway 79 East, Fordyce, Ark. 71742. Telephone 501-352-7423. Contact Benny or Sherry Roark. Open Monday through Thursday, 8 a.m. to 5 p.m., 8 a.m. to 6 p.m. on Friday, 8 a.m. to 1 p.m. Saturday. Customers may browse yard unsupervised. Specializes in all makes from the '60s and '70s, particularly Chryslers. Approximately 1,500 vehicles in yard. In scrap iron and metals business. In business four years.

James Lasiter Cars & Parts: Rt. 2, Box 39, Wilmar, Ark. 71675. Telephone 501-469-5453. Contact James Lasiter. Open Monday through Friday, 5 p.m. to 9:30 p.m., Saturday 9 a.m. to 5:30 p.m., Sunday 1 p.m. to 6 p.m. Limited mail-order service. Specializes in 1950-80 Fords, including trucks and flathead parts, 1959-79 GM products, 1949-76 Chrysler products, several AMC products, and Corvairs. Approximately 980 vehicles in yard. Will tow within 100-mile radius. In business 30 years.

CALIFORNIA

Aase Bros. Inc.: 701 E. Cypress St., Anaheim, Calif. 92805. Telephone 714-956-2419 or 1-800-444-7444. Contact Dave or Dennis Aase. Open Monday through Friday 8:30 a.m. to 5:30 p.m. Mail-order service available. Yard specializes in Porsche and Mercedes. Approximately 200 vehicles in the yard. In business 22 years.

Allchevy Auto Parts: 4999 Vanden Rd., Vacaville, Calif. 95687. Telephone 707-437-5466, FAX 707-437-6821. Contact Billy Marks. Open Monday through Friday, 8:30 a.m. to 5:30 p.m. Customers may browse yard supervised. Mail-order service. Specializes in Chevy cars and trucks, 1955-93. Approximately 200 vehicles in yard. Computerized inventory, parts locating system nationally. In business 9 years.

Best Deal Inc.: 8171 Monroe, Stanton, Calif. 90680. Telephone 1-800-354-9202 or 714-995-0081. Contact John Waner. Open Monday through Friday, 8:30 a.m. to 5 p.m., Saturday 9 a.m. to 3 p.m. New and used parts and accessories for Porsche enthusiasts. Mail-order service. Catalog available upon request. In business since 1975.

Capital Auto Parts: 15326 S. Figueroa, Gardena, Calif. 90248. Los Angeles area. Telephone 213-323-4242.

Coast G.M. Salvage: 1400 West Anaheim, Long Beach, Calif. 90813. Telephone 213-437-1247. Contact David

R. Hensch, Monday through Friday 8 a.m. to 5 p.m., Saturday 9 a.m. to 2 p.m. Specializes in Chevy pickups 1960-up, Camaros 1967-up, Corvettes 1968-up, GM cars, trucks, vans 1978-up. Approximately 1,500 vehicles in yard. In business 14 years.

Crossroads Classic Mustang: 12421 Riverside Ave., Mira Loma, Calif. 91752. Telephone 714-986-6789, 1-800-Giddy-Up for catalog. Contact Paul Nusbaum or Norm Stepnick. Open Monday through Friday, 8 a.m. to 5 p.m., Saturday 8:30 a.m. to 2 p.m. Inventory list available. Customers may browse yard supervised. Mail-order service. Specializes in 1964 1/2 and up Mustangs. Approximately 250 Mustangs in yard. New and reproduced parts, rebuilt parts. In business since 1967.

E & H Auto Wreckers: 595 Trade Zone Blvd., Milpitas, Calif. 95035. Telephone 408-262-4500..

Kalend's Auto Wrecking: 8237 E. Hwy. 26, Stockton, Calif. 95215. Telephone 209-931-0929. Contact George DeYoung or Ken Aman. Open Monday through Friday, 8 a.m. to 5 p.m., Saturday 9 a.m. to 2 p.m. Mail orders accepted. Customers may browse yard unsupervised. Specializes in 1980 to 1990 all makes and parts, domestic and foreign. Approximately 400 vehicles in yard. In business 40 years.

Lee's Auto: Route 1, Box 1632, Orland, Calif. 95963. Contact Lee Carter. Open normal business hours. Stocks 300-plus vehicles, with most older than 1970. Many commercial vehicles in the 5.5-acre yard, including a number of restorable units. In business under current management for 10 years.

Mather's Auto Dismantlers, Inc.: 4095 Happy Lane, Sacramento, Calif. 95827. Telephone 916-366-8211.

M.A.T.S.: 701 Straugh Rd., Rio Linda, Calif. 95673. Telephone 916-991-3033. Contact Darin Moore. Open Monday through Friday, 9 a.m. to 5 p.m., Saturday 9 a.m. to 3 p.m. Inventory list available to interested parties at no charge. Customers may browse yard unsupervised. Mail orders accepted. Specializes in 1948-85 pickups and cars up to and including 1975. Approximately 1,500 vehicles. In business 7 years.

McHughes Auto Parts: 1969 Arnold Industrial Way, Concord, Calif. 94520. Telephone 415-686-2343.

Memory Lane Collector Car Dismantlers: 1131 Pendleton, Sun Valley, Calif. 91352. Telephone 818-504-3341. Calif. only 800-AT-1-YARD. Contact Tony Martinez. Open Monday through Saturday 8 a.m. to 5 p.m., Sunday 9 a.m. to 3 p.m. Customers may browse yard supervised. Mail order services. Yard specializes in cars from '40s to '70s. Approximately 700 vehicles in yard. Offers towing, movie car rentals and prep.

Old Car Parts Store: 6305 Manchester Blvd., Buena Park, Calif. 90621. Telephone 213-693-6673, 714-670-6517.

Papke Enterprises, Inc.: 17202 Gothard St., Huntington Beach, Calif. 92647. Telephone 714-843-6969 (shop), 714-839-3050 (recording). Contact Bill Papke. Open Monday through Saturday by appointment only. Inventory list is available. Mail-order service. Specializes in 1949-51 Mercurys and Fords. Many other Ford and Mercury parts, chrome accessories and custom items. In business 19 years.

Pearson's Auto Dismantling & Used Cars: 2343 Hwy. 49, Mariposa, Calif. 95338. Telephone 209-742-7442. Contact A.G. Pearson. Open Wednesday through Friday, 9 a.m. to 6 p.m., Saturday 9 a.m. to 5 p.m. Mail-order service for small items. Customers may

browse yard supervised. Specializes in all makes and models of '40s, '50s, and '60s. No classics. Approximately 1,500 vehicles in yard. In business 38 years.

Phelp's Auto Wreckers: 2640 Eden Rd., San Leandro, Calif. 94607. Telephone 415-638-9909.

Tressar's Auto Salvage: 120 S. Amphlett's Blvd., San Mateo, Calif. 94401. Telephone 415-343-6754.

Turner's Auto Wrecking: 4248 S. Willow Ave., Fresno, Calif. 93725. Telephone 209-237-0918. Mail-order service. In business 31 years.

Withers Auto Wrecking: 138AAA Rt. 2, Tulelake, Calif. 96134. Telephone 916-664-2204.

Z & Z Auto Salvage: 233 N. Lemon, Orange, Calif. 92666. Telephone 714-997-2200. Open normal hours weekdays, weekends by appointment only. Specializing in Camaros & Firebirds, and offering restorations. In business 19 years.

COLORADO

Eddie Paul: 9150 Boone Road, Yoder, Colo. 80864. Telephone 719-478-2723. Monday through Friday 8 a.m. to 9 p.m., Saturday 8 a.m. to 9 p.m. by appointment only. Customers may browse yard supervised. Mail-order service. Specializes in '33 to '51 Chevy cars, '36 to '41 trucks, 1936 Olds, 1941 and 1951 Cadillacs, 1940, 1950 and 1953 Buicks, 1946, 1947 and 1955 Dodges, 1940 Hudsons, 1942, 1948 and 1950 Plymouths, 1939, 1951 and 1959 Chryslers, 1953 Fords, and 1938 International pickups. Approximately 35 vehicles in yard. In business 16 years.

Martin Supply & Salvage Yard: 8405 U.S. Hwy. 34, Windsor, Colo. 80550. Telephone 303-686-2460.

Morgan Auto Parts: 722 Kennie Rd., Pueblo, Colo. 81001. Telephone 303-545-1702. Contact Dennis Morgan. Open Monday through Friday 8 a.m. to 5 p.m., Saturday 8 a.m. to 1 p.m. Customers may browse yard supervised. Mail-order service. Specializes in all makes and models. Approximately 450 vehicles in yard. In business 30 years.

Red Canyon Truck Center: 3764 Hwy. 82, Glenwood Springs, Colo. 81601. Telephone 303-945-0140. Contact Kerry "Stretch" Bustad. Open Monday through Friday 9 a.m. to 5 p.m., Saturday 9 a.m. to 2 p.m. Customers may browse yard unsupervised. Specializes in all years, mostly '70s, early '80s, including Ford, Chevy, Dodge, Jeep, and International. Approximately 400 vehicles in yard. Conversions on trucks offered. In business 5 years.

West 29th Auto Inc.: 3200 W. 29th St., Pueblo, Colo. 81003. Telephone 719-543-4247 or 543-4249. Contact Glenn Kittinger. Open Tuesday through Saturday 8 a.m. to 5 p.m. Mail-order service. 80 acres, 30-year accumulation, old to new merchandise, all makes. Approximately 4,000 vehicles in yard. In business 30 years.

Woller Auto Parts, Inc.: 8227 Road SS, Lamar, Colo. 81052. Contact Don Woller. Telephone 719-336-2108. Open Monday through Friday 8 a.m. to 5:30 p.m., Saturday 8 a.m. to noon. Mail-order service. Specializes in 1955-84 models, mostly domestic and pickups. Approximately 4,000 vehicles in yard. Offers paint, body, glass and mechanical work, etc. In business 20 years.

CONNECTICUT

Mt. Tobe Auto Parts: Mt. Tobe Auto Parts, R.F.D. 1, Plymouth, Conn. 06782. Yard is located on Mt. Tobe Rd. Telephone 203-753-0332.

CONNECTICUT *continued*

Leo Winakor & Sons, Inc.: 470 Forsyth Rd., Salem, Conn. 06420. Telephone 203-859-0471 or 203-859-0422. Contact Art Winakor. Open Saturday 10 a.m. to 3 p.m., Sunday 10 a.m. to 2 p.m., or by appointment. Mail orders accepted. Customers may browse yard unsupervised. Specializes in all makes and models from 1930 to 1981. Parts, complete vehicles and restorables. Over 30 acres of cars with approximately 4,000 vehicles in yard. 24-hour towing within 50-mile radius. Information on interchanges given for a small fee. No chrome or ornamental parts sold unless major parts purchased through firm.

FLORIDA

Alley Auto Parts: Rt. 2, Box 551, Immokalee, Fla. 33934. Telephone 800-282-7728 or 813-657-3541. Contact John Dinunzio. Open Monday through Sunday, 8 a.m. to 5 p.m. Inventory list available to interested parties for $4. Customers may browse yard supervised. Mail-order service. Specializes in cars and trucks from 1948 to 1975. Over 800 vehicles in yard. Towing services. Helps in locating hard to find parts. In business 24 years.

B & B Used Auto Parts: Rt. 1, Box 691, Industrial Rd., Big Pine Key, Fla. 33043. Telephone 305-872-9761 or 305-745-3517. Contact Bob Kieber or Bonnie Hall. Open Monday through Friday 9 a.m. to 5:30 p.m., Saturday 9 a.m. to ?. Customers may browse yard supervised. Yard specializes in Cadillacs, Chevys, Chryslers, Buicks, Internationals, and Fords of the '50s and up, also 1968 and up Volvos. Approximately 1,200 vehicles in yard. In business 11 years.

Holder's Auto Salvage: 12404 Highway 231, Youngstown, Fla. 32466. Telephone 904-722-4993. Contact Carlos Holder. Open Tuesday through Saturday 8 a.m. to 5 p.m. Closed Sunday and Monday. Specializes in pre-'75 cars, with some from the '20s. In business 8 years.

J and B Auto Parts, Inc.: 17105 E. Hwy. 50, Orlando, Fla. 32820. Telephone 305-568-2131. Contact N.C. or N.L. Horton Sr. Open Monday through Friday 8 a.m. to 5:30 p.m., Saturday and Sunday 8 a.m. to 4 p.m. Mail orders accepted. Customers may browse supervised. Specializes in all years and makes American and foreign, cars and trucks. Approximately 1,500 vehicles in yard. Firm has radiator shop, service department, installs glass and has towing service. In business 39 years.

Old Gold Cars & Parts: Rt. 2 Box 1133, Old Town, Fla. 32680. Telephone 904-542-8085. Contact Steven or Shannon. Open Monday through Friday 8 a.m. to 6 p.m. Mail order services. Yard specializes in 1948-78 American make only. Approximately 3,500 vehicles in yard. In business 6 years.

Out Of The Past Parts: 3720 S.W. 23rd St., Gainesville, Fla. 32601. Telephone 904-377-4079. Open Monday through Saturday, 8 a.m. to 6 p.m., phone hours, 8 a.m. to 10 p.m. Monday through Sunday. Contact Jay White. Customers may browse yard supervised. Mail-order service. Specializes in Buicks, Cadillacs, Chevrolets, Pontiacs, Plymouths, Dodges, LaSalles, Olds, and Fords of 1935 and later vintage. Car hauling service. Have 1936-48 Chevrolet restoration, parts-locating service (free) with access to over 2,000 '30s through '60s cars. Approximately 150 vehicles in yard. In business 12 years.

Sunrise Auto Sales and Salvage: Rt. 3, Box 6, Aero Ave., Lake City, Fla. 32055. Telephone 904-755-1810. FAX 904-755-1855. Contact William Lockwood. Monday through Friday 8 a.m. to 5:30 p.m., Saturday 8 a.m. to 1 p.m. Customers may browse yard supervised. Mail-order service. Specializes in '40s through early '70s cars and trucks. A few '30s. Over 1,000 autos. In business 4 years.

Umatilla Auto Salvage: 19714 Saltsdale Rd., Umatilla, Fla. 32784. Telephone 904-669-6363. Contact Thomas Lee. Monday through Friday 8 a.m. to 5 p.m. Saturday 8 a.m. to 2 p.m. Customers may browse supervised. Mail-order service. Yard specializes in '50s through '70s, all makes, a few imports and luxury. Approximately 1,000 vehicles in the yard. Auto repair offered. In business 7 years.

GEORGIA

Bayless Fiat Lancia Heaven: 1111 Via Bayless, Marietta, Ga. 30066. Telephone 404-928-1446. Contact Art Bayless. Open Monday through Friday 8 a.m. to 5:30 p.m. Exclusively Fiat and Lancia Beta automobiles since 1988.

Clark's Auto Parts: Hwy. 23 near Georgia Highway Patrol barracks, Helena, Ga. 31037. Firm has nearly 2,500 vehicles, including cars and light trucks from '30s to late '70s.

Embee Parts: 4000 Lee Rd., Smyrna, Ga. 30080. Telephone 404-434-5686. Contact George Wolfes. Open Monday through Friday 9 a.m. to 6 p.m., Saturday 9 a.m. to noon. Customers may browse yard supervised. Mail-order service. Specializes in 1934-88 Mercedes. Approximately 500 vehicles in yard. In business 10 years.

Old Car City, USA: 3098 Hwy. 411 NE, White, Ga. 30184. Telephone 404-382-6141 or 404-974-6144 (Atl.). Contact Dean Lewis. Open Monday through Friday, 8:30 a.m. to 5 p.m., Saturday 8:30 a.m. to noon. Call for appointment. Mail inventory list available for $4.Customers may browse yard supervised. Mail-order service available. Specializes in 1969 and earlier American cars and pickups, restorables. Offers professional appraising and restoration. Approximately 4,000 vehicles in yard. In business 59 years.

Park's Used Auto Parts: Friendship Rd., Eatonton, Ga. 31024. Contact Richard Park. Telephone 706-485-9905; 706-485-4511. Open 2 p.m. to 6 p.m. All day Saturday. Mail-order service. Specializing in muscle, antique and street rod cars & parts. Also trucks and mobile home axles.

Waugh's Auto Parts: Hwy. 27 North, Rt. 6, Box 1598, LaGrange, Ga. 30240. Contact Charlie Waugh. Open Saturday 9 a.m. to noon. Many auto and light-truck parts from the '40s through the '60s. Approximately 800 vehicles in yard. In business 40 years.

IDAHO

Classic Auto Parts: 2945 1/2 Government Way, Coeur d' Alene, Idaho 83814. Telephone 208-667-3428. Open Monday through Friday 9 a.m. to 3 p.m.

Desert Sky: 2742 State Highway 46, Wendell, Idaho 83355. Telephone 208-536-6606. Owner Larry Harns, sales Glenn Mott.

Highway 30 Auto Wrecking: 960 Sunset Strip, Highway 30 W, Mount Home, Idaho 83647. Telephone 208-587-4429. Contact Cort Braithwaite, owner. Open Monday through Friday 9 a.m. to 5 p.m. Saturday 9 a.m. to 1 p.m.

Hopkins Antique Autos and Parts: 24833 Highway 30, Caldwell, Idaho 83605. Telephone 208-459-2877.

Morris' Antique and Classic Cars & Parts: Indian Valley, Idaho 83632. Telephone 208-256-4313. Contact Lynn Morris, owner.

Vintage Automotive: P.O. Box 958, 2290 N. 18th E., Mtn. Home, Idaho 83647. Telephone 208-587-3743. Contact Jim Hines. Open Monday through Friday 9 a.m. to 6 p.m. Saturday 10 a.m. to 5 p.m. Inventory list available for $1. Customers may browse supervised. Mail-order service available. Specializes in all makes prior to 1970. Specializing in Metropolitan. Good stock of new parts for pre-'70 cars, trucks, and equipment. Approximately 900 vehicles in yard. Offering sand blasting and parts locating. In business 20 years.

ILLINOIS

Ace Auto Salvage: Hwy. 51, Tonica, Ill. 61370. Telephone 815-442-8224 or 815-442-8225. Contact Mitchell Urban. Open Monday through Friday 8 a.m. to 5 p.m., Saturday 8 a.m. to noon. Customers may browse yard supervised. Specializes in antique, collectible, convertibles, and muscle cars. Tours of these vehicles in 3 storage buildings are available Saturdays at noon, by appointment. Approximately 4,000 vehicles in yard. In business 29 years.

Auto Parts City: 3570 Washington, Waukegan, Ill. 60085. Telephone 312-244-7171. Open Monday through Friday, 8 a.m. to 5 p.m., Saturday 8 a.m. to 3 p.m. Customers may browse yard unsupervised. Approximately 1,500 vehicles in yard. In business 25 years.

B.C. Automotive, Inc.: 2809 Damascus, Zion, Ill. 60099. Telephone 312-746-8056. Contact Steve Slocum. Open Monday through Saturday, 8:30 a.m. to 5 p.m. Customers may browse yard unsupervised. Mail-order service available. Specializes in 1960-82 domestic and 1970-84 foreign. Approximately 600 vehicles in yard. Towing services. In business 10 years.

Bryant's Auto Parts: RR 1, Westville, Ill. 61883. Telephone 217-267-2124. Contact Wayne, Mike or Keith. Open Monday through Friday, 8 a.m. to 5 p.m. Saturday 8 a.m. to noon. Inventory list available. Customers may browse yard supervised. Mail-order service. Vehicles available as far back as 1939. Approximately 5,000 vehicles in yard. In business 28 years.

Casner Motor Co.: RR 1, Box 217, Oakley, Ill. 62552. Telephone 217-864-2162. 9 miles east Decatur on U.S. Rt. 36. Contact Crista K. Hjort. Open Monday through Friday 9 a.m. to 5 p.m., Saturday by appointment only. Customers may browse yard supervised. Some NOS, various makes and years. Used motor vehicle sales, new and used parts, repairs. In business over 70 years.

E & J Used Auto & Truck Parts: P.O. Box 6007, 315-31st Ave., Rock Island, Ill. 61204. Telephone 309-788-7686, toll-free 800-728-7686. Contact Rick, Jon, Marc or Tiny. Open Monday through Friday, 8 a.m. to 4:30 p.m., Saturday 8 a.m. to 1 p.m. Customers may browse yard supervised. Specializes in all American and foreign cars and trucks from 1937-93. Mail-order service. Approximately 3,500 vehicles in yard. In business 42 years.

Gus Miller: Box 634, Heyworth, Ill. 61745. Telephone 309-473-2979. For specific information send SASE with letter. Open by appointment only. Customers may browse yard unsupervised. Specializes in cars from the '40s and '50s, some '30s and '60s. Approximately 450 vehicles in yard. In business 25 years.

INDIANA

Auto Heaven: 103 W. Allen Street, Bloomington, Ind. 47401. Telephone 812-332-9401, WATS 1-800-777-0297. Contact Chuck Forney. Open Monday through Friday 8:30 a.m. to 5:30 p.m., Saturday 8:30 a.m. to noon. Customers may browse yard supervised. Mail-order service available. Approximately 700 to 1,000 vehicles in yard. In business 14 years.

BSIA Mustang Supply.: 0278 S. 700 E., Millcreek, Ind. 46365. Telephone 219-326-1300, FAX 324-3879. Contact William S. Chalik or Carol M. Chalik. Open Monday through Friday 9 a.m. to 5 p.m. Saturday open by appointment only. Customers may browse yard supervised. Mail-order service. Specializes in 1964 1/2-1973 Mustangs, 1928-31 Model A Fords. Approximately 100 vehicles. Sales of new and reproduction parts. In business 20 years.

Canfield Motors: 22-24 Main, New Waverly, Ind. 46961. Telephone 219-722-3230. Contact Wanda Canfield. Open Monday through Friday 8 a.m. to 4 p.m., Saturday by appointment only. Customers may browse yard supervised. Mail-order service. Specializes in 1940-up American made vehicles. Approximately 1,000 vehicles in yard. In business 40 years.

Robinson's Auto Sales: 200 New York Ave., New Castle, Ind. 47362. Telephone 317-529-7603. Contact Brent or Charlie Robinson. Open Monday through Friday 8 a.m. to 6 p.m., Saturday 8 a.m. to 4 p.m. Customers may browse yard supervised. Mail-order service. Specializes in Cadillacs, Corvairs, 1960-70. Approximately 25-30 vehicles in yard. Many NOS parts 1950-60, wheel covers and hubcaps 1940 on up. In business 47 years.

Bill Shank Auto Parts: 14648 Promise Rd., Noblesville, Ind. 46060. Telephone 317-776-0080. Contact William Shank. Open by appointment only. Inventory list available. Mail-order service. Specializes in all makes 1948-90. Approximately 2,500 vehicles in yard. In business 30 years.

Webb's Classic Auto Parts: 5084 West State Road 114, Huntington, Ind. 46750. Telephone 219-344-1714. Open Monday through Friday 8 a.m. to 5 p.m., weekends by appointment only. Mail-order service. NOS, used and repro parts for Rambler and AMC, 1950 and newer. Large line of AMX-Javelin parts. Technical service manuals and parts books. Send SASE with your needs. Discover, VISA, Mastercard and American Express accepted.

Wright's Auto Service: 102 S. Shelby, Indianapolis, Ind. 46202. Telephone 317-638-4482. Contact Arthur or Edith Wells. Open Monday through Friday, 9 a.m. to 5 p.m. Mail orders accepted with prepaid check. Specializes in parts from 1930 to 1959 and cars of early vintage. Services include repairs to older cars (transmissions, motors and brakes). Many rebuilt items available. No body work. In business since 1939.

IOWA

Becker's Auto Salvage: Hwy. 30 West, Atkins, Iowa 52206. Telephone 319-446-7141. Contact Mike Becker. Open Monday through Friday, 8 a.m. to 5 p.m., Saturday 8 a.m. to noon. Customers may browse yard. Mail-order service. Specializes in AMCs, Fords, Studebakers, Edsels, Chevys, and more. Yard consists of 10 acres. In business 26 years.

Kelsey Auto Salvage: Rt. 2, Iowa Falls, Iowa 50126. Telephone 515-648-3066. Located on 00 Avenue southeast of Iowa Falls, in north central Iowa. Take Rocksylvania Ave. and turn right on 00 Avenue; the yard will be two miles away. Contact Dean or Chuck. Open Tuesday through Friday, 8 a.m. to 5 p.m., Saturday 8 a.m. to noon. Mail orders accepted. Customers may browse yard unsupervised. Specializes in American cars from 1965 to 1980. 250 vehicles in yard. Started in 1974.

IOWA continued

Meier Auto Salvage Inc.: RR 1, Box 6L, Sioux City, Iowa 51108. Telephone 712-239-1344. Contact Dan and Mike Goosmann. Open Monday through Friday 8 a.m. to 5 p.m., Saturday 8:30 a.m. to 4 p.m. Inventory list available. Customers may browse yard supervised. Mail-order service. Specializes in 1935-65 (250), 1965-88 (700). Approximately 1,000 vehicles in yard. In business 25 years.

Norm's Antique Auto Supply: 1921 Hickory Grove Rd., Davenport, Iowa 52804. Telephone 319-322-8388. Contact Norm Miller. Open Monday through Friday 9 a.m. to 5 p.m., Saturday 9 a.m. to noon. Customers may browse yard unsupervised. Mail-order service. Specializes in 1917 to 1969 Fords, 1923 to 1953 Chevys, 1929 to 1955 Chrysler products, 1923 to 1932 Durant products, 1935 to 1952 Packards, and GM products. Approximately 150 vehicles in yard. Offers speedometer, cable, starter, generator and distributor services, vacuum tanks rebuilt. In business 26 years.

North End Wrecking, Inc.: 55 West 32nd St., Dubuque, Iowa 52001. Telephone 319-556-0044. Contact Don Dick. Open Monday through Friday, 8 a.m. to 5 p.m. Mail-order service. Miscellaneous late-model parts only. Approximately 1,200 vehicles in yard. In business 40 years.

Parmer Studebaker Sales: 408 S. Lincoln, Van Wert, Iowa 50262. Telephone 515-445-5692. Contact Eddie L. Parmer. Open Saturday 9 a.m. to 4 p.m. by appointment only. Customers may browse yard unsupervised. Mail-order service. Many new parts in stock; parts locating service. Specializes in Studebakers only, 1947-66 autos, 1946-64 trucks. Approximately 70 vehicles in yard, others dismantled in bins. In business since 1971.

Ron's Auto Salvage: R.R. 2, Box 54, Allison, Iowa 50602. Telephone 319-267-2871. Contact Ronald Saathoff. Open Monday through Friday, 8 a.m. to 5 p.m., Saturday 8 a.m. to noon. Customers may browse yard unsupervised. Mail-order service. Specializes in all makes 1949-85 cars and pickups. Approximately 2,000 vehicles in yard. In business 25 years.

Terry's Auto Parts: Box 131, Granville, Iowa 51022. Telephone 712-727-3273. Open Monday through Friday, 8 a.m. to 5 p.m., Saturday 8 a.m. to 1 p.m. Customers may browse yard supervised. Mail orders accepted. Specializes in 1940-84 Buicks, including 1963-84 Rivieras with all assembly and miscellaneous body parts available. Approximately 100 vehicles in yard. In business 29 years.

VanderHaag's, Inc.: Box 550, Sanborn, Iowa 51248. Telephone 712-729-3268. Contact John Van Dyke. Open Monday, Tuesday & Thursday 8 a.m. to 5 p.m., Saturday 8 a.m. to noon. Customers may browse yard supervised. Mail-order service. Specializes in 1975 and older cars, 1939 and newer trucks, 1/2-ton through diesels. Approximately 500 vehicles in yard. In business 52 years.

KANSAS

Dixon's Body Shop & Auto Salvage: 1901 No. A' St., Wellington, Kan. 67152. Telephone 316-326-8783. Contact Mike Dixon or Howard. Open Monday through Friday 8 a.m. to 6 p.m., Saturday 8 a.m. to noon. Customers may browse yard unsupervised. Mail-order service. All makes in yard, some old and new. Approximately 100 vehicles in yard. Offers complete body rebuilding and painting services. In business 27 years.

"Easy Jack" & Sons Auto Parts: 2725 South Milford Lake Rd., Junction City, Kan. 66441. Telephone 913-238-7541 or 913-238-7161. Contact "Easy Jack," Joe or Jamin. Located 6 miles west of Junction City on Interstate 70 at Exit 290. Open Monday through Friday 8 a.m. to 5:30 p.m., Saturday 8 a.m. to 2 p.m. Mail-order service. Large collection of antique and collector-type cars from 1912 through 1982, most makes. Convertibles, hearses, two-doors, four-doors, buses, limousines, drivable units, restorable units, parts cars, trucks, etc. Large quantity of antique new and used parts. Services include used cars, towing, storage, shop work and parts location. In business since 1963, but trying to phase out antique, collector-type vehicles. Thirty-five acre inventory.

Edmonds Old Car Parts: P.O. Box 303, 307 East Pearl, McLouth, Kan. 66054. Telephone 913-796-6529 or 913-796-6529 (home). Contact Jim Edmonds. Open Monday through Friday 5 p.m. to 9 p.m., Saturday 9 a.m. to 5 p.m. Open by appointment only. Customers may browse yard supervised. Mail-order service. Specializes in Chevrolets from 1928-57, Chevy pickups from 1928-66. Approximately 35 vehicles in yard.

Hall's Oldsmobile Salvage: 20849 F. Rd., Soldier, Kan. 66540. Telephone 913-924-3748, 913-924-3315. Open Monday through Saturday 8:30 a.m. to 5:00 p.m. Customers may browse yard. Over 2,000 Oldsmobiles from 1936 to 1984 and 400 Chevrolets, Buicks, Pontiacs and Cadillacs from 1940 to 1972. Also has new GM parts. Mastercard and VISA accepted. Satisfaction guaranteed.

Jim's Auto Sales: Rt. 2, Inman, Kan. 67546. Telephone 316-585-6648. Contact James D. White. Open Monday through Saturday, 9 a.m. to 6 p.m. Open Sunday by appointment. Mail orders accepted. Customers may browse yard supervised. Firm specializes in Studebakers 1935-66. Over 250 cars in stock. Has Mopars from the late '30s to mid-'70s, and a few Ford and GM products of the '40s to early '70s. Approximately 40 restorable or parts vehicles for sale. Stock includes remains of more than 15 defunct Studebaker dealerships. NOS Studebaker parts, mostly mechanical (motor, transmission, drivetrain, suspension, instruments, etc). In business 25 years.

Bob Lint Motor Shop: Antique Cars & Parts, Old License Plates, P.O. Box 87, 101 S Main, Danville, Kan. 67036. Telephone 316-962-5247. Contact Bob Lint, (prefers letters). Open Monday through Friday, 8 a.m. to 5 p.m., Saturday 8 a.m. to noon. Customers may browse yard supervised. Inventory list available for $2. Mail-order service. Specializes in all makes and parts, but have lots of wire wheels, radiators, transmissions, etc. Approximately 70 vehicles in yard. Some restoration services. In business for 40 years at this location.

Schuster Auto Wrecking: 406 Benton, Box 31, Wathena, Kan. 66090. Telephone 913-989-4719. Contact John E. Schuster. Open Monday through Friday 8 a.m. to 4 p.m., Saturday 8 a.m. to noon. Inventory list available with SASE. Customers may browse yard unsupervised. Mail-order service. Specializes in Chevrolet, Ford and all pickups, 1938-82. New and used hubcaps. In business 40 years.

Vintage Tin Auto Parts: 4550-A Scotty Lane, Hutchinson, Kan. 67502. Telephone 316-669-8449. Open Tuesday through Saturday 9 a.m. to 6 p.m. Customers may browse yard unsupervised. Mail-order service. Specializes in 1940 through 1970 makes including Chevy, Ford, Chrysler, Dodge, Plymouth, Oldsmobile, Pontiac, Cadillac, Packard, Hudson, Nash, Rambler, and DeSoto. Approximately 1,200 vehicles in yard. In business since 1948.

KENTUCKY

Classic Auto Parts: c/o Antique Auto Shop, 603 Lytle Ave., Elsmere, Ky. 41018. Telephone 606-342-8363. Contact Terry Kesselring. Open Monday through Friday 8 a.m. to 5 p.m.

Ellington Auto Parts: 5840 Contest Rd., Paducah, Ky. 42001. Telephone 502-554-2685. Contact Tom or Randy Ellington. Open Monday through Friday 8 a.m. to 6 p.m., Saturday 8 a.m. to 4 p.m. Mail-order service. Large stock of new older parts including fuel pumps, exhaust systems, mufflers, '53 to '62 patch panels, curved auto glass, etc. Approximately 400 vehicles in yard 1970 and up. In business 20 years.

Nolley Auto Sales, Inc.: South Central Ave., Campbellsville, Ky. 42718. Telephone 502-465-2306 at the shop, or 502-465-4413 at home. Contact Charles Nolley. Walk-in is okay, but it's best to call ahead. Prefers to sell whole units, either as restorable vehicles or parts cars, but some parts can be acquired individually off selected units.

R.C. Van Cleave & Son Used Cars & Trucks: 344 Salem Church Rd., Campbellsville, Ky. 42718. Telephone 502-465-2329. Open by appointment. Randall Van Cleave is the sole proprietor. Prefers to sell whole units, either as restorable vehicles or parts cars, but some parts can be acquired individually off selected units.

LOUISIANA

Fannaly's Auto Exchange: P.O. Box 23, 701 Range Rd., Ponchatoula, La. 70454. Telephone 504-386-3714. Contact Marion Fannaly, Jr. Open by appointment only. Customers may browse yard supervised. Mail-order service. Specializes in 125 Cadillacs 1939-77, 85 Buicks 1927-74, 25 Lincolns 1946-78, 18 Packards 1946-56. Most popular makes represented. Large NOS inventory. Always 25 or more collector cars for sale; also contemporary used cars. Approximately 475 vehicles in yard. In business since 1954.

MAINE

Collectible Cars and Parts: P.O. Box 52, Limestone, Maine 04952. Telephone 207-325-4915. Contact Jack McLean. Open Monday through Saturday 8 a.m. to 5 p.m., Sunday 8 a.m. to 2 p.m. Closes in late November for the winter. Customers may browse yard unsupervised. Mail order services. Approximately 5,000 cars in the yard, from '35 to '60s. In business 3 years.

MARYLAND

Chuck's Used Auto Parts: 4722 St. Barnabas Rd., Marlow Heights, Md. 20748. Telephone 301-423-0007. Contact Chuck Ryan or Chuck Pounds. Open Monday through Friday 8 a.m. to 5 p.m., Saturday 8 a.m. to 2 p.m. Mail-order service. Specializes in all Corvettes, late model GM cars and trucks. Car sales of rebuildable vehicles. Parts location service. Approximately 250 vehicles in yard. In business 12 years.

Faggelli's Auto Parts: 5850 Oakland Rd., Skyesville, Md. 21784. Telephone 301-795-3007. Contact Joe Faggelli. Open Monday through Friday, 9 a.m. to 6 p.m., Saturday 9 a.m. to 5 p.m. Customers may browse yard supervised. Mail-order service. Specializes in domestic cars and trucks from the late '40s to current. Approximately 150 vehicles in yard with a large supply of inventory shelved. In business 26 years.

Petry's Junk Yard, Inc.: 800 Gorsuch Rd., Westminster, Md. 21157. Telephone 301-876-3233 or 301-848-8590. Contact Tom Runaldue, Tom Petry or Harry. Open Monday through Saturday, 8 a.m. to 5 p.m. Open Sundays by appointment only. Inventory list available. Customers may browse yard supervised. Mail orders accepted. Specializes in all makes and models of the '40s through the '70s. Approximately 400 to 500 vehicles in yard. Towing services. In business 25 years.

Smith Brothers Auto Parts: 2316 Snydersburg Rd., Hampstead, Md. 21074. Telephone 301-239-8514 or 301-374-6781. Contact Ray Messersmith or Ed Lucke. Open Monday through Friday 8 a.m. to 5 p.m., Saturday 8 a.m. to 4 p.m. Customers may browse yard unsupervised. Specializes in all types of vehicles from 1935-80. Approximately 400 to 500 vehicles in yard.

Vogt's Inc.: 2239 Old Westminster Rd., Finksburg, Md. 21048. Telephone 1-800-492-1300. Contact Jake. Open Monday through Friday 8:30 a.m. to 5 p.m., Saturday 8:30 a.m. to noon. Customers may browse yard unsupervised. Mail-order service. Specializes in all 1935-90. Approximately 2,500 vehicles in yard. In business 35 years.

MASSACHUSETTS

Arthur's Junkyard: 147 Fremont St., Taunton, Mass. 02780. Telephone 617-822-0801.

Auto Save Yard Corp.: 800 West Roxbury Pkwy., Chestnut Hill, Mass. 02167. Telephone 617-739-1900, 6 p.m. to 9 p.m. Contact Edward R. Schwartz. Send SASE for reply. Mail-order service. Yard is closed but has many parts, carbs and ignition, little sheet metal. In business 60 years.

Curboy's Used Auto Parts: Meshapaug Rd., Sturbridge, Mass. 01566. Telephone 508-347-9650. Customers may not browse yard. Inventory of cars and parts 1960 to present.

L & L Auto Parts: 2091 Cedar St., Dighton, Mass. 02715. Telephone 617-669-6751.

Standard Auto Wrecking: 257 Grant St., Worcester, Mass. 01600. Telephone 617-755-8631, 755-5246 or 756-2786.

Stevens Auto Wrecking: 160 Freeman Rd., Charlton, Mass. 01507. Telephone 508-832-6380 or 508-248-5539. Contact Fred Stevens. Open Monday through Friday 8 a.m. to 5 p.m., Saturday 8 a.m. to 2:30 p.m. Customers may browse yard unsupervised. Mail-order service. Specializes in early and late model cars and trucks. Also used & reconditioned cars for sale. Approximately 3,000 vehicles. In business 35 years.

Ventura's Auto Parts: 917 Somerset Ave., Taunton, Mass. 02780. Telephone 617-824-9711.

Westport Auto Salvage: American Legion Hwy., Rt. 177, Westport, Mass. 02790. Telephone 617-636-8201.

MICHIGAN

Bartnik Sales & Service: 6524 Van Dyke, Cass City, Mich. 48726. Located at the corner of M-53 & M-81. Telephone 517-872-3541. Contact Jerry or Henry Bartnik. Open Monday through Friday, 8 a.m. to 5:30 p.m., Saturday 8 a.m. to 5 p.m. Customers may browse yard unsupervised. Mail orders accepted. Specializes in cars and trucks from the '60s and '70s. Approximately 375 vehicles in yard. In business 38 years.

Bob's Auto Parts: 6390 N. Lapeer Rd., M-24 and M-90, Fostoria, Mich. 48435. Telephone 313-793-7500. Contact Robert T. Zimmerman. Open by appointment only. Please include SASE with inquiries. Mail-order service. Specializes in all makes from 1930-75. Approximately 2,000 vehicles in yard. In business 35 years.

MICHIGAN continued

Doc's Auto Parts: 38708 Fisk Lk. Rd., Paw Paw, Mich. 49079. Telephone 616-657-5268. Contact Walter or Mary Jane Lula. Open Thursday and Friday, noon to 6 p.m., Saturday 8 a.m. to 3 p.m. Customers may browse yard supervised. Mail-order service available on small parts. Specializes in '30s through '70s, most makes. 600 vehicles in yard. Antique shop on premises. In business 40 years.

Hillard's Scrapyard: 11301 Crystal N.E., Vestaberg, Mich. Telephone 517-268-5262.

Joe's Auto Wrecking: 14718 M 104, Spring Lake, Mich. 49456. Telephone 616-842-6940. Contact Gary Bisacky. Open Monday through Friday 8 a.m. to 2 p.m.

Schultz's Auto Salvage: 10101 N. Belsay Rd., Millington, Mich. 48746. Telephone 517-871-3165. Contact Wayne or Angela Schultz. Open Monday through Saturday, 9 a.m. to 5 p.m. Customers may browse yard supervised. Specializes in GM products of the mid-'60s and up. Approximately 500 vehicles in yard. 24-hour wrecking service. In business 15 years.

Super Auto Parts: 6162 Lapeer Rd., Clyde, Mich. 48049. Telephone 313-982-6895. Contact Bernell Henderson. Open Monday through Saturday, 11 a.m. to 5 pm., but closed on Tuesdays. Customers may browse yard supervised. Handles all makes and models with majority of '50s and '60s, through most '75s. Approximately 600 vehicles in yard. In business 53 years.

Tri County Sales Inc.: 7625 Marsh Rd., Marine City, Mich. 48039. Telephone 313-765-3114. Contact John. Open Monday through Friday 9 a.m. to 4 p.m., Saturday 9 a.m. to noon. Call in advance. Mail-order service. Specializes in Chevrolets, 1967-69 Camaro parts, '73 & up Chevy pickups. One-tons bought and sold. Will buy or trade. Porsches wanted, any condition. Chevy big-block engines wanted. Approximately 100 vehicles in yard. Also towing and damage-free car hauling. In business 16 years.

MINNESOTA

Cedar Auto Parts: 1100 Syndicate St., Jordan, Minn. 55352. Telephone 612-492-3300, 1-800-755-3266. For information contact Pat Skelley or Dave Miller. Open Monday through Friday, 8 a.m. to 6 p.m., Saturday 8 a.m. to noon. Will put names on mailing list. Customers may browse yard at owner's discretion. Mail-order service. Specializes in 1949 to current makes and models with many special-interest cars and 4x4 parts. Approximately 1,000 vehicles in yard. Offers complete body shop, transmission rebuilding, hotline, new and rebuilt parts. In business 20 years.

Doug's Auto Parts: Hwy. 59 North, Box 811, Marshall, Minn. 56258. Telephone 507-537-1487. Contact Doug. Open Monday through Friday 8 a.m. to 5 p.m. Mail-order service. Specializes in 1932-48 Fords, 1937-68 Chevys, '32-up big trucks (Fords & Chevys); have many other cars. Carries a complete line of new sheet metal and rust-repair panels. Charge of $5 for photos. Approximately 200 vehicles in yard. In business 19 years.

Joe's Auto Sales: 5849-190th Street East, Hastings, Minn. 55033. Telephone 1-800-359-0970 or 612-437-6787. For information contact Joe Kummer, Fred Weiland or Steve Robben. Open Monday 9 a.m. to 5 p.m., Tuesday through Friday, 8 a.m. to 5 p.m., Saturday 8 a.m. to noon. Customers may browse yard supervised. Mail-order service. Specializes in Ford and Mercury cars and light trucks from 1939-83 with real heavy inventory of 1955-75 Fords and decent inventory of 1950 to 1955 Fords. Many parts stored away along with NOS parts. Approximately 1,500 vehicles in yard. Services include rebuilt and used parts sales, rebuilding of some parts and some customer repair work. In business 27 years.

Mopar Mel's: RR 2 Box 6B1, Hwy 32 North, Fertile, Minn. 56540. Telephone 218-945-6920. Contact Mel Bohnenkamp. Open Monday through Friday 8 a.m. to 6 p.m. Closed weekends. Visitors by appointment only. Mail-order service available. Specializing in '57-62 Mopars. Approximately 310 vehicles in yard. Services include restorations for '57-62 Mopars and parts sales for '56-66 Mopars. In business for 26 years.

Pine River Salvage: Hwy. 371 North, Pine River, Minn. 56474. Telephone 218-587-2700, 1-800-642-2880. Open Monday through Saturday 8 a.m. to 6 p.m., Sunday by appointment only. Customers may browse yard unsupervised. Mail-order service, please enclose SASE. Specializes in variety of makes and models 1940-80. Approximately 3,500 vehicles in yard.

Rick's Towing, Auto Parts & Sales: Box 92, 124 Hwy. 10, Royalton, Minn. 56373. Telephone 612-584-5586, 612-654-1302, Minn. Watts 800-245-5588. Contact Richard T. Kowalczyk or Jaime Hoff. Open Monday through Friday 7:30 a.m. to 5:30 p.m., Saturday 8 a.m. to 3 p.m. Inventory list available. Customers may browse yard supervised. Specializes in late-model domestics, cars and trucks, 4x4s. Towing available. New and used parts. Approximately 300 vehicles in yard. In business 13 years.

Sleepy Eye Salvage Co.: RR 4, Box 60, Sleepy Eye, Minn. 56085. Telephone 507-794-0073. Contact Glen Jr., Gary or Glen Sr. Open Monday through Friday 8:30 a.m. to 6 p.m., Saturday 8:30 a.m. to 4 p.m. Customers may browse yard supervised. Mail-order service. Specializes in 1937-77 vehicles. Approximately 600 vehicles in yard. Towing available. In business 25 years.

Windy Hill Auto Parts: 9200 240th Ave. NE, New London, Minn. 56273. Telephone 612-354-2201. Contact Allan, Dave, or Hannah. Open Sunday through Saturday 7 a.m. to 5 p.m. Mail-order service. Customers may browse unsupervised. Specializes in American-made cars and trucks from 1915-90. Mostly older cars and trucks with nearly 8,000 cars pre-1968 and military trucks. Approximately 12,000 vehicles in yard. In business 27 years at this location.

MISSOURI

Hillside Auto Salvage: Rt. 4, Box 179B, Joplin, Mo. 64801. Telephone 417-624-1042. Contact Johnny Rawlins. Open Tuesday through Saturday, 8 a.m. to dark. Customers may browse yard unsupervised. Specializes in vehicles from 1941-81, including Ford products, Camaros, Corvettes, Firebirds, etc. Approximately 200 vehicles in yard. In business 4 years.

J and M Vintage Auto: two miles West on B Hwy., P.O. Box 297, Goodman, Mo. 64843. Telephone 417-364-7203. Contact Jim Burrowes. Open Monday through Saturday 8 a.m. to 5 p.m. Customers may browse yard unsupervised. Mail-order service. Specializes in 1930-68 cars and pickups. Approximately 1,200 vehicles in yard. Offers towing and auto repair. In business 20 years.

Lorenz Service: RR 1 Box 70, Corder, Mo. 64021. Telephone 816-394-2423. Contact Roy Lorenz, owner. Open Monday through Friday 8 a.m. to 6 p.m. Yard specializes in '30s to '70s, all makes. Approximately 600 vehicles in yard. In business 43 years.

R & R Auto Salvage: Highway 60, Aurora, Mo. Open Monday through Saturday 8 a.m. to 5 p.m. Mailing address: Route 2, Box 196G, Verona, Mo. 65769. Order line: 1-800-426-HEMI; info line: 417-678-5551; fax: 417-678-6403.

Trimble Farmer's Salvage, Inc.: P.O. Box 53, Trimble, Mo. 64492. Telephone 816-357-2515. Contact V.L. Anderson. Open by appointment only Monday through Friday 8 a.m. to 5 p.m. Mail-order service. Specializes in some old Packard parts and trim, 1956 1/2 Packard parts cars. In business 25 years.

Versailles Auto Salvage: Rt. 4, Box 255, Versailles, Mo. 65084. Telephone 314-378-6278. Contact G. E. Molloy. Open Monday through Friday 8 a.m. to 5 p.m., Saturday 8 a.m. to noon. Customers may browse yard supervised. Specializes in 1964 1/2 to 1973 Mustangs, Chevelles, and other older cars. Approximately 1,900 vehicles. In business five years.

MONTANA

Dutton's Restorables: 179 Ricketts Rd., Hamilton, Mont. 59840. Telephone 406-363-3380. Contact Allan Dutton, owner.

Flathead Salvage and Storage: 495 Highway 82, Box 128, Somers, Mont. 59932. Telephone 406-857-3791. Contact Dick Lawrence, owner. Open Monday through Friday 9 a.m. to 5 p.m. Saturdays call. Customers may browse yard supervised. Mail order services. Yard specializes in vintage 1932-50 and '70s through current year. Approximately 600 vehicles in yard. Towing and storage available. In business 9 years.

Kelly Auto Salvage: 1568 Highway 93, Arlee, Mont. 59821. Telephone 406-726-3400. Contact Kelly Wolcott, owner. Open 9 a.m. to 6 p.m. daily.

Medicine Bow Motors, Inc.: 5120 Hwy. 93 South, Missoula, Mont. 59801. Telephone 406-251-2244. Contact Otis Gilliland. Open Monday through Friday 8:30 a.m. to 6 p.m., Saturday by appointment only. Customers may browse yard supervised. Mail-order service. Specializes in 1928 to 1948 Fords. Approximately 500 vehicles in yard. Purchased business in November 1985.

Neal's Wrecking: 4300 Songer Rd., Ronan, Mont. 59864. Telephone 406-676-8111 or 676-8112. Contact Neal Talsma. Open 9 a.m. to 5 p.m. Closed Sunday.

Polson Auto Salvage: 54826 Highway 93, Polson, Mont. 59860. Telephone 406-883-6860. Contact Duane Olsen.

Marshall Sanders: Box 1195 Shalkaho Hwy., Hamilton, Mont. 59840. Telephone 406-363-5328.

Wisher's Auto Recycling: 2190 Airport Rd., Kallispell, Mont. 59901. Telephone 406-752-2461. Contact Clem or Jerry Wisher. Open Monday through Friday 8:30 a.m. to 5:30 p.m., Saturday 8:30 a.m. to 1 p.m. Inventory list available at no charge. Specializes in all makes from 1950-88. Approximately 1,200 vehicles in yard. Towing, MII satellite systems hot line. Offers frame work, mechanical, body and paint services. In business 30 years.

Young's Enterprises: 2870 Highway 2 West, Kalispell, Mont. 59901. Telephone 406-755-6043. Contact Dennis Young, owner. Open 9 a.m. to 5 p.m., Saturday by appointment. Closed Sunday.

Zimp's Enterprises: 2800 So. Montana, Butte, Mont. 59701. Telephone 406-782-5674. Contact Ed or Yvonne Zimpel. Open Monday through Saturday 8 a.m. to 6 p.m. Inventory list available. Customers may browse yard supervised. Specializes in antiques. Approximately 60 antique vehicles for parts and 100 later models from 1950-79. In business 10 years.

NEBRASKA

Eastern Nebraska Auto Recyclers: Mile Marker 351 on Hwy. 34, P.O. Box 266, Elmwood, Neb. 68349. Telephone 402-994-4555 or 402-475-1135. Contact Dan Buckner or Roger Pickering. Open Monday through Friday, 9 a.m. to 6 p.m., Saturday 9 a.m. to 4 p.m. Customers may browse yard supervised. Mail-order service. Specializes in postwar cars, late '40s through '80s. Has restorable complete cars and parts cars. Approximately 1,500 vehicles in yard. Offers towing and repair work. In business 13 years.

W.L. Wally Mansfield: P.O. Box 237, 526 E. 2nd, Blue Springs, Neb. 68318-0237. Telephone 402-645-3546. Contact Wallace L. Mansfield. Open by appointment only. Customers may browse yard supervised. Mail-order service. Specializes in Ford Model As and Ts 1917-31, prewar V-8s, Chevrolets from 1925-48, Dodges from 1920-26, and most other makes up to 1952. Approximately 90 to 100 prewar vehicles in yard. In business 40 years.

Osintowski's Repair: RR 1, Box 107, Genoa, Neb. 68640. Telephone 402-678-2650. Contact Pat Osintowski. Open Monday through Saturday 8 a.m. to 8 p.m. Customers may browse yard with supervision. Specializing in Mopar and Chrysler cars & parts '50-70s, Pontiacs from '60s & '70s. Assorted cars from '60s. Approximately 250 cars in yard. Hauling service offered. In business 9 years.

Sullivan Salvage & Recycling: Hemingford, Neb. 69348. Telephone 308-487-3755. Contact Gil Sullivan. Approximately 100-150 cars in yard.

NEVADA

All Auto Inc or Mustang Auto Wrecking: Rural Route 1, Mustang, Sparks, Nev. 89431. Telephone 702-342-0225. Open Monday through Friday 9 a.m. to 5 p.m. Saturday 9 a.m. to 1 p.m.

K & L Auto Wrecking: 4540 Hammer Lane, Las Vegas, Nev. 89115. Telephone 702-644-5544.

Ken's Auto Wrecking: 5051 Coppersage St., Las Vegas, Nev. 89115. Telephone 702-643-1516. Contact Ken Phillips. Open Monday through Friday 10 a.m. to 4 p.m., Saturday 10 a.m. to 1 p.m. Customers may browse yard supervised. Mail-order service. Specializes in AMCs from 1953-80, T-Birds from 1958-78, Chrysler products from 1956-80. Approximately 360 vehicles in yard. Custom motor rebuilds for restorations. In business 14 years.

Larry's Auto Wrecking: 4160 Studio St., Las Vegas, Nev. 89115. Telephone 702-644-1671. Contact Larry M. Whittaker. Open Monday through Saturday 8 a.m. to 5 p.m. Customers must be escorted, and parts are generally pulled by the staff. Shipping available throughout the U.S. Approximately 600 vehicles in yard.

S & M Vintage Auto: 2560 Solari Dr., Reno, Nev. 89509. Telephone 702-826-0257. Contact Mike or Sandy Tackett. Open by appointment. Customers may browse yard supervised. Mail-order service. Specializes in Ford Products, mid '50s to early '70s. Approximately 150 vehicles in yard. Offers mechanical parts, both new and used. Towing anywhere. In business since 1983.

Southwest Auto Wrecking: 4515 E. Smiley Rd., Las Vegas, Nev. 89115. Telephone 702-643-1771. Contact Robert Dippner. Open Monday through Friday, 8 a.m. to 4:30 p.m., Saturday 8 a.m. to 2:30 p.m. Customer may browse yard supervised. Approximately 4,500 vehicles in yard. Older American rust free-sheet metal. Offers auto glass, new aftermarket sheet metal, and accessories. In business 12 years.

NEW HAMPSHIRE

Lane's Garage & Auto Body: RFD 8, Box 365, Loudon, N.H. 03301. On Rt. 106, 10 miles north of Concord. Telephone 603-783-4752. Open Monday through Friday, 8 a.m. to 6 p.m., weekends by appointment only. Handles all makes and models of 1930s through late '60s. Has restorable cars and parts cars.

NEW JERSEY

Studebaker Sanctuary: 425 Washburn Ave., Washington, N.J. 07882. Contact Ralph Banghart. Specializing in Studebakers.

NEW MEXICO

Discount Auto Parts: 4703 Broadway S.E., Albuquerque, N.M. 87105. Telephone 505-877-6782. Open Monday through Friday, 8 a.m. to 5:30 p.m., Saturday 8 a.m. to 1 p.m. Customers may browse yard supervised. Specializes in new and used VW parts day one through 1985. Approximately 1,400 vehicles in yard.

NEW YORK

Adler's Antique Autos Inc.: 562 Main St., Stephentown, N.Y. 12168. Telephone 518-733-5749. Contact Bob Adler. Monday through Friday 8:30 a.m. to 5 p.m., Saturday 8:30 a.m. to 5 p.m. Customers may browse yard supervised. Mail-order service. Specializes in vintage Chevrolets. Cars and trucks in 1940s, '50s, '60s, and '70s. Extensive coverage of '47-54 Chevy and GMC trucks. Approximately 575 vehicles in yard. Towing, restoration and consultation services available. All work & parts guaranteed. In business since 1975.

Bob & Art's Auto Parts: 2641 Reno Rd., Schodack Center, Castleton, N.Y. 12033. Telephone 518-477-9183. Contact Bob Jeannin or Art Carkner. Open Monday through Sunday 1 to 5 p.m. Customers may browse yard by special arrangement only. Mail-order service. Specializes in late '40s to late '60s, AMCs to '80s (especially Ramblers), many Hudsons, also Studebakers, Fords, GM models and Mopars. Approximately 1,000 vehicles in yard. In business since 1958.

British Auto: 600 Penfield Rd., Macedon, N.Y. 14502. Telephone 315-986-3097. Contact Mark Voelckers. Open Monday through Friday, 8 a.m. to 5 p.m. Specializes in English cars only, 1950 to present. Represents Austin, Austin-Healey, English Ford, Jaguar, Jensen, Lotus, MG, Sunbeam, Triumph, TVR, etc. Approximately 700 cars, parts from another 400. Complete expert repair service. Importer. Information source and parts locator. Large inventory of new, used and NOS. In business 18 years.

Fleetline Automotive: P.O. Box 291, Highland, N.Y. 12528. Telephone 914-895-2381. Contact E.M. Martin. Open by appointment only. Mail-order service. Approximately 2,000 vehicles in yard including 1935 to 1975 Chevrolet, Buick, Olds, Pontiac, Cadillac, Corvair & Chev-GMC trucks. 1937-70 Chrysler Corp. original engines, trans, & running gear, seats, dashboards, body hardware and moldings. In business 35 years.

Mountain Fuel: RFD #2, Gilboa, N.Y. 12076. Contact Russell Van Aken. Open dawn to dusk weekends only. Appointments requested. Customers may browse yard supervised. Approximately 200 vehicles in yard. In business 40 years.

Nash Auto Parts: Pump Rd., Weedsport, N.Y. 13166. Telephone 315-252-5878. Toll free 1-800-526-6334. Contact Joseph Nash. Open Monday through Friday 9 a.m. to 5 p.m., Saturday

9 a.m. to 1 p.m. Customers may browse yard unsupervised. Mail orders and phone orders accepted, Mastercard and Visa welcome. Handles all makes 1920-1990, NOS, used and NORS parts available. Firm offers teletype locating of parts, bead blasting and cleaning to over 1,500 other salvage yards. Approximately 3,000 vehicles in yard. In business since 1952.

Red Praetorius: 1935 Rt. 32, Saugerties, N.Y. 12477 (mailing address). Telephone 914-246-9930. Open by appointment only. Customers may browse yard supervised. Will sell whole parts cars, 1920-1960 available. Approximately 1,000 vehicles in yard. In business 35 years.

Saw Mill Auto Wreckers: 12 Worth St., Yonkers, N.Y. 10701. Located two blocks off North Lockwood Ave. Telephone 914-968-5300.

Sil's Foreign Auto Parts, Inc.: 1498 Spur Dr. So., Islip, N.Y. 11751. Telephone 516-581-7624. Contact Yulands Dilovc. Open Monday through Friday, 8 a.m. to 4:30 p.m., Saturday 9 a.m. to 3 p.m. Mail orders accepted. Specializes in late-model European and Japanese cars.

Tucker's Auto Salvage: RD, Box 170, Burke, N.Y. 12917. Telephone 518-483-5478. Contact Richard J. Tucker. Open Monday through Friday 8 a.m. to 5 p.m., Saturday, 8 a.m. to noon. Mail orders accepted. Customers may browse yard unsupervised. Approximately 1,000 vehicles in yard. Firm has several parts cars from the postwar era and a line of Studebaker cars and trucks. NOS and used parts available. Mechanical repairs, body work, and sandblasting services available. In business 20 years.

NORTH CAROLINA

City Salvage: 3700 Statesville Ave., Charlotte, N.C. 28206. Telephone 1-800-532-0116. Owner Darryl Burriss. Located about 25 miles east of Charlotte off Hwy. 601, 10 miles south of Concord. Approximately 800 cars, mostly '50s-'70s.

Richard's Auto Sales & Salvage: Rt. 3, Box 140, Denton, N.C. 27239. Telephone 919-857-2222, FAX 919-857-3222. Open Monday through Friday 8 a.m. to 5 p.m., Saturday 8 a.m. to 3 p.m. Customers may browse yard. Mail-order service. Specializes in '50s, '60s and '70s, also have some '30s and '40s. Approximately 3,500 vehicles in yard. Pull your own parts.

Thunderbird Barn: Rt. 5, Box 18-A, North Wilkesboro, N.C. 28659. Telephone 919-667-0837. Contact Don Hayes. Open Monday through Friday, 9 a.m. to 5 p.m., Saturday 9 a.m. to noon. Customers may browse yard supervised. Mail-order service. Specializes in 1958 through 1969 T-Birds. Approximately 50 vehicles in yard. In business 5 years.

NORTH DAKOTA

East End Auto Parts: 75-10th Ave. E, Box 183, Dickinson, N.D. 58601. Telephone 701-225-4206. Open Monday through Friday, 8 a.m. to 5 p.m., Saturday 8 a.m. to noon. Inventory list is available for $5. Customers may browse yard supervised. Mail-order service. Specializes in '40s, '50s, '60s, '70s and '80s Chevys, Fords, Dodges and foreign. Over 1,200 vehicles in yard. Towing services. In business 30 years.

Porter Auto Iron & Metal: Rt. 1, Box 180, Park River, N.D. 58270. Telephone 701-284-6517. Contact Kenneth Porter. Open Monday through Friday, 8 a.m. to 5 p.m., Saturday 8 a.m. to noon. Specializes in buying aluminum cans, all kinds of metals. Older vehicles in yard. Offers towing AAA and welding. In business 27 years.

OHIO

Arlington Auto Wrecking: 445 North Arlington St., Akron, Ohio 44305-1687. Telephone 216-434-3466. Contact counterman on duty. Open Monday through Friday, 8 a.m. to 5 p.m., Saturday 8 a.m. to 4 p.m. Customers may browse yard supervised. Mail-order service. Specializes in standard transmissions, both used and rebuilt, plus many hard to find driveline parts. Approximately 500 vehicles in yard. Over 51 years in the recycling business.

Bob's Auto Wrecking: 12602 Rt. 13, Milan, Ohio 44846. Telephone 419-499-2005. North off Rt. 250 1/2 mile south of Ohio turnpike. Contact Bob or Mark Reer. Monday through Friday, 8 a.m. to 5:30 p.m., Saturday, 8 a.m. to noon. Customers may browse yard unsupervised. Specializes in all makes from 1946-90 cars & small trucks. Approximately 5,000 in yard. In business 32 years.

Cherry Auto Parts: 5650 N. Detroit Ave., Toledo, Ohio 43612. Telephone 419-476-7222, 1-800-537-8677. Contact Mark and Nevin Liber. Monday through Friday 7 a.m. to 5 p.m., Saturday 8:30 a.m. to noon. Mail-order service available. Specializes in Asian cars and trucks '85-91 and European cars '80-91. Full machine shop. Approximately 800 vehicles in yard. In business 44 years.

Del-Car Auto Parts: 5501 Westerville, P.O. Box 157, 5501 Westerville Rd., Westerville, Ohio 43081. Telephone 614-882-0220, fax 614-895-1399. Contact John or Ken Parrish. Open Monday through Friday, 8 a.m. to 5 p.m. Mail-order service. Specializes in American cars and trucks, 1983 to current. Approximately 1,300 vehicles in yard. Offers towing services. In business 22 years.

Del-Car Auto Wrecking: 6650 Harlem Rd., Westerville, Ohio 43081. Telephone 614-882-0777, fax 614-895-1399. Contact John or Ken Parish. Open Monday through Friday, 8 a.m. to 5 p.m. Mail order services. Specializes in American cars and trucks from 1965-92. In business 22 years.

Ron's Auto Parts: 3590 Center Rd., Zanesville, Ohio 43701. Telephone 614-453-7234. Contact Ron or Kathy Hall. Open Monday through Friday 8 a.m. to 5 p.m., Saturday 8 a.m. to 2 p.m. Customers may browse yard supervised. Specializes in all makes from early '40s to present. Approximately 3,000 vehicles in yard. In business 25 years.

Frank Sibal's Salvage Yard: 10635 Shanks Down Road, Garrettsville, Ohio 44234. Hours are 9 a.m. to 5 p.m., Monday through Saturday, 9 a.m. to 4 p.m. on Sunday. Sibal requests no phone calls, please.

Stark Wrecking Co.: 7081 Germantown Pike, Miamisburg, Ohio 45342. Telephone 513-866-5032. Contact Clarence Witte. Open 9 a.m. to 5 p.m., Monday through Saturday. No mail order. "Self-service" pull your own parts. About 3,000 cars from '20s-80s. In business at the same location for 70 years.

Twilight Taxi Parts, Inc.: 14503 Old State Rd. Rt. 608, Middlefield, Ohio 44062. Telephone 216-632-5419 noon to 4 p.m. Contact Ben Merkel. Monday through Friday 9 a.m. to 4 p.m. By appointment only on weekends. Customers may browse yard supervised. Specializes in Checker motors products, mostly 1960-82. Approximately 160 vehicles in yard. In business 3 years.

OKLAHOMA

Aabar's Cadillac & Lincoln Salvage: 9700 N.E. 23rd, Oklahoma City, Okla. 73141. Telephone 405-769-3318, FAX 405-793-4044. Open Monday through

Friday 8:30 a.m. to 5 p.m. Customers may browse yard supervised. Specializes in 1939-up Cadillac and Lincoln parts, NOS, NORS, reproduction and used. Seven acres of parts, with approximately 600 cars standing. Loads of parts warehoused. Ship anywhere — Visa, MasterCard & American Express. Guarantee all parts to suit. In business 33 years.

Classic Auto Parts: 2040 N. Yale, Tulsa, Okla. 74115.

Hauf Auto Supply: Box 547, Stillwater, Okla. 74076. Telephone 405-372-1585. Contact Gene or Jo Hauf. Open Tuesday through Friday, 8 a.m. to 5 p.m., Sunday open by appointment only. Customers may browse yard supervised. Specializes in American and foreign cars, pickups and trucks from 1928-70. Approximately 3,500 vehicles on 67 acres. In business for 47 years; fourth generation of Haufs in salvage business.

North Yale Auto Parts, Inc.: Rt. 1, Box 707, Sperry, Okla. 74073. Telephone 1-800-256-NYAP, 918-288-7218. Contact Walt or Bobby Ward. Open Monday through Friday, 8 a.m. to 5 p.m. Saturday 9 a.m. to noon. Customers may browse yard unsupervised. Mail-order service. Specializes in '84 and older models of Chrysler, Ford, and GMs. Approximately 1,000 vehicles in yard. In business 29 years.

31 Auto Salvage: Rt. 5, McAlester, Okla. 74501. Telephone 918-423-2022. Open Monday through Friday 8 a.m. to 5 p.m., Saturday 8 a.m. to noon. Customers may browse yard supervised. Mail-order service. Specializes in 1960-72 General Motors. Approximately 250 vehicles in yard. In business 15 years.

OREGON

Brad's Auto & Truck Parts: 2618 S. Highway 97, Redmond, Ore. 97756. Telephone 503-923-2723; FAX 503-923-3113. Contact Brad and Sharon Carrell, owners. Open Monday through Friday 8 a.m. to 5 p.m. Saturday 10 a.m. to 2 p.m.

Carrell's Collectibles: P.O. Box 865, Redmond, Ore. 97756. Contact Mark Carrell.

D & R Auto Sales: Rt. 2 Box 2080, Hermiston, Ore. 97838. Telephone 503-567-8048, outside Oregon 1-800-554-8763. Contact David Spangenberg. Open Monday through Friday 9:30 a.m. to 6:30 p.m. Saturday 10:30 a.m. to 6 p.m. Inventory list available for $2. Customers may browse yard unsupervised. Yard specializes in all makes and models, preferably pre-1970 vehicles through 1926. Selling whole vehicles, not parting out, but can sell many vehicles as a whole for less than parts cost. Approximately 500 vehicles in yard. Also offers towing, delivery, restoration, and location of special interest autos.

Faspec British Parts: 1036 SE Stark St., Portland, Ore. 97214. Telephone 800-547-8788 (except Oregon), 503-232-1232 (in Oregon). Contact Larry Mosen. Open Monday through Friday, 9 a.m. to 6 p.m., Saturday 9 a.m. to 12:30 p.m. Mail orders accepted. Specializes in new and used parts. Catalogs available for all models of MG and Spridget. Approximately 100 vehicles in yard. Firm also sells British used cars. Also parts for Austin America, Marina, Riley, etc. In business 24 years.

Ira's Sales and Service: 181 S.W. Merritt Lane, Madras, Ore. 97741. Telephone 503-475-3861. Contact Ira Merritt, owner. Open Monday through Friday 8 a.m. to 5 p.m.

Klamath Auto Wreckers: 3315 Washburn Way, Klamath Falls, Ore. 97603. Telephone 503-882-1677; 1-800-452-3301 (Ore., Nev., and Calif. only). Open Monday through Friday 8 a.m. to 5 p.m. Saturday 9 a.m. to 1 p.m.

OREGON *continued*

McCoy's Auto and Truck Wrecking: 80820 Pacific Hwy 99N, Creswell, Ore. 97426. Telephone 503-942-0804. Open Monday through Friday 8:30 a.m. to 5:30 p.m. Saturdays 8:30 a.m. to 3 p.m. Mail order services. Inventory list available. Customers may browse yard supervised. Yard specializes in all makes and model, 1950-85. Approximately 1,000 vehicles in yard. In business 10 years.

Rainbow Auto Wreckers: 25850 Tidball Lane, Veneta, Ore. 97487. Telephone 503-935-1828, 1-800-303-1828. Contact Leo and Emma Hecht. Open Monday through Saturday 8:30 a.m. to 5:00 p.m. Specializing in 1955-64 Chevy cars and pickup parts, also other makes, models and years.

Willie's Auto Salvage: 34415 State Highway 58, Eugene, Ore. 97405. Telephone 503 746-1816, or leave message 503-741-3531. Call in advance. Specializing in '30s to present. Selling whole cars and some parts. Approximately 400 cars in yard.

PENNSYLVANIA

The Junkyard: 201 Cedar St., Allentown, Pa. 18102. Telephone 215-435-7278. Open Monday through Friday 9 a.m. to 6 p.m., Saturday 9 a.m. to 4 p.m. Customers may browse yard unsupervised. Specializes in all makes 1980 and older. Over 1,000 vehicles in yard. In business 4 years.

Klinger's Used Auto Sales: RD 3, Box 454, Pine Grove, Pa. 17963. Telephone 717-345-8778. Contact Dean H. Klinger. Open Monday, Wednesday through Friday 9 a.m. to 5 p.m., Saturday 8 a.m. to 4 p.m., closed Tuesday and Sunday. Inventory list available. Customers may browse yard supervised. Specializes in 1941-56 Chevrolet cars and trucks, later models 1963-80 Ford and Chevy cars and trucks. Approximately 2,500 vehicles in yard. 24-hour roll-back truck service, radiator repair. In business 11 years.

Ed Lucke's Auto Parts: RR 2, Box 2883, Glenville, Pa. 17329. Telephone 717-235-2866. Contact C. Edwin Lucke. Open Monday through Friday 9 a.m. to 5 p.m., Saturday 9 a.m. to noon. Customers may browse yard supervised. Specializes in 1939-56 Packards, Chrysler products 1939 and later, many Corvairs, some Fords in '50s and '60s. Approximately 1,800 vehicles in yard. In business 25 years (formerly Ed's Auto Sales, Westminster, Md.).

Fritz Used Cars: RD 3, Box 233, Birdsboro, Pa. 19508. Telephone 215-582-3310; home 215-582-3160. Contact John M. Fritz, Sr. Monday through Saturday, 9 a.m. to 7 p.m. Customers may browse yard supervised. Specializes in vehicles from 1940 to 1970. Approximately 200 vehicles in yard. In business 18 years.

Secco Auto Parts: Box 271-B, Hayes Rd., Kersey, Pa. 15846. Telephone 814-885-6370. Contact Leroy Secco. Open by appointment only. Customers may browse yard with supervision. Mail orders accepted. Yard specializes in makes from the '50s, '60s and early '70s, also parts for 1941-49 and 1953 Ford flathead engines. Interested in selling out. Everything goes at the right price. Approximately 1,000 vehicles in yard. In business 30 years.

Winnick's Auto Sales & Parts: Rt. 61, P.O. Box 476, Shamokin, Pa. 17872. Telephone 717-648-6857. Located on Rt. 61 between Shamokin & Kulpmont. Open Monday through Friday, 8 a.m. to 5 p.m., Saturday 8 a.m. to noon. Inventory list available. Customers may browse yard supervised. Mail-order service. Specializes in '65 to '75 Mustangs and Camaro cars & all old make vehicles. Parts for American & imported cars and trucks. Approximately 500 vehicles in yard. In business 50 years.

RHODE ISLAND

Arnold's Auto Parts: 1484 Crandall Rd., Tiverton, R.I. 02878. Telephone 401-624-6936. Contact Doug Waite. Open Monday through Friday 8 a.m. to 5 p.m., Saturday 8 a.m. to 3 p.m. Customers may browse yard unsupervised. Mail-order service. Specializes in American cars and trucks from '30s to '70s. Approximately 1,000 vehicles in yard. Towing, referrals. In business since 1952.

Bill's Auto Parts: 1 Macondry St., Cumberland, R.I. 02864. Telephone 401-725-1225. Open Monday through Friday 8 a.m. to 4:30 p.m., Saturday 8 a.m. to 4 p.m. and Sunday 9 a.m. to 3 p.m. Inventory list is available for $5. Customers may browse yard unsupervised. Yard specializes in foreign and domestic, mostly '70s and early '80s with some '50-60s. Approximately 1,000 vehicles in yard. New parts can be ordered. In business 30 years.

Wilson's Auto Parts: Mill Rd., Foster, R.I. 02825. Telephone 401-647-3400.

SOUTH CAROLINA

Cook's Garage: Rt. 1, Callison Hwy., Box 289, Greenwood, S.C. 29646. Telephone 803-227-2731 (business). Contact J.P. Cook after 6 p.m., at 803-227-9415. Open Monday through Friday, 8 a.m. to 6 p.m., Saturday by appointment only. Mail orders accepted. Customers may browse in yard supervised. Specializes in many makes and models from T's of the '20s through makes of the '70s. Some cars complete, some for parts, some pickups, plus a huge stock of NOS and NORS parts. Firm offers engine rebuilding services, sandblasting, towing and partial to complete restorations. Approximately 300 vehicles in yard. In business 25 years.

Marshall Royston: 316 Hwy 221 S, Greenwood, S.C. 29646. Telephone 803-227-2598. Cars in the yard range from '40s to late 60s. Approximately 200 vehicles in the yard. In business 30 years.

SOUTH DAKOTA

Howard's Corvettes: RR 3, Box 162, Sioux Falls, S.D. 57106. Telephone 605-368-5233. Contact Howard Goehring. Open Monday through Friday 9 a.m. to 5:30 p.m., Saturday 9 a.m. to 4 p.m. Inventory list available. Mail-order service. Specializes in 1968-88 Corvettes. Approximately 40 vehicles in yard. In business 19 years.

Jim's Auto Salvage: HC 75 Box 4, Sturgis, S.D. 57785. Telephone 605-347-2303, 605-347-5636. Contact Jim and Cyndi Dempsey. Open Monday through Friday 8 a.m. to 5:30 p.m. Saturday 8 a.m. to 2 p.m. Approximately 1,200 cars and trucks in yard.

Sinner Auto: RR 1 Box 12A, Waubay, S.D. 57273. Telephone 605-947-4121. Contact Jack Sinner. Open Monday through Friday 8 a.m. to 5 p.m., Saturday 8 a.m. to noon. Inventory list available at $2. Customers may browse yard supervised. Mail-order service. Specializes in 1925 to 1982 (most makes). Approximately 300 vehicles in yard. Offers body repair, glass work and trans. rebuilding. In business 30 years.

Wayne's Auto Salvage: RR 3, Box 41, Winner, S.D. 57580. Telephone 605-842-2054. Contact Wayne Myers. Open Monday through Friday, 9 a.m. to 6 p.m., Saturday 10 a.m. to 4 p.m. Customers may browse yard supervised. Mail-order service. Specializes in 1937-70 Fords, Chevys, Plymouths, Dodges, etc., 1946-48 Ford coupes, plus Hudsons, Studebakers, Kaisers, Frazers, Nashes, etc. Approximately 1,500 vehicles in yard. Offers mechanical and muffler shop. In business 26 years.

Ziegler King Salvage: Box 451, Scotland, S.D. 57059. Telephone 605-583-4507. Located west of Scotland, S.D. in the southeastern corner of state. Open by appointment only. Used cars, trucks, farm tractors and machinery of pre-'62 vintage. Sells complete vehicles or parts. Approximately 2,000 cars in yard.

TENNESSEE

Cars and Parts: Rt. 1, Dyer, Tenn. 38330. Telephone 901-643-6448. Contact Ernest Lumpkin. Open Monday through Saturday, 6 a.m. to 8 p.m. Customers may browse yard supervised. Mail-order service. Specializes in Model A and T Fords, early V-8 Fords, some dating back to the '30s. Four barns full of parts. Over 30 vehicles in yard. In business 20 years.

Holt's Auto Salvage: Hwy 431, Fayetteville, Tenn. Telephone 615-433-2501; 615-433-2900. Contact Claude Holt. Call before visiting. Approximately 3,000 vehicles in yard. In business for 33 years.

Lane Auto Salvage: Highway 127, Jamestown, Tenn. 38556. No phone calls. No mail-order business. Contact J.C. Lane for appointment to visit.

LeMance AUTOWORKS: P.O. Box 449, 914 Old Mill Rd., Wartburg, Tenn. 37887. Telephone 615-346-3194. Contact P.A. LaMance. Open by appointment only. Inventory list available for $5. Customers may browse yard unsupervised. Mail-order service. Specializes in domestic cars, mid-'60s and older, including 1970-76 Porsche 914's (over 75) 1963-64 Rambler (over 40) 1958-59 Edsels (over 25) and 1959 Fords (over 10), plus Kaisers, Nashes, Dodges, Corvairs, etc. Also 1969-70 Buick Electra 225s and 1971-73 Buick Rivieras. Also, now collecting auto related toys from '50s and '60s. Approximately 175 vehicles in yard. In business 17 years.

Gale Smyth Antique Auto: 8316 East A.J. Hwy., Whitesburg, Tenn. 37891. Telephone 615-235-5221. Contact Gale Smyth. Open Monday through Saturday 8 a.m. to 6 p.m. Inventory list available for $5. Customers may browse yard supervised. Mail-order service. Specializes in 1935 to 1972 American makes. Approximately 1,300 vehicles in yard. Offers re-chromed bumpers. In business 20 years.

Sonny's Auto Parts: 10058 Rutledge Pike, Carryton, Tenn. 37721. Telephone 615-932-2610 or 615-933-9137. Contact Robert Reeser. Open Monday through Saturday 9 a.m. to 6 p.m. Customers may browse yard. Cars from the '30s to '60s. Approximately 3,000 vehicles in yard.

Volunteer State Chevy Parts: P.O. Drawer D, Greenbrier, Tenn. 37073. Telephone 615-643-4583. Contact Paul or Don. Open by appointment only, Monday through Friday 8 a.m. to 5:30 p.m., weekends and holidays by chance. Call before visiting. Specializing in early '50s-'70s Chevy cars and trucks, few '40s. Less than 100 Chevys only with no Corvairs, no Corvettes, and no tire kickers.

Waldron Auto Salvage: 5356 Murfreesboro Rd., La Vergne, Tenn. 37086. Telephone 615-793-2791. Open Monday through Friday 8 a.m. to 5 p.m., Saturday 8 a.m. to noon. Customers may browse yard supervised. Specializes in 1960 to 1975 American cars and pickup trucks. Approximately 1,200 vehicles in yard. In business 38 years.

TEXAS

Chevy Craft: 3414 Quirt, Lubbock, Tex. 79404. Telephone 806-747-4848. Contact Wm. R. Clement. Open Monday through Friday, 9 a.m. to 6 p.m. by appointment only. Color catalog is available for $5. Tours of yard cost $25, refundable on purchase. Mail-order service. Specializes in V-8 fully framed Chevrolets 1955-63, 1964-72 Chevelles, Corvettes to 1971, factory power packs and 409 models. No trucks or Novas. Approximately 400 vehicles in yard. Offers show-quality chrome plating and a video about '57 Chevys. In business for 27 years.

City Wrecking Co.: P.O. Box 1188, Waco, Tex. 76703. Telephone 817-829-1665. Open Monday through Friday 8 a.m. to 5 p.m., Saturday 8 a.m. to noon. Closed Sundays. Mail order services. Approximately 6,000 cars and trucks. Offers rebuilding and installation of motors and transmissions.

Henderson Auto Parts: P.O. Box 54, Seagoville, Tex. 75159. Telephone 214-287-4787. Contact Edmond Dwight Baker. Open Monday through Saturday 8 a.m. to 6 p.m. Inventory list available. Customers may browse yard. Specializes in all makes of 1976 and earlier. Approximately 750 vehicles in yard. In business 15 years.

Honest John's Caddy Corner: P.O. Box 741, Justin, Tex. 76247. Located at FM 407 West. Telephone 817-566-5066; FAX 817-566-3590. Contact John Foust. Open Monday through Friday 9 a.m. to 6 p.m. Mail-order service. Specializing in all Cadillacs 1936-80. Approximately 300 vehicles. Offering restoration, service, NOS parts, and reproduction parts. In business eight years.

South Side Salvage: Rt. 2, Box 8, U.S. Hwy. 83 South, Wellington, Tex. 79095. Telephone 806-447-2391. Contact David or Marshall Peters. Open Monday through Friday, 8 a.m. to 6 p.m., Saturday 8 a.m. to 5 p.m. Customers may browse yard supervised. Approximately 1,000 vehicles in yard. In business 40 years.

Texas Acres, Mopar Parts: 1130 FM 2410, Harker Heights, Tex. 76543. Telephone 817-698-4555. Contact Ronald E. Stitt or leave message. Open Monday through Friday 8:30 a.m. to 5:30 p.m. Saturday by appointment only. Mail-order service. Customers may browse yard supervised. Specializes in '40 to '80 Chrysler, Plymouth, Dodge, DeSoto cars and parts. Approximately 50 vehicles in yard. Offering major collision and partial restorations. In business 9 years.

VIRGINIA

Glade Mountain: R 1 Box 360, Atkins, Va. 24311. Telephone 703-783-5678. Take exit off I-81, west 1 mile on U.S. 11, south 1 mile on Va. 708, east on Va. 615, new exit 54. Open 1 p.m. to 8 p.m. Sunday afternoons, May thru August. Special hours by appointment or chance. Over 200 parts cars and most parts are for sale.

Philbates Auto Wrecking, Inc.: Hwy 249, P.O. Box 28, New Kent, Va. 23124. Telephone 804-843-9787. Contact George A. Philbates. Open Monday through Friday, 8 a.m. to 5 p.m., Saturday 8 a.m. to 3 p.m. Mail-order service. Customers may browse yard supervised. Specializes in makes from 1940 through 1978. Parts locating service for hard to find parts. Approximately 6,000 vehicles in yard. Towing services. In business 37 years.

VIRGINIA continued

Ralph's Auto Salvage and Repair: Route 1, Box 322, Linville, Va. Telephone 703-833-6111. Contact Ralph Frank. Open Monday through Friday 8 a.m. to 6 p.m., closed Saturday and Sunday. Approximately 200 vehicles on 10 acres. Several makes represented with majority in Fords and Chevrolets ranging from the 30s to the 70s. Sells whole cars and parts. Visitors may browse unsupervised. In business since 1941.

WASHINGTON

A-1 Auto Wrecking: 13818 Pacific Ave., Tacoma, Wash. 98444. Telephone 206-537-3445. Open 9 a.m. to 5 p.m., six days a week. Offers transmission parts (new and used), used axles, drums, fenders, hub caps, cylinder heads, starters, and generators for makes 1928 and newer. In business since 1948 at same location with same owner.

Antique Auto Items: S. 1607 McCabe Rd., Spokane, Wash. 99216. Telephone 509-926-0987. Contact Darrell or Donna Rosenkranz. Inventory lists available with SASE. Open by appointment only. Send specific list of items needed with SASE. Small items from closed yard. Mail-order small parts for 30 years.

Antique Auto Ranch: N. 2225 Dollar Rd., Spokane, Wash. 99212. Telephone 509-535-7789. Contact Tom or Gary. Open Monday through Friday, 8 a.m. to 5 p.m., Saturday 8 a.m. to 2 p.m. Customers may browse yard unsupervised. Mail-order service. Specializes in American makes, 1962 and older. Large inventory of new old stock (NOS). Extensive antique vehicle library maintained. Over 200 vehicles in yard. Offers chassis restoration including all sub components. In business 33 years.

Dan's Garage: 508 E. Bruneau Ave., Kennewick, Wash. 99336. Telephone 509-586-2579. Contact Dan Stafford, owner.

Ferrill's Auto Parts, Inc.: 18306-Hwy. 99, Lynnwood, Wash. 98037. Telephone 1-800-421-3147; 206-778-3147; FAX 206-771-3147. Open Monday through Friday, 8 a.m. to 5:30 p.m., Saturday 8 a.m. to 5 p.m. Customers may browse yard supervised. Mail-order service. Specializes in domestic and import models from 1976-92. Approximately 1,600 vehicles in yard. Three locations. Computerized inventory. In business 39 years.

Fitz Auto Parts: 24000 Hwy. 9, Woodinville, Wash. 98072. Telephone 206-483-1212. Open Monday through Saturday, 8:30 a.m. to 5 p.m. Mail-order service. Specializes in products from Ford, GM, Chrysler/Jeep, plus European and Japanese vehicles. Approximately 2,500 vehicles in yard. In business 60 years.

I-5 Auto & Truck Parts: (also known as Classic Cars, Ltd.) 190 Estep Rd., Chehalis, Wash. 98532. Telephone 206-262-3550, 1-800-551-4489. Contact: Sam or Dave Clark, or Frank Carson. Mail order services. Open Monday through Saturday 9 a.m. to 5:30 p.m.

Part Time Auto Wrecking: HC 01, Box 620, Ilwaco, Wash. 98624. Telephone 206-642-4852. Open Monday through Friday, 9 a.m. to 5 p.m., Saturday 9 a.m. to noon. Customers may browse yard unsupervised. Yard specializes in 1970-80 models. Anyone wishing older parts for '50s iron should submit a specific parts list. Approximately 300 vehicles in yard with a flow of about 250 per year. In business since 1980.

Rick's Auto Wrecking: 12526 Aurora N., Seattle, Wash. 98133. Telephone 206-363-8800. Contact Rick Rennebohm. Open Tuesday through Saturday, 9 a.m. to 5 p.m., closed Sundays and Mondays. Customers may browse yard unsupervised. Mail-order service. Specializes in American vehicles from the '60s, '70s and '80s, foreign vehicles and trucks. Approximately 1,000 vehicles in yard. In business 17 years.

Vintage Auto Parts: 24300 Hwy 9, Woodinville, Wash. 98072. Telephone 206-486-0777. Outside Wash. 1-800-426-5911. Open Monday through Saturday 8 a.m. to 5 p.m. Customers may browse yard. Specializing in late '40s to late '60s American cars and parts from the teens. Approximately 500 vehicles in yard.

WEST VIRGINIA

Antique Auto Parts: P.O. Box 64, Elkview, W. Va. 25071. Telephone 304-965-1821. Contact C.A. Smith, Jr. Open Monday through Saturday 9 a.m. to dusk. Inventory list available. Customers may browse yard supervised. Mail-order service. Specializes in 1935-69, most makes. Approximately 134 vehicles in yard.

WISCONSIN

All Auto Acres: W3862 Hwy. 16, Rio, Wis. 53960. Telephone 414-992-5362, or 800-637-4661(WI). Contact Roger or Renee Gavitt. Open Monday through Friday, 8 a.m. to 5 p.m., Saturday 8 a.m. to noon. Customers may browse yard unsupervised. Mail orders accepted. Specializes in 1955-85 American cars and light trucks. New replacement fenders, doors, etc., in fiberglass and metal. Approximately 2,000 vehicles in yard. In business nine years.

Bradley Auto Inc.: 2026 Hwy. A., West Bend, Wis. 53095. Telephone 414-334-4653 or 334-4066. Contact Ken Wegener. Open Monday through Friday 8 a.m. to 5 p.m., Saturday 8 a.m. to noon. Mail-order service. Specializes in American, imports, light-duty trucks, 1975-current. Approximately 1,000 vehicles in yard. Special interest and collectibles bought, sold, and traded.

C.L. Chase Used Auto and Truck Parts: Rt. 1, Box 291, Camp Douglas, Wis. 54618. Telephone 608-427-6734. Contact C.L. Chase. Open Monday through Saturday 8 a.m. to 6 p.m. Customers may browse yard supervised. Specializes in all makes and models from teens through '90s, cars, pickups, semis. Approximately 5,000 vehicles in yard. Has eight light and heavy-duty wreckers available and 100-ton crane service. In business 25 years.

Golden Sands Salvage: 501 Airport Rd., Boscobel, Wis. 53805. Telephone 608-375-5353. Contact Keith Swenson, owner. Open Monday through Friday 8:30 a.m. to 5:30 p.m., Saturday 8:30 a.m. to noon. Inventory list available. Customers may browse yard. Mail order services. Specializing in all makes, '30s to '70s. Approximately 300 collectible cars. Approximately 1,000 cars in yard. In business 5 years.

Helgesen Antique Auto Parts: Rt. 6, Janesville, Wis. 53545. Telephone 800-356-0006 or 608-756-0469.

Northern Tire & Auto Sales: N. 8219 Hwy. 51, Irma, Wis. 54442. Telephone 715-453-5050. Contact Arden Menge. Open Monday through Friday, 8 a.m. to 5 p.m., Saturday 8 a.m. to 3 p.m. Customers may browse yard supervised. Mail orders accepted. Specializing in all

makes from the '20s to '70s. Approximately 1,500 vehicles in yard. Offers towing services. In business for 20 years.

Ray's Automotive Ent., Inc.: 605 W. Bayfield St., Washburn, Wis. 54891. Telephone 715-373-2669. Contact Ray. Open Monday through Saturday 8 a.m. to 5 p.m. Customers may browse yard supervised. Specializes in all foreign and domestic cars, trucks 1960s and up. Approximately 1,500 vehicles in yard. Towing, body repairs, frame work offered. In business 22 years.

Ray's Auto Repair/Salvage: Rt. 1, Box 85, Sanborn Ave., Ashland, Wis. 54806. Telephone 715-682-6505. Contact Ron Parent. Open Monday through Friday 9 a.m. to 5 p.m., Saturday 9 a.m. to 2 p.m. Customers may browse yard unsupervised. Specializes in 1964 and up. Approximately 250 vehicles in yard. Services offered are exhaust shop, rebuilding brake shoes. In business 30 years.

Dale Remington Salvage Yard: Corner of C & TT, Eau Claire, Wis. 54701. Telephone 715-834-2560.

Seward Auto Salvage, Inc.: 2506 Vincent Rd., Milton, Wis. 53563. Telephone 608-752-5166. Contact Henry Seward. Open Monday through Saturday, 8 a.m. to 5 p.m. Customers may browse yard. Mail-order service. Specializes in 1937 to 1992 autos and trucks, some complete cars for sale. Approximately 1,500 vehicles in yard. In business 15 years.

Somerset Auto Salvage & Repair: Rt. 1, Box 39A, Somerset, Wis. 54025. Telephone 715-247-5136. Contact Dana J. Bentz. Open Monday through Saturday 8 a.m. to 5 p.m. Customers may browse yard unsupervised. Specializes in all cars from old to new, foreign and domestic, pickups and big rigs also. Approximately 300 vehicles in yard. Complete service on engines and drive trains, body work and painting. In business 15 years.

Van's Auto Salvage: Rt. 2, Box 164, Waupun, Wis. 53963. Telephone 414-324-2481. Contact Ted or Larry Vander Woude. Open Tuesday through Friday, 9 a.m. to 5 p.m., Saturday 8 a.m. to noon. Customers may browse yard unsupervised. Mail-order service. Specializes in makes and models from 1947-76, plus a few in the '30s. Approximately 4,000 vehicles in yard. In business 27 years.

Wiese Auto Recycling, Inc.: Rt. 1, Box 32, Hwy. T.W., Theresa, Wis. 53091. Telephone 414-488-3030. Contact Bob, Chuck or Gail Wiese. Open Monday through Friday, 8 a.m. to 5 p.m., Saturday 8 a.m. to noon. Partial inventory list available for $2. Customers may browse yard unsupervised. Mail-order service. Specializes in mostly American models from the late '60s to present; some foreign. Approximately 500 vehicles in yard. Offers repair, body and frame work, plus towing service and storage. In business 21 years.

Zeb's Salvage: 2426 Bernitt Rd., Tigerton, Wis. 54486. Telephone 715-754-5885. Contact Mike Kasperek. Open Monday through Saturday, 8 a.m. to 5 p.m. One hour video available at $14.95. Customer may browse yard unsupervised. Mail order services for small items only. Specializes in most makes and models '30s to '70s. Approximately 900 vehicles in yard. Offers engine work, valve jobs, snow plowing and welding. In business nine years (yard has been here over 30 years).

CANADA

A & H Used Auto Parts: R.R. 3, Sawmill Rd., Oliver, British Columbia, Canada V0H 1T0. Telephone 604-498-3188. Contact Herb or Wayne Pinske. Open Monday through Friday, 8 a.m. to 5 p.m. Inventory list available for $1. Mail orders accepted. Customers may browse yard. Specializing in all makes from the '40s to the '60s, some '30s. Firm has a full repair shop. Approximately 400 vehicles in yard. In business 24 years.

Aldon Auto Salvage Ltd.: Hwy 831, Lamont, Alberta, Canada T0B 2R0. Telephone 403-895-2524; FAX 403-895-7555. Contact Carter family. Open Monday through Friday 8 a.m. to 5:30 p.m. Saturday 8:30 a.m. to 3 p.m. Customers may browse yard unsupervised. Mail-order services. Yard specializes in all domestic autos and light trucks 1940-92. Approximately 4,000 vehicles in yard. Offering towing, engine rebuilding, parts locating & delivery service. In business 22 years.

C.R. Auto: Box 237, Hay Lakes, Alberta, Canada T0B 1W0. Located 38 miles southeast of Edmonton, Alberta, Canada. Telephone 403-878-3263. Contact Randy Berfelo. Open Monday through Friday, 8 a.m. to 7 p.m., Saturday 9 a.m. to 6 p.m. Mail-order service. Specializes in Cadillacs only, 1947-79. Bumpers for most Cadillacs. Accepts Visa and MasterCard. Firm offers restoration work for Cadillacs only. Approximately 240 vehicles in yard. In business 5 years.

Elliott Auto Parts: 4752 Highway 2, near Newtonville, Ontario, Canada. Take Highway 401 to exit 448 (Newtonville Road) and travel north to Highway 2. Turn east and go one mile to Elliott Auto Parts. Open weekdays 8 a.m. to 6 p.m. and Saturday 9 a.m. to 1 p.m. The phone number is 416-786-2255.

Fawcett Motor Carriage Co.: 106 Palmerston Ave., Whitby, Ontario, Canada L1N 3E5. Telephone 416-668-4446; from Toronto 416-686-1412; FAX 416-668-3203. Open 7 a.m. to 5 p.m. Monday through Saturday. Visitors are welcome to tour the yard, but only with permission. In business 40 years.

Roy Graham's Studebaker Parts: RR No. 4, Marmora, Ontario, Canada K0K 2M0. Telephone 613-395-0353. Visitors are asked to call in advance.

Minaker's Auto Parts: King St., Milford, Ontario, Canada K0K 2P0. Telephone 613-476-4547. Contact Paul Minaker. Open Monday through Friday 9 a.m. to 5 p.m., Saturday 9 a.m. to 4 p.m. Closed Thursdays at noon. Customers may browse yard unsupervised. Specializes in mostly North American cars from 1930 to 1980, sedans of the '40s, light trucks of the '50s, trim parts, and those hard-to-get parts. Thousands of NOS parts. NOS parts specialties include brakes and suspension, thousands of brake shoes, wheel and master cylinders. Require sample of part, schematic or photo to fill order. Basically walk-in trade business. Approximately 3,000 plus vehicles in yard, 1,500 pre-1970. Buy and sell cars and parts. Founded in 1925.

Reg's Storage: 10920 Winterburn Rd. N.W., Edmonton, Alberta, Canada T5S 2C3. Telephone 403-447-3610. Open Monday through Friday 8 a.m. to 6 p.m., Saturday 8 a.m. to 4 p.m. Inventory list available for $5. Customers may browse yard supervised. Mail-order service. Specializes in all makes of North American cars and light trucks from 1940 to 1976. Approximately 400 vehicles in yard. In business 30 years.